Praise for
The Fearless Cross-Examiner

"How often do you see a law book that is both revolutionary and laugh-out-loud funny? *The Fearless Cross-Examiner* is. Chock-full of innovative tips, real trial transcript examples, and fresh approaches to cross-examination, Malone's book takes the panic out of cross-examination and puts you back in the driver's seat. This one is a winner."

—Zoe Littlepage, 2015 winner of the American Bar Association's Pursuit of Justice Award; Top Ten Jury Verdict in 2007, 2009, and 2010; member of the Inner Circle of Advocates

"In this definitive Bible on the most effective truth-revealing tool in a lawyer's arsenal, Pat Malone rewrites Irving Younger's ten rules of cross-examination for the modern courtroom. The lesson? If you are still crossing witnesses the way you learned in law school, you are probably doing it wrong. Whether you have been a practicing lawyer for years or are brand new to the profession, this book is a must-read."

—Randi McGinn, president of the Inner Circle of Advocates, author of *Changing Laws, Saving Lives*

"As usual, Patrick Malone challenges the traditions many trial lawyers have inherited and forces us to examine whether there is a better way. He brings tools that will heighten anyone's game, from beginner to seasoned pro, and I heartily recommend this book."

—Mark Lanier, Trial Lawyer of the Year 2015, AAJ Lifetime Achievement Award

"*The Fearless Cross-Examiner* is a really excellent book. Despite having taught the art of cross-examination for more than forty years, I learned a lot from Malone about how to become a more strategic, analytical, and effective cross-examiner."

—Stephen Wizner, William O. Douglas clinical professor emeritus and professorial lecturer at Yale Law School, dean of the faculty at the National Board of Trial Advocacy, and recipient of the Richard S. Jacobson Trial Advocacy Teaching Award and the Theodore I. Koskoff Award

"Pat Malone, a gifted trial lawyer, teacher, and author, adds to his list of excellent trial strategy books with one that is destined to become a classic. I will keep it close at hand during deposition and trial preparation, and our clients will benefit from his willingness to share what he has learned."

—Roxanne Conlin, past president of the
American Association for Justice

"This down-to-earth book features practical tips and helpful examples of proven, effective cross-examination methods that even experienced lawyers will benefit from knowing."

—Paul Luvera, member emeritus of the Inner Circle of Advocates,
listed in *Best Lawyers in America*

"Malone once again takes 'conventional wisdom,' shows how unwise it is, and makes us all better trial lawyers with his new approach. He makes the journey useful, readable, and even fun."

—Bart Dalton, president elect of the
American College of Trial Lawyers

"[It's] the bible to twenty-first-century cross-examination. Any attorney, or any person for that matter, who is asking questions and searching for information must read this book. This is what they should be teaching in law school."

—Jordan Merson, listed in the *New York Law Journal* Hall of Fame
for medical malpractice, obtained the largest verdict in Westchester
County in 2014, listed as a *Super Lawyers* "Rising Star" for 2015

"This is the finest book on cross-examination I have ever read."

—Mark Mandell, member of the Inner Circle of Advocates,
author of *Case Framing*

"I was skeptical before I opened this book. What could be added to a subject covered almost as much as the presidential campaigns? Then Malone grabbed my attention and never let go. Now, having read through it, I can only say this is brilliant, genuinely insightful, and thought provoking."

—Hon. Marcus Z. Shar, judge, Baltimore City (Md.)
Circuit Court, and former trial lawyer

THE FEARLESS CROSS-EXAMINER
Win the Witness, Win the Case

PATRICK MALONE

TRIAL GUIDES, LLC

Trial Guides, LLC, Portland, Oregon 97210

Copyright © 2016 by Patrick Malone. All rights reserved.

TRIAL GUIDES and logo are registered trademarks of Trial Guides, LLC.

ISBN: 978-1-941007-44-0

Library of Congress Control Number: 2015959785

These materials, or any parts or portions thereof, may not be reproduced in any form, written or mechanical, or be programmed into any electronic storage or retrieval system, without the express written permission of Trial Guides, LLC, unless such copying is expressly permitted by federal copyright law. Please direct inquiries to:

> Trial Guides, LLC
> Attn: Permissions
> 2350 NW York Street
> Portland, OR 97210
> (800) 309-6845
> www.trialguides.com

TRIAL GUIDES and logo and RULES OF THE ROAD are registered trademarks of Trial Guides, LLC.

Editor: Tina Ricks

Production Editor: Travis Kremer

Assistant Editor: Melissa Gifford

Interior Designer: Laura Lind Design

Jacket Designer: Miroslava Sobot

Copyeditor: Patricia Esposito

Proofreader: Karin Mullen

Indexer: Lucie Haskins

Printed and bound in the United States of America.

Printed on acid-free paper.

Also by Patrick Malone

Books

Rules of the Road: A Plaintiff Lawyer's Guide to Proving Liability by Rick Friedman and Patrick Malone

Winning Medical Malpractice Cases: With the Rules of the Road Technique by Patrick Malone with Rick Friedman

The Life You Save: Nine Steps to Finding the Best Medical Care—and Avoiding the Worst by Patrick Malone

Video

Rules of the Road: Roadmap to a Winning System by Patrick Malone

To Vicki, always

There are only two mistakes one can make along the road to truth: not going all the way, and not starting.

—Anonymous (wrongly attributed to the Buddha)

Contents

Publisher's Note xiii
Introduction. 1

PART I: You, the Cross-Examiner 9
  1. Laying the Mental Foundation. 11
  2. Freeing Yourself from the Ten Commandments
     of Cross. 23
  3. Choosing the Weapons Right for You. 47

PART II: Building the Case with Cross-Examination. . .65
  4. Cross-Examination with Case-Building Rules 67
  5. Witness Self-Interest and Case-Building Cross. . . .89
  6. Using Treatises to Get to Yes 107

PART III: Tearing Down the Witness 119
  7. Planning: The Essential Weapon for Speed 123
  8. Cross-Examination with Witness
     Tear-Down Rules 145
  9. Fixing Contradictions Cross 171
 10. Exposing the Ignorant Witness 199
 11. Shooting It Out with the Hired-Gun Witness . . .211
 12. Polarizing the Extreme Witness. 231
 13. Fundamental Attribution 243
 14. Mining for Dirt 261

PART IV: PROBLEMS AND SOLUTIONS 277

15. EVIDENCE RULES EVERY CROSS-EXAMINER
    MUST KNOW 279
16. CALLING THE ADVERSE PARTY. .297
17. TECHNIQUE PROBLEMS AND THEIR CURES 317
18. CONTROLLING THE RUNAWAY WITNESS. 337

PART V: BRINGING IT HOME 353

19. PULLING TOGETHER WHAT WE'VE LEARNED 355

APPENDICES 381

APPENDIX A: TRUISMS AND RULES 383
APPENDIX B: WRITING BETTER RULES FOR
              CROSS-EXAMINATION .395

ACKNOWLEDGMENTS. 401

SOURCES. 403

INDEX. 405

ABOUT THE AUTHOR. 417

Publisher's Note

This book is intended for practicing attorneys. This book does not offer legal advice and does not take the place of consultation with an attorney or other professional with appropriate expertise and experience.

Attorneys are strongly cautioned to evaluate the information, ideas, and opinions set forth in this book in light of their own research, experience, and judgment; to consult applicable rules, regulations, procedures, cases, and statutes (including those issued after the publication date of this book); and to make independent decisions about whether and how to apply such information, ideas, and opinions to a particular case.

Quotations from cases, pleadings, discovery, and other sources are for illustrative purposes only and may not be suitable for use in litigation in any particular case.

The majority of cases described in this book are real cases and are cited appropriately. Sample questions and testimony, if not cited, spring from the author's brain only.

All references to the trademarks of third parties are strictly informational and for purposes of commentary. No sponsorship or endorsement by, or affiliation with, the trademark owners is claimed or implied by the author or publisher of this book.

The author and publisher disclaim any liability or responsibility for loss or damage resulting from the use of this book or the information, ideas, or opinions contained in this book.

Introduction

The Old Way, and a Better Way

In the scary, thrilling roller-coaster ride that we lawyers call "trial by jury," no moment has our hearts seized in our throats more than when we stand up to cross-examine a difficult witness. We teeter between humiliation and triumph, abject failure and heroic rescue. And because humiliation and failure seem a lot worse than the possible rewards, we often give up long before the witness might give us what we seek.

It doesn't have to be this way. Cross-examination can be exhilarating, fun, and productive. Never easy, but nothing worthwhile is easy. With the right strategy and sound methods, we can conduct cross-examinations that bring us a lot closer to the victory line than the usual mediocre, cautious crosses we have been taught to do. And there's the problem—we grew up with bad advice.

Cross-examination has always nagged at me. It never felt natural, the way it was taught by the usual rules. It felt like putting on a massive suit of armor and hardly being able to walk under the mass of all the rules—not just rules, but commandments! Engraved in stone!—about never doing this and always doing that. Now and again, if I left the suit of armor in the closet and just engaged with the witness on a subject I knew well and felt passionately, the cross would turn out fine. Why is that? Is it possible that the conventional wisdom is all wrong?

THE OLD WAY

The teachers who have indoctrinated the modern conventions of cross-examination are a dour, cheerless, self-absorbed lot. They start with the idea that the cross-examiner is always about to screw up, and the main task is for the lawyer to avoid looking bad. Not much solace there for your client. What could be worse than losing the case? Well, according to the commandment teachers, the lawyer looking like a buffoon on cross-examination. So they teach a hyper-cautious, superficial approach. Forget about trying to actually establish positive points for your case through the witness. All that stuff about cross-examination being the greatest invention for the discovery of truth—that works only for the genius lawyers. You ordinary souls: Concentrate instead on trying to rough up the witness with a few trick jabs, then sit down quickly before anyone realizes what you're up to.

Probably the worst aspect of the old cross teaching is the way it feeds lawyer egos by insisting that it's the lawyer's words that count in cross—that the best cross is all lawyer talk, punctuated by the occasional timid "yes" from the witness. This technique can be persuasive, if you can pull it off, but it's just about impossible to do for anything longer than three to four questions. Yet we're taught that we fail if we do not maintain rigid control with all-leading questions that demand simple one-word responses and that do not—ever!—tolerate explanations from the witness.

A BETTER WAY

After many years of trying cross-examination the commandment teachers' way, and then venturing to try it the way I see real trial lawyers win cases, I think these teachers are all wrong. I think we can do a lot better. I think we can win cases by preparing ourselves and preparing our cases in a different way, liberated from the usual restraints. And effective cross-examination is a central piece of the new way of conducting trials.

I see the trial lawyer as a builder. We build our cases out of all the materials on hand, including whatever we can borrow or steal from our adversaries. Of course, every builder also does demolition work, so we do some of that too, but fundamentally, we are builders, not destroyers. That's especially true of lawyers on the plaintiffs' side, but it's true for defense attorneys too.

The first and fundamental mistake we make launching any cross-examination is thinking of the cross as demolition work, tearing down the witness. No, if we want to win the case, we must build, not simply tear down.

Ten Truths

Here are ten truths I plan to demonstrate in this book:

1. Cross-examination is important. It may not turn around an otherwise losing case, but a good cross can lock in a victory margin and a bad one can seal your case's fate.

2. Much of the received wisdom about cross-examination—"don't ask one question too many," "ask only leading questions," and the like—is wrong, impossible to follow, and ill-focused.

3. Any smart, hardworking lawyer can become a good cross-examiner.

4. Cross-examination is a game of skill, not chance, that rewards practice and preparation. See number 3.

5. Excessive caution has ruined far more cross-examinations than excessive vigor.

6. An excess of ambition, on the other hand, can make a cross fall short, where more modest goals could have produced a successful result. Judgment and humility are important assets for the cross-examiner. They're difficult to cultivate because,

at the same time, to be a good cross-examiner you must develop the self-confidence to face any witness without fear.

7. There is no such thing as an overly planned cross. Yet the peril and exhilaration of the process is the inability to plan everything. All the same, you can usually anticipate the witness's answers and plan for good rejoinders.

8. A case-specific, witness-tailored strategy for cross-examination is far more important than obsessing over the style you use to ask questions.

9. Cross-examination is a game of wits, something like a tennis match, but one the jury scores not on points but on the overall impression you and the witness create. Thus, the need to focus hard on your best topics, hit each sharply, and not waste time on the petty stuff.

10. Instead of the old lawyer-talk, always-leading approach, what's far more persuasive, I believe, is when we can get witnesses to agree with what we want, and to say that in their own voices with their own words. Leading questions are an overrated tool.

Note that these are truths, not commandments. I reject the idea that anyone can distill a subject as complex as cross-examination to simple Must and Never commandments. I preach advice. Yes, there are some rules to follow, but you can profitably break these rules on occasion, except for the rules of evidence and procedure that the courts impose.

Speaking of rules, the Rules of the Road® method that I've written about twice before has much applicability to cross-examination.[1] Rules, as described in the prior two books, are nothing more than simple truths of human behavior. When we can boil our cases down to a set of simple rules and the principles behind them, winning

---

1. Rick Friedman and Patrick Malone, *Rules of the Road, A Plaintiff Lawyer's Guide to Proving Liability* 2nd ed. (Portland, OR: Trial Guides, 2010) and Patrick Malone with Rick Friedman, *Winning Medical Malpractice Cases: With the Rules of the Road Technique* (Portland, OR: Trial Guides, 2012).

concessions from opposing witnesses on cross-examination can become more straightforward in execution. As readers will see, the Rules of the Road method also helps us clarify our goals in cross-examining any witness. Even when this is a witness who will give up no agreements with our case, the Rules method can help guide the destructive cross-examination we must do.

A good way to see cross-examination, I've come to believe, is as a game of chess or tennis. You're playing to win, and your adversary is playing to win. No need to get agitated; it's better to try to anticipate the witness's next move and plan what you can do to forestall and frustrate that move, just like a good chess player tries to think ahead as many moves as she can crowd into her neural networks. And by the way, just as in a high-level chess match, we need to understand that this game of cross is a whole-body and whole-brain experience, not just an exercise in logic. Just as tennis is more than muscles at work, so too chess and cross-examination are more than brains at work. They involve the whole body too.

You will know this when you have just finished a successful cross-examination and, as your heart begins to slow, you realize you are bone-tired and will sleep well that night.

Here is how I've structured the book.

- Part 1, "You, the Cross-Examiner," is about you: the mental preparation needed to reach your full potential, the old ways that need to be thrown off and why, and an introduction to how to select and execute the type of cross-examination that fits each witness.

- Part 2, "Building the Case with Cross-Examination," is about building your case through cross-examination by winning witness agreement to important liability Rules of the Road that mean your client deserves to win. After exploring how we construct these case-building Rules, I will also focus on how to analyze the witness's self-interest and turn that to our advantage.

- Part 3, "Tearing Down the Witness," looks at the four ways we can tear down a witness's credibility, by showing lack of fit for the case, ignorance and mistakes about key facts, bias, and contradictions. Each of these four strategies works well with a Rules of the Road approach.

- Part 4, "Problems and Solutions," studies the common problems that derail cross-examination and the solutions to get our cross back on track: key evidence rules, bogus objections, the adverse party in our case-in-chief, runaway witnesses, and technique issues and their cures.

- Part 5, "Bringing It Home," pulls together some overall lessons.

A side note about transcripts and names: Trial lawyering is an imperfect art, as I can see all too well when I look back over some of my own cross-examination transcripts, like some I have featured in this book. Too many books about trial practice make it seem all triumph and no trial, all glory and no stumbling. In some of these texts, transcripts are bleached of all blemishes and starched of all wrinkles. The cross-examiner slices up witnesses with effortless eloquence. We admire these practitioners and wonder why our own efforts seem so feeble and inarticulate in comparison. But do awe and discouragement really help anyone do better? I think not. So my antidote in this book is to present raw transcripts, edited only with an occasional ellipse of irrelevant material, sidebars at the bench and such.

I also try to always use real names except when there is a very good reason to protect someone's identity. In those cases, I have indicated the name alteration. My fetish for real names probably stems from my days as a newspaper reporter, when editors would say mean things to us if we tried to slip anonymous people into our stories. For teaching lawyers, the reason I like real names is because it reassures us that these are real cases and real cross-examinations. In a few instances (and at my publisher's insistence), I've omitted the names of the witness being cross-examined. Other than that, these are real, unedited transcripts from real cases.

Before we dive into the chapters, here is a blunt but fair question: Why listen to Malone? I've practiced this craft of trial lawyering for thirty years, doing cross the old way and then the better way, and I know by painful experience what doesn't work and what does. For the last decade, I've taught the Rules of the Road method all over the country, and I've consulted with many trial lawyers building their cases. I have also reached out to some of the most successful trial lawyers I know to send me transcripts of cross-examinations that worked for them, and I've spent a lot of time studying their secrets of success. In this book, you will see many examples from these other lawyers of fine cross-examinations, with comments from me about how they work and why. The before-and-after difference for me boils down to two three-letter words:

- "Meh . . ." for the old-style cross that scores a few points but leaves the witness basically intact.
- "Wow!" for the new-style cross where the witness seems to mutate into a whole new person.

This book will give you the tools for more Wows and fewer Mehs.

PART I

You, the Cross-Examiner

Let's begin by holding up a mirror to you, the reader. I said in the introduction, "Any smart, hardworking lawyer can become a good cross-examiner," but not without some introspection and honest self-study. This comes first because the rest of the book counts for little if I cannot help you tap into your core strengths and weed out the self-destructive habits and bad old learning that hold you back.

- So chapter 1, "Laying the Mental Foundation," starts with the person you must control in the courtroom before you can control any other: yourself. I show some effective techniques to manage stress and remain genuine in the heat of the battle. I look at the elements of a winning trial lawyer personality. And I harness the power of positive thinking and show how to set specific goals to help you get the most from this book.

- Chapter 2, "Freeing Yourself from the Ten Commandments of Cross," takes on all our deeply engrained but self-defeating attitudes about cross, the ones we think we know, like "Never ask a question you don't know the answer to," or "Always ask leading questions," but which I show to be wrong much of the time. We have to do "out with the old" before we're ready for "in with the new."

- Chapter 3, "Choosing the Weapons Right for You," starts us down the path of building new methods of effective cross-examination. It shows how all of cross-examination falls into case-building or witness-destroying, how to choose the weapons to achieve each of these goals, and how to know when you've succeeded. This chapter will complete part 1 of the book and move us directly into case-building (part 2) and witness-destroying (part 3).

1

Laying the Mental Foundation

If you know the enemy and know yourself, you need not fear the result of a hundred battles. If you know yourself but not the enemy, for every victory gained you will also suffer a defeat. If you know neither the enemy nor yourself, you will succumb in every battle.

—Sun Tzu, *The Art of War*

Since this is at heart a self-improvement book, we start with the "self," as in yourself. Why does mastering self-control come before you can master control of the witness? And why can we see our own worst enemies only by looking without flinching into the mirror? Answering those questions with some practical mental housecleaning advice is my first goal in this book.

If you read only one thing in this book, please make it these next few pages. Because a big question looms now that you've invested in this book: Is this going to be yet another how-to-be-a-better-lawyer book that winds up on your bookshelf, half-read and fully forgotten? Or will you invest the time and sweat equity needed to pull this book's lessons into your daily routine and take your practice to a higher level? We retreat from good advice just like we abandon New Year's resolutions, quietly and without really meaning to, but with the same self-destructive effect as if we'd set our hair on fire. Why do we give up, and what can we do to block the self-surrender and unlock our true potential?

It's not laziness and lack of resolve that defeat our efforts to improve cross-examinations (or any other aspect of lawyering). Probably the biggest obstacle is fear. Cross-examination is, after all, the one moment in trial when we face three opponents, each very vocal. We must fend off not only the opposing lawyer and the sometimes difficult judge, but a third adversary: a witness who wants to frustrate our efforts to make points out of his or her mouth. Facing three opponents at the same time can be pretty scary. Add to this the fact that cross-examination, even in the best of circumstances, is a high-risk, high-reward game, with ever-present opportunities for humiliation and triumph.

If you've thought about all this and still have never felt sheer terror when standing up to cross-examine a witness, you're a better human than I am, Gunga Din.

One way to respond to the fearful prospects is to retreat into a hyper-cautious style of cross-examination. This is the style that counsels, "never ask a question you don't know the answer to," and "save your point for closing," and other misplaced warnings that inhibit effective cross.

A better way to respond to Fear-of-Cross is to confront the fear and defeat it with emotional calisthenics and honest introspection. That may be even more important than exercises in the techniques of cross-examination, the technical aspects of which are not hard to learn. Oliver Wendell Holmes said, "The life of the law has not been logic: it has been experience," and we can now say that the life of the cross-examiner is not logic but the confronting of our own fears. Let's explore this idea in more depth by looking at stress and self-control. Then I will focus on stress-reduction techniques, a plan for motivating success, and some thoughts on positive thinking.

STRESS, SELF-CONTROL, AND CROSS-EXAMINATION

One way to look at cross-examination is through the lens of stress. Physiological stress—pounding heart, dry mouth, trembling hands—happens when we face a threat and need to figure out a response. Fight or flight? The answer depends on whether you are facing a threat you can control. Charging rhino bearing down on you? Unlikely you will control this threat, unless you're holding a high-powered rifle. Yapping witness whose own lawyer has just said, "No further questions," and now it's your turn? Maybe.

Cross-examination is at its core something much more profound than a clash of two brains, questioner versus witness. It's a stressful body-and-brain activity that we cannot understand until we know something about the biology of stress and risk-taking, and risk avoidance too.

All humans have a basic need to reduce stress. One effective way to do that is to take control whenever you can. It doesn't matter so much how demanding your job is; if you can control the situation, you do much better with stress. High-level corporate executives typically have less stress than mid-level managers, by objective biological markers, because they have more control.

As any cross-examination starts, one basic issue involves who will control the proceedings. It's a given that the lawyer wants control; that's an instinctive, self-preserving, stress-reducing reaction to the threat that any serious cross-examination situation poses.

Another important element of control in cross-examination is the judges' and jurors' *perception* of control. Judges and jurors generally like it when *you* stay in control, as long as you seem even-handed and fair. If you keep a loose hand on the reins, you'll do much better, by and large, than if you constantly jerk the bit tightly and fight the witness forever. That attorney, by the way, has lost the battle of perception even if he technically keeps the witness from straying too far from his tightly barked commands.

Jurors who are only paying half-attention to the *content* of the cross can see and instantly judge the *context* of the back-and-forth. Who shows calmer self-control? Jurors generally see that person as the winner of the cross, as long as the answers don't blatantly contradict the perception. Who shows more stress? There shuffles the loser of the cross.

The lesson is that as hard as you work to control the witness, you must work even harder to control yourself.

One way to reduce stress as a cross-examiner is to just stop, or not even start: "No questions for this witness, Your Honor." But unless the witness hasn't hurt your case, you *must do something* to undermine the witness or the other side's case through this witness. When you stand up to do that, you are taking a risk that you will lose the match. And that thought is stressful. Your adrenal glands are squirting out cortisol, and this ancient fight-or-flight response is preparing your body to move, and fast, to either fight like hell or run as fast as your legs can carry you.

But right now your body is moving nowhere. You are in the middle of a courtroom, deciding what to do with a witness whom you now can ask any question you want. You want to venture forth in a way that takes some measured risk (otherwise you will just sit down), controls your own stress, and takes the witness where you want to go. Confronting your own internal demons is a first step to maximizing your returns by getting the right balance between risk and reward. Knowing what the witness will say is one way to stay in control and reduce stress, but that also minimizes your chances of obtaining a surprising, helpful concession from the witness. So one thing I teach in this book is plotting a cross-examination to deal with the unknown and surprising answer.

Stress plays a different, important role in cross-examination—enhancing the memory of the points you score in the brains of the jurors. They may not feel the same levels of stress that you and the witness feel in a hard-fought cross-examination. But bystanders engaged in watching verbal combat feel their own stress, and that's a good thing for us cross-examiners, because stress is the brain's memory drug. When our hearts begin to pound, our memory centers of the brain kick into work.[1] Bottom line: a cross

---

1. The studies on stress and memory (which at its extreme is the root cause of PTSD) are summarized neatly in James McGaugh's book *Memory & Emotion,*

that looks stressful, especially for the witness, is a physiologically memorable cross.

WALKING THE STRESS TIGHTROPE

How do we walk the stress tightrope, without making the cross such a low-stress event that we lose its memory-enhancing core? Here are some basic rules for modulating stress and achieving better self-control. These rules make sense when we understand the balancing act between risk, stress, and control that makes for the best cross-examination.

1. *Work hard to stay polite.* Yes, there are a few times that provocation is so bad that you have permission to drop the politeness and go bare-knuckled. But this happens less than you think. One big reason to stay polite is that it shows control and lack of stress. When you interrupt, yell, slam papers—you are showing that you've lost control over yourself. You get a big demerit, not because Miss Manners and Emily Post sit in the jury box, but because when you get mad, it looks like you're losing.

2. *Don't get mad.* See above. The general rule is this: whoever gets mad first in a cross-examination is the loser of the bout. You do have permission to get mad second, but only rarely.

3. *Keep your tone and volume even.* It's so easy to veer into sarcasm, or pump our volume up to eleven on our internal amplifier when we want to best a nonresponsive witness. Those methods don't work! When the witness grows louder, you grow softer. When the witness gets nasty, you stay even. This will help keep your stress down and show that you're the winner.

The Making of Lasting Memories (New York: Columbia University Press, 2003). McGaugh is founding director of the Center for the Neurobiology of Learning and Memory at the University of California, Irvine.

4. *Stay your genuine self.* Some lawyers like to cuddle up to an adverse witness at the start of the cross. "Good morning, Mrs. Cleaver, I hope you're having a wonderful day," oozes lawyer Eddie Haskell, with elaborate and phony sincerity. Polite is one thing; obsequious is something else. Jurors know you're there to undermine the witness, so get on with it. You can do it in a courteous, businesslike way without the fake preamble.

5. *Listen, listen, listen.* You ask a carefully honed yes-or-no question, and the witness responds with a narrative. You go into a slow burn and don't even hear the answer, you're so mad. Finally, you bark: "That was a yes-or-no question!" The witness responds, "But I was agreeing with you, counsel." Guess who just lost that exchange? The antidote: Listen to every answer, and build from the answer. Don't so obsess with tight control that you lose track of when you are getting meaningful agreement.

6. *Embrace risk in measured doses.* Throughout this book, I will show you how to take prudent risks in your cross-examinations that will get you much better results than the overcautious, risk-avoidant style that baby lawyers learn. Some level of stress, in you and the witness and hence in your bystanders, is necessary.

7. *Don't accuse the witness of lying.* Let jurors reach their own conclusions. If it's obvious the witness is lying, your accusation will add nothing, except to ratchet up everyone's stress level. If it's not obvious, you will look bad.

8. *You can start nice and finish mean, but you can never start mean and finish nice.* I stole that line from San Francisco attorney Mike Kelly. When you start mean and finish nice, you expose yourself as a phony. Let the witness give you a reason to turn mean, and it has to be something pretty flagrant, approaching out-and-out perjury. When you start nice, you are calm and in control.

9. *Hit the reset button when you feel yourself losing control over your own emotions.* Ask for a recess, pour yourself a

glass of water, whisper a few words to co-counsel—a timeout of even a few seconds usually works.

10. *Be aware of your stress level and manage it.* Pay as much attention during trial to reducing your stress level as you do to deposition digests and proposed jury instructions. There are lots of reasons for this. For starters, chronic stress is bad for your health in an amazing variety of ways, from your heart to your digestive system to your sex life. But as a cross-examiner, stress modulation is simply an important element for victory, because it makes for calmer, more in-control examinations. Figure out what works for you: jogging, meditation, a few deep regular breaths, prayer, timeouts during trial—whatever it takes to blow off the steam and bring you to calm. And once you're in that quiet place of mindfulness, you may just discover a whole new level of insight into your work.

Building a Better You, and a Better Cross-Examiner Too

The place where I want you to come out, before we get to the law stuff, is being true to yourself and true to your mission at the same time. Think about it this way.

The successful cross-examiner is:

- **Self-confident.** But self-confidence without truth is just cockiness, and reckless too.
- **Persistent.** But persistence without a worthy goal is just bullying.
- **Humble.** Because self-knowledge keeps us tethered to the ground and connected to the jury.
- **Genuine.** The sum of all the above.

Getting there is a balancing test that takes a while to master and that you must revisit in every trial, and from moment to moment within the trial.

The Winning Trial Lawyer Personality through the Ages

In his 1903 classic, *The Art of Cross-Examination*, Francis Wellman said this about lawyer personality and demeanor in the courtroom:

> The counsel who has a pleasant personality; who speaks with apparent frankness; who appears to be an earnest searcher after truth; who is courteous to those who testify against him; who avoids delaying constantly the progress of the trial by innumerable objections and exceptions to perhaps incompetent but harmless evidence; who seems to know what he is about and sits down when he has accomplished it, exhibiting a spirit of fair play on all occasions—he it is who creates an atmosphere in favor of the side which he represents, a powerful though subconscious influence with the jury in arriving at their verdict.
>
> On the other hand, the lawyer who wearies the court and the jury with endless and pointless cross-examinations; who is constantly losing his temper and showing his teeth to the witnesses; who wears a sour, anxious expression; who possesses a monotonous, rasping, penetrating voice; who presents a slovenly, unkempt personal appearance; who is prone to take unfair advantage of witness or counsel, and seems determined to win at all hazards—soon prejudices a jury against himself and the client he represents, entirely irrespective of the sworn testimony in the case.[2]

Wellman paced some of the toughest courtrooms in New York City for many decades. He must have done something right in stress control, because he lived to age eighty-seven.

---

2. Francis L. Wellman, *The Art of Cross-Examination*, (1903; repr., New York: Touchstone, 1997), 34.

SUCCESS STARTS WITH GOALS

So how do we move past the failed New Year's resolutions and begin improving our lawyerly selves? Let's look way, way outside the law for some tips: to bodybuilders. Not that I find their overly muscled bodies all that attractive, but in a society like ours bloated with an obesity epidemic, when you find a group of people who have the self-discipline to diet and exercise their way to chiseled transformations, attention must be paid. Tom Venuto, a personal trainer, wrote a popular book, *Burn the Fat, Feed the Muscle*,[3] with four steps: the second, third, and fourth of which are nutrition, cardio exercise, and weight training. No surprise there. But his first step, before all those, is mental training. I borrowed and adapted the following how-to-succeed list from Venuto and other sources:

1. Set specific, measurable goals.

    In cross-examination, this means moving beyond the vague "I want to be a better lawyer." Your goals can vary depending on the strengths and weaknesses you start with, but could include, for example, "I will get one witness within the next ___ months to admit the truth of a major element of my case." The goals need to be specific enough that you can measure results.

2. Set big but attainable goals.

    There's no sense being modest about what you want to achieve. Tiny, partial victories aren't enough. Look at some of the transcripts in this book that you want to emulate, and then do it. (And send me your own transcripts for the second edition!)

3. Set realistic deadlines, and break them down into short-term and long-term goals.

    Ask yourself: What am I going to do today to start the journey of becoming a better cross-examiner? Every day, or at least every week, you should have some specific new habit or technique you're working on. Then there are longer-term goals: every three months, or six months, or at least in

---

3. Tom Venuto, *Burn the Fat, Feed the Muscle* (New York: Harmony Books, 2013).

a year—what is the goal at each interval? Set the goals and write them down.

Some of the chapters in this book are self-contained enough to lend themselves to short-term goals. For example, chapter 6, "Using Treatises to Get to Yes," and chapter 15, "Evidence Rules Every Cross-Examiner Must Know," each gives you the opportunity to cross some technical hurdles in the Rules of Evidence. These chapters will equip you with new, specific weapons for better cross, all in the time it takes to read the chapter and try it out once or twice in your own cases. It starts with a goal as simple as, "I will learn how to effectively use an adverse witness to put in front of the jury literature quotations that help my side."

A more medium-term goal might be, "I will master the elements of 'contradictions cross' and how and when to deploy this type of cross." This requires pulling together organizational skills (chapter 7), contradictions-cross techniques (chapter 9), witness analysis (chapter 5), and witness control methods (chapter 18), so it's going to take a little longer than mastering a specific evidence rule for cross.

And a long-term goal could be, "When I stand up to cross-examine, I will feel less anxiety and more eagerness." When that happens, you will know you have absorbed some of the major lessons of this book, but it won't happen overnight.

4. Establish the emotional reasons why you want to achieve your goals.

We have both positive and negative reasons why we want to do better. A simple list for the trial lawyer could include:

» I want to avoid being humiliated when I stand up to cross-examine.

» I want to be admired.

» I want to make more money.

» I want to win more cases.

» I want to do a better job for my client in my next trial.

This list is intended to be frank, and so I'm not censoring out the less admirable goals. If we cannot be honest with ourselves, it's hard to be honest with others.

5. Write out a list of goals. Make them positive affirmations. Read them to yourself regularly.

What's the point of reaffirming our goals repeatedly and sounding them out?

Now we wax a little woo-woo: the power of positive thinking. But it happens to work. So bear with me.

Positive Thinking: It Works for Cross-Examiners Too

We all know, yet mightily resist, the truth that, to quote Pogo, "We have met the enemy and he is us." We defeat ourselves because secretly we don't think we deserve success. What other explanation is there for the choices we regularly make: to persist in bad habits, to put off to some rainy day the self-improvement that we know would make us happier than we are now? You don't have to be an apostle of Freud to know that our subconscious has a way of undermining our best intentions.

So what do we do about it? Simple:

- We change the soundtrack that loops through our brains by setting simple, concrete, positive goals.
- We put our goals in the present.
- We visualize them as having already occurred.
- We remind ourselves of them over and over.
- We let the body follow the mind.

There—I've just summarized a library's worth of self-improvement books, all of which preach the same basic message. Why? Because it's effective if you follow it. From Napoleon Hill's Depression-era classic *Think and Grow Rich*[4] to Norman Vincent Peale and motivational speakers like Tony Robbins and Zig Ziglar, all espouse the same basic secret: focusing on the positive will help you get there. We're not talking about giddy self-delusion, but making the most of what you know you have.

Takeaways

- Cross-examination is a skill that you can learn, just like judo or playing the guitar. It takes persistence, practice, and attention.
- Learning to keep your own emotions under control is even more important than learning to control the witness. The jurors' perception that you are under better self-control than the witness is key to the impression you want to create.
- The skilled cross-examiner is self-confident and persistent, yet humble. And genuine too.
- Set realistic, measurable goals concerning what you want to achieve as a cross-examiner. That applies to each witness you cross-examine, and to your growth as a better cross-examiner. Keep a positive attitude, practice, and watch yourself grow.

Exercise

Decide on a goal for improving your cross-examination in the next thirty days. Make it as specific as you can. (Suggestion: Look over the table of contents and pick a chapter that deals with something you know you're weak in. Stress and fear are a good place to start.) Stick this goal in your calendar and review it a month from now. Then set another goal.

---

4. Napoleon Hill, *Think and Grow Rich* (Cleveland: The Ralston Society, 1937).

2

Freeing Yourself from the Ten Commandments of Cross

Education: a succession of eye-openers each involving the repudiation of some previously held belief.

—George Bernard Shaw

We just learned some positive steps we can take to conquer stress and fear as cross-examiners. Now for the underside: a tour of all the demons of cross-examination advice, which we must exorcise before we can grow. Like many demons, they masquerade as something positive: in this case, as the famed ten commandments of cross-examination. They were handed down on tablets from Mount Justice by renowned law lecturer Irving Younger. He in turn had received them from other trial lawyering scribes from ages past.

Here they are:

1. Be brief.

2. Use short questions, plain words.

3. Ask only leading questions.

4. Don't ask if you don't know the answer.

5. Listen to the witness's answers.

6. Don't quarrel with the witness.

7. Don't allow the witness to repeat.

8. Don't allow the witness to explain.

9. Don't ask one question too many.

10. Save the ultimate point for closing.

Whatever religion promulgated these commandments is a joyless, repressive, down-at-the-mouth faith. The big message to the budding cross-examiner: Kid, shut up and sit down, before you make a fool of yourself.

The next thing you may notice: these are all about *how* to ask questions, not *what* to ask. In this book, I teach that the *what* of cross—that is, the strategy—is far more important than the *how*. We will come back to that many times.

Let's seek out what works in these commandments, while making careful note of what is not just wrong, but dangerous. Then I'll attempt to rewrite them in ways that I think are more helpful.

Be Brief

Insecure lawyers want firm advice. They hate it-all-depends. But the admonition to "be brief" in cross-examining witnesses is a good example of advice that is occasionally correct, but often is not, and when it's not, is dangerously wrong.

Younger's brevity tip started with an inarguable truth: juries can only absorb so much detail. So he advised cross-examiners to limit their questioning to no more than three points to undermine the witness's testimony. Why three? Well, it's as good a number as any, and to those of us who grew up with tripartite intonations like "mea culpa, mea culpa, mea maxima culpa," it's got a good beat that you can dance to.

Roy Black tells a story on Younger that shows how wrong *be brief* can be. Black is a renowned Miami criminal defense lawyer who writes an excellent blog on trial practice. Black remembers attending one of Younger's lectures years ago and being dazzled by the professor's showmanship. Younger, with his horn-rimmed glasses, comb-over hair, bow tie, Italianate gestures, and multiple voices, was an A-plus continuing education lecturer. Here was Younger's story about the virtues of the technique to *be brief*, as remembered by Roy Black:

> Younger represented the *Washington Post* when it was sued for libel by the president of the Mobil Oil Corporation. The plaintiff called a trucking executive to the stand. The trucking executive gave testimony helpful to the plaintiff. Younger's cross-examination consisted of four questions:
>
> MR. YOUNGER: Mr. Hoffman, did you just get into Washington just about an hour ago?
>
> MR. HOFFMAN: About an hour and a half, I would think.
>
> Q: Did you come up from Florida?
>
> A: No, I did not.
>
> Q: Where did you come from?
>
> A: Indianapolis.
>
> Q: How did you get from Indianapolis to Washington?
>
> A: On the Mobil corporate jet.
>
> "It was a hand grenade in the courtroom," Younger enthused, "the kind of moment a trial lawyer savors for the rest of his life."

Black's reaction, after pointedly noting that the jury went on to hand down a sizable verdict against Younger's client, was less enthused:

Okay, so the plaintiff had the witness flown in on its private jet to testify. This was one of the world's richest corporations and no doubt this is how they did business, especially when a witness was needed quickly. This was not a great benefit to the witness since he probably didn't want to testify anyway. So the point is dubious, but to make it the only impeachment of a major witness? Bizarre at best.

I agree with Roy Black's conclusion:

> Brief keeps you safe but also denies you any rewards. Perhaps one can be brief if it involves a minor case with a short witness, but it is otherwise unworkable and bad advice. When the witness batters you and destroys your case, what choice do you have except to go to war?[1]

If you really need commandments to practice cross-examination by, then *be brief* could be rewritten to *be proportional*. Mete out your cross as the testimony deserves. If the witness hasn't hurt your case, "no questions" might be the best cross. If the witness is the mother or daughter of the opposing party, then maybe one question: "You love your [son or father] and want him to win this case?" (Bear in mind, of course, that if there is one single question that you can anticipate your adversary has trained the witness to have a good response to, it's that one.) But if it's an expert witness who has just consumed most of a day telling the jury why you have no case, then you must join battle.

● The Rewrite: *Be brief* becomes *Be proportional*.

---

1. The Younger story and Black's comment both appear in Black's excellent trial lawyering blog. See "Irving Younger's Ungodly Ten Commandments," posted on July 18, 2012. http://www.royblack.com/blog/irving-youngers-ungodly-ten-commandments/.

USE SHORT QUESTIONS, PLAIN WORDS

This is good advice. Short questions have fewer escape hatches for the witness than long ones. They're also easier on the ear for everyone in the courtroom. Plain words are good words. Here might be a good place to ask why lawyers have such trouble with the plain parts of the English language. Why say, "directing your attention to the night of . . ." instead of "let's talk about the night of . . ."? What's with all the "pursuant to" and "contemporaneously" and "with respect to" that litter so many of our questions to witnesses?

My theory involves nudity—and fear thereof. Plain is naked. Plain puts us right in front of judge, jury, and witness without our protective lawyer garb. We went to law school to sound educated, right? In our defense, we're far from the only profession that uses a professional patois to distance ourselves from the lay public and justify high fees. The doctor who intones, "The patient went into cardiac arrest, with an idiopathic etiology," sounds so much finer than the one who says, "The poor guy's heart stopped, and we have no idea why." Finer, but not more persuasive. A Rutgers group studied persuasiveness of expert witnesses with mock jurors and found that technical jargon was a real turnoff for the jurors.[2] When jurors cannot understand what someone is saying, they judge credibility on what they can see and measure, and that is when side traits like timbre of voice and sculpt of chin come to the fore. Jurors have a hunger to understand what the witness is saying. When they can't, they judge the person.

So, yes, plain is naked, but if you're trying to communicate with and persuade regular folk, you need to get past the fear of public nudity.

- No Rewrite: *Use short questions, plain words* stays as it is.

---

2. Joel Cooper and Isaac M. Neuhaus, "The 'Hired Gun' Effect: Assessing the Effect of Pay, Frequency of Testifying, and Credentials on the Perception of Expert Testimony," *Law and Human Behavior* 24, no. 2 (April 2000): 149–171.

Ask Only Leading Questions

This is one of those hoary maxims of trial law passed down through so many generations that its paternity has been lost. Which is good, because it's self-evidently wrong, and I don't want to be sued for libel by the parent of the idea. A leading question is not simply a yes-or-no question. A leading question technically is one that suggests an answer.

It's a declarative statement, followed by a variation of these:

- "True?"
- "Correct?"
- "Am I right?"
- "Is that fair?"
- Or silence, coupled with a gesture or a voice inflection that tells the witness this statement has a question mark at the end.

This last type of leading question—a plain statement without "true," "correct," "right," or "fair" added on—is probably the best way to ask a leading question: most controlling and least annoying of the variations. And to be clear, I have no objection to leading questions. It's just that using them constantly and exclusively is counterproductive and impossible to achieve.

Any lawyer who tries to ask only leading questions on cross will drive everyone in the courtroom crazy and risk physical violence to his person. It's not a normal method of asking questions, at least not as an exclusive means of dialogue. If you doubt me, try it at home sometime with your spouse. After five minutes of leading questions from you followed by increasingly gape-jawed responses, you will be prostrate on the floor, and your only rejoinder then will be, "But you still love me, true?" And your spouse, if he or she is the forgiving type, will say, with flared nostrils, "True. But never do that again."

Here is another problem with an all-leading menu of questions. At least in the courtrooms where I practice, it's routine for the judge to give preliminary instructions before the first witness, one of which is to the effect that *questions from lawyers* are not evidence; only the *answers from the witness stand* are evidence. Any juror trying to follow this has a mighty struggle with all-leading questions, because the judge instructed that the only evidence is the one-word response from the witness stand. And how memorable can long strings of "yes" and "true" and "correct" ever be?

And a final problem with all-leading questioning: it's boring! Except to the lawyer and his acolytes, all of whom have the mistaken impression that the lawyer is the star of this show.

Now, there is a kernel of truth in this so-called commandment. Leading questions help direct the witness down the path you want to take and keep the witness under control. That's true at least until the witness sees an opening for a more expansive answer, which won't be long for any witness who has an IQ above room temperature. And this expansive answer tends to flummox and irritate any lawyer who hasn't considered why it's nearly impossible to confine the witness with a series of leading questions. The better solution is to be ready for the witness's predictable dodges and excursions, and have the next question ready.

Controlling the witness is a good, essential tool, of course, as I discuss in chapter 18, "Controlling the Runaway Witness." But leading questions are not and should not be the only means of exercising control. In fact, let me go out on a limb: I have seen not a single example of a real cross-examination that stretches for more than a page of transcript using only leading questions. Has anyone else? Remember, seeing it in a book of cross-examination advice doesn't count; those transcripts tend to be massaged. My point is this: The advice to ask *only* leading questions is akin to telling a lawyer to walk on water. It would be great if you could pull it off, but pretty much impossible for ordinary mortals, at least for more than three or four questions in a row.

If this chestnut was rewritten to say, *Ask simple questions with narrow answers*, it would be correct, most of the time. That means the lawyer should mostly be eliciting facts, one at a time. Yes, you can use leading questions, but never exclusively.

There is a big difference between "ask only leading questions" and "ask only narrow questions." Asking questions with only narrow answers still keeps the lawyer in charge of the back-and-forth.

But it has the added advantage of making the witness speak facts and not merely agree with the lawyer over and over. A witness impeached with his own words, and not merely agreement with the lawyer's words, is much better destroyed.

Here's an example. You're cross-examining a professional damages expert whose mission is to minimize the dollars needed to provide lifelong care for your paralyzed client. You want to show this is a lawsuit expert, not someone with substantial real-life experience helping paralyzed people. So how do you ask the question?

Old, leading-only way: "Isn't it true you have very little experience working with paralyzed people outside litigation?"

Better, simple-narrow way: "In the last _____ years, tell us how many paralyzed people you have worked with to line up medical and rehab care?"

The first, leading question is only going to buy you an argument. The second, non-leading question is going to get you a fact you can work with. Let's say the answer is "none," or "I cannot recall at this time." Now, you could have shoved the same answer down the witness's throat with a leading version, like "Isn't it true that in the last ___ years, you haven't helped a single paralyzed person get resources for their care needs?" But isn't it much better hearing that word "none" come from the witness's mouth?

A last thought on this one: The maxim, "Ask simple questions with narrow answers," is so close to the prior point to "use short questions, plain words," that we ought to combine them.

- The Rewrite: *Ask only leading questions* becomes *Ask simple, plain questions with narrow answers.*

Don't Ask If You Don't Know the Answer

Here is another wrong piece of advice that has a kernel of truth. The kernel is that it's risky to venture into areas where you have no idea what the witness is going to say. But the advice as phrased is wrong on several levels. Worse, it has caused much mischief and has set back trial lawyering.

The corollary to don't-ask-if-you-don't-know is to obsessively learn in discovery everything that the witness will say, if you're lucky enough to work in a jurisdiction that still allows discovery. This approach is responsible for the all-day depositions in civil cases that exhaust and bewilder witnesses, who wonder why the questioner kept circling around them asking if they agreed with this or that but never asked what the witness really thought. By the end of these marathons, everyone in the deposition room can see the script for the trial cross, and of course the witness and his attorney will then busily set about preparing their answers to outwit the script. These depositions are pretty boring stuff, and mostly an ineffectual tactic for the deposition taker faced with an intelligent and prepared adversary.

The other thing that makes this piece of advice wrong is something that dawns late in the game on every lawyer preparing for trial in any case of consequence: *There are questions I wish I knew the answer to, but I don't. And the opposing witness might know.*

So what do you do?

The safe, Younger-esque thing to do is surrender. Don't ask the question. It's too risky.

The better approach, which talented cross-examiners know, is to analyze the issue and figure out what the answer *must be*, based on logic, common sense, and everything else you know about the case. *Or* work out a series of questions that lead the witness to a place where his answer to the next question is fine, no matter what, because you have a good retort whichever way the witness goes.

Here's an example from Houston lawyer Jason Itkin, whose client was hurt when he slipped on an oil-slickened deck of a drilling rig in the Gulf of Mexico. By the time this witness, the rig's safety investigator, got to the scene and took photographs, the deck was clean, with just a thin film of a watery substance. The company took the position that the plaintiff had made up the story about the oil on the deck. Itkin had never deposed the witness, but he did have the witness's report and the company's manual about how to do accident investigations. Those showed him that the investigator hadn't interviewed anyone who could have cleaned the deck, that the witness had arrived at the scene hours after it happened, so there was plenty of time for a cleanup, and, in the photograph taken by the investigator at the scene, you could see the edge of a deck power washer sitting near the place where the man had slipped.

After establishing *all* these facts in his cross, it was safe for Itkin to jump to the $64,000 question. And as you will see, when he got the wrong answer, he persisted, and quickly turned the witness around. Watch:

Mr. Itkin: Can you tell us for a fact under oath here today in court that after Nigel's fall nobody came to use that hose and that power washer to clean that area?

Accident Investigator: I can tell you that 100 percent, sir.

Q: You can?

A: Yeah.

Q: Even though the fall happened at 8:15?

A: Yeah.

Q: He saw the medic from 8:20 to 8:40?

A: Uh-huh.

Q: You didn't interview him for almost three hours later?

A: Possibly.

Q: And you can tell us 100 percent for a fact that nobody used that power washer?

A: No. I can't tell you that. Nobody did. I suppose—excuse me. I will take that back. But [for] me to check the area and to say that there was oil there and somebody suggested that somebody cleaned it, I would say no. One hundred percent that that happened, I can't say that.

Q: There is a slick spot of oil there—

A: Yeah.

Q: —and someone saw it, they should clean it up, right?

A: Yeah. Sure.[3]

So there you have a lawyer using an adverse witness to eat his own words and destroy the other side's theory of the case—all by asking questions that he didn't know the answer to. Doing it this way takes courage and persistence, but most of all, a close study of the facts so you can be ready for whatever answers you get.

> The Rewrite: *Don't ask if you don't know the answer* becomes *Ask only questions that you know the answer to, OR for which you know what the answer should be, OR that you have a good response to no matter what the witness says.* Or more simply: *Ask only questions whose answers you can deal with.*

LISTEN TO THE WITNESS'S ANSWERS

I like this one. But doesn't it almost contradict the one right before it? Why do we need to listen, if we already know the answer to every question we're posing? True, if the witness blatantly contradicts what we know the correct answer to be, we must be ready to impeach the new answer. But that's not the best reason why we should listen intently to the witness's answers. The best reason is that answers given in the heat of the moment can provide the best fodder for new lines of questions.

Some lawyers mute their listen button as soon as the witness has strayed beyond the one-word answer the lawyer wanted to hear. Then they turn sour on the witness or whine to the judge for help. Then they're embarrassed when it turns out all the witness was doing was agreeing with the question, but in a narrative style instead of a narrow yes-or-no. They're also missing great fruit for follow-up.

Or, if the witness has dodged a sharp-edged question, it may be more important to follow up on the dodge and deflate it, than to pummel the witness with his failure to answer the yes-or-no.

---

3. *Bryant v. Cal Dive International Inc.*, Case No. 2011-57457, Harris County, Texas District Court, May 6, 2013.

Denver attorney Jim Leventhal did that in this exchange with a defendant doctor who had just testified that if the patient had told him the chest pain had come on suddenly, he would have ordered different tests that could have found the heart problem that killed him. When the doctor tried to blame the patient for the missing detail, Leventhal asked this:

Mr. Leventhal: But you're the doctor. You're the one that understands the significance. He comes in and says, I got this pain this morning, and I'm here, and I'm concerned. That's basically what he said, right?

Defendant Doctor: Yes.

Q: And you're the doctor. You're saying that if he had told you it was a sudden onset, that it would have made a big difference. What stopped you from asking him whether it was sudden?

A: In getting the history, I asked, When did it start? I asked the severity of it. That's where the eight out of ten came from. I asked, Does it go anywhere? In that, the patient will usually elicit—if it is there, they will tell me it was a sudden onset.

Q: I understand you don't have that written down, and you don't know whether he said sudden or not; but what stopped you from asking him anything?

A: I just knew it started that morning.

Q: But there was no reason that you couldn't have asked him, was this sudden?

A: I could have asked him, yes.[4]

See what happens when a good cross-examiner listens carefully to each answer? The witness did not directly answer the question, so asking it again kept the witness on the hook, and finally the witness admitted the key fact: *I could have asked him.*

---

4. *Epperly v. Perez,* Case No. 08CV165, 13th Judicial District, Colorado, January 15, 2009.

So yes, listening to each answer is vitally important. The entire answer. And what goes with that is to follow up when the answer hands you something to work with.

- The Rewrite: *Listen to the witness's answers* becomes *Listen to the witness's entire answer, and follow up.*

Don't Quarrel with the Witness

Another good one. We have a trend going here! But it's important to know why and also important to sense when this rule needs to be broken.

As explained in more detail in chapter 1 on self-control and stress, a quarrelsome style with the witness, especially with a polite witness, usually signals to bystanders in the jury box that you feel you are losing the match. The aphorism goes, "He whom the gods wish to destroy, they first make angry." Also, fighting with the witness and, especially, trying to cut off answers that seem responsive to everyone but you, makes you look like you're trying to hide stuff from the jury.

But if you maintain your cool composure and the witness shows clear bias or evasiveness, you can be justified in removing the white gloves. After all, juries expect a certain degree of combat in cross-examination. And better yet for our side is the knowledge from neurobehavioral research that emotion-laden memories stick much stronger in the mind than nonemotional memories. So turning up the emotional heat at judicious intervals can be very effective, especially if you have a strong point to make for the ultimate truth of your side in the case. Still, elaborate courtesy can destroy an evasive witness just as well as indignation, maybe better.

- The Rewrite: *Don't quarrel with the witness* becomes *Don't quarrel with the witness, except when it's obvious the witness really deserves it.*

And when I say "obvious," that means obvious to others on your side, not just you. You cannot trust your own sense of umbrage in the thick of combat.

Don't Allow the Witness to Repeat

This is a truism of cross-examination but one which amateurs violate. They earnestly take elaborate notes of the witness's direct testimony and then go over their notes with the witness on all the points that puzzled the cross-examiner and which the witness is now only too happy to repeat and elaborate on. The apparent tactic here is to hope that some weakness in the testimony will turn up on its own. Fat chance. So it's a decent rule as far as it goes.

The one famous exception to the no-repeat rule, written up in every cross-examination book since the 1903 edition of Francis Wellman's, is Max Steuer's cross-examination of the woman who gave vivid and elaborate testimony in the Triangle Shirtwaist Factory case about how she had seen one of the victims try to escape the fire. On a hunch, Steuer asked her to go back over one piece of her story. He saw how she mentally seemed to advance her story to that portion and then how she repeated word for word what she had said on direct. Then he asked for another, and another, and another, all with the same result, until it was obvious that the witness had memorized her story and could not deviate from it in the slightest detail.

That tactic should be rarely deployed, since it likely will work only with witnesses who show great fragility of mind, which your opponent has tried to navigate around by excessive coaching.

Still, every witness will repeat what was said on direct if you give him or her half a chance, and many cross-examiners have rued that a line of questions they found too late gave their witness a platform to say more than the cross-examiner intended.

- The Rewrite: *Don't allow the witness to repeat* becomes *Stick with narrow, simple questions that deny witnesses an opportunity to repeat their core message.*

Don't Allow the Witness to Explain

This goes with the no-repeat rule, but it's easier said than done. When the witness responds to what you thought was a careful, narrow question with a cheerful, "I disagree with you, counselor, and here's why," just what exactly does this commandment teach the cross-examiner to do? Interrupt the response and say, "I don't want your explanation; save it for when your lawyer does redirect"? Even if the judge allows your interruption, over the heated cry of opposing counsel, and allows the witness's explanation to be squashed, you haven't won that exchange in the eyes of the jury, have you? More often, the judge will allow the witness to explain the answer. And you will stand by grinding your teeth.

But here's another way to meet and defeat the explaining witness. Let me turn over the floor again to Roy Black:

> Younger says the examiner must prevent the witness from wandering from the direct question asked and add damaging comments. Of course I would love to be able to do this, as all trial lawyers would. Unfortunately, Younger fails to allow for the third party involved in the examination—the judge. As soon as you try to cut off the witness who is demanding to explain, the friendly judge always tells the witness to answer the question first then explain. Gee, thanks for nothing.
>
> The rule stipulates that the witness shall only answer the question asked, but judges rarely enforce it. Some witnesses insist on repeating their side of the story no matter what you do. Clever witnesses like experts and cops have an agenda and will take advantage of judge's laxity to beat you at your own game.
>
> The classic advice is to ask the judge for help since the answer is nonresponsive. Bad idea. This sounds like whining and defeat. Instead embrace the fight. Let the witness refuse to answer simple questions. Keep repeating the same question until you get an answer. Let the

jury see how biased they are. You will score more points with that approach than whining about the rules of evidence. And any begrudging admissions you wrest from the witness will seem even more valuable since the witness is so obviously hostile.[5]

The don't-allow-the-witness-to-explain rule also is wrong, dangerously so, to the extent it suggests you should never ask a witness to explain anything. On the contrary, some of the strongest cross-examinations set up a conflict between the witness and common sense. Then, you ask the witness to explain, which if it's a genuine weakness, the witness cannot do. A great fictional version of this is the grits scene from *My Cousin Vinny*, at the end of this chapter.

- The Rewrite: *Don't allow the witness to explain* becomes *Stick with narrow, simple questions that deny witnesses a chance to explain or to repeat their core message. If a witness insists on explaining anyway, then join battle.*

Don't Ask One Question Too Many

This tidbit might be the best known of the list and, in my opinion, the most wrongheaded. It has ruined many cross-examinations and squelched the good instincts of far too many otherwise good lawyers.

The advice often given, by Irving Younger and other supposed cross-examination experts before him, is never to ask one question too many. The idea behind the advice was that with careful and delicate questioning, the cross-examiner could set up a good argument for why the jury should discount the witness's testimony, only to see it blow up in his or her face by asking that famous one question too many, and the whole construct collapses.

Two stories, one true and one apocryphal, are often trotted out to illustrate the advice.

---

5. Roy Black, *supra* note 1 previously in this chapter, "Irving Younger's Ungodly Ten Commandments," quoted with permission.

Freeing Yourself from the Ten Commandments of Cross   39

True story: The artist Whistler was under cross-examination in his London libel trial against the art critic John Ruskin, who had written of two of Whistler's *Nocturne* paintings, "I . . . never expected to hear a cockscomb ask 200 guineas for flinging a pot of paint in the public's face."

Ruskin's lawyer to Whistler:

RUSKIN'S LAWYER: Can you tell me how long it took you to knock off that *Nocturne*?

WHISTLER: Two days.

Q: The labor of two days then is that for which you ask 200 guineas?

A: No, *I ask it for the knowledge of a lifetime.*

Ouch. Good answer, Jimmy.

Whistler went on to win the jury's verdict, for a symbolic one farthing, and Ruskin resigned his art professorship in disgust. The *Nocturne* in question subsequently sold for ten times Whistler's asking price and was given to London's National Gallery, where it hung in honor. So much for two days' labor.

Apocryphal story: A lawyer defending a man for allegedly biting off someone's ear has just established that the witness didn't actually see the defendant bite off the ear. But then the lawyer asks the fatal question:

Q: So then, how can you be so sure my client bit off the victim's ear?

A: Because I saw him spit it out.

Clever and funny, but what do these anecdotes prove? Not much. The advice against asking the one question too many suffers from at least three fatal flaws:

- First, the advice-givers forget about the right of redirect examination. If you don't ask that next fatal cross-examination question, your opponent certainly will on redirect, and then you will look even lamer than if you had asked it yourself.

- ♦ Second, the advice-givers are hindsight sages. Sure, they can see the fatal misstep reading the transcript in their lounge chairs long after the fact, but what about in real time, when you can't peek ahead to the answer to see if it was one too many?

- ♦ Third, they confuse poor strategic planning for a mere tactical error. The point of all these examples is not that the cross-examiner asked one question too many, but that the cross-examiner made a poor choice of subjects to put to the witness, trying to make a clever point whose premise was so fragile a single question could blow it up. So all the questions along that line were one too many.

And there's the heart of the issue. When we decide what to ask in our cross-examinations, we need to plan it through. We need to select only those subjects where the witness is most vulnerable, where the witness lacks the killing retort, and where the other side can't easily patch the hole on redirect. Then it doesn't matter how many questions we ask, as long as we are pounding home that one weakness.

In the James Whistler example, the questioner waded into an issue that Whistler had obviously spent a long time thinking about. The published review that he sued over had sneered at the 200-guinea price for the painting, and his whole motive for suing was to proclaim to the world, "I'm worth the prices I charge!" So of course he's going to have a smart answer to a question that focuses on the heart of his case.

The worst thing about one-too-many is it casts a pall over the entire work of any cross-examiner. It suggests we're always about to mess up, always about to lose the exchange in some disastrous way. And so we hesitate; we stop; we leave points underdeveloped. Cross-examiners need to be self-confident, not hesitant. We need to finish the point, not leave it dangling.

And what does this one-too-many nostrum say about the ethics of our profession? It's not pretty, is it? The advice suggests that cross-examiners are playing a game of trickery, fundamentally dishonest because the flimflam always risks exposure by that fateful one-too-many question, but worth trying because—well, because why exactly? I guess it's because so many cross-examiners lack the imagination and energy to work for the tough but valid points with the witness and instead play for the cheap score.

I'm far from the first trial lawyer to wonder at the staying power of Younger's commandments, especially this one. Among the most cogent critiques, Los Angeles lawyer Michael Doyen wrote:

> Time and again, Younger brings us face to face with the same unintelligible and wrong lesson: that your job as cross-examiner is, through some means Younger does not explain, to create a false appearance of weakness in the witness's testimony, and then to sit down before you inadvertently ruin it.[6]

So: We need to bury once and for all the nonsense advice to not ask one question too many. A light edit cannot save this commandment. I would delete it from the list.

The Rewrite: Don't ask one question too many becomes Don't chase cheap points on your cross that the witness or redirecting counsel can easily crush.

SAVE THE ULTIMATE POINT FOR CLOSING

This final, tenth commandment is also a bad piece of advice, depending on what it means. And that's the trouble, because it's not clear. If this commandment means only that you should not tell

---

6. Michael R. Doyen, "On Breaking Commandments," *Litigation,* Spring 2008. I commend this article to all readers for, among other things, Doyen's virtuoso effort at setting the record straight on one of Younger's best-known stories about Abraham Lincoln's last major criminal trial, *People v. Armstrong.* The future president impeached the key prosecution witness with a farmers' almanac showing that the witness could not have had a full moon on the night he claimed to have watched the defendant kill the victim. As Doyen shows, Lincoln trapped the witness by getting him to commit to a story of seeing the killing late at night without a candle and despite being 150 feet away, all because of the bright moon. Then he pulled out the almanac.

the witness in so many words that his testimony makes no sense for the following reasons, then yes, you don't need to argue ultimate points like that with the witness. But Younger seemed to mean much more. Just as with his admonition not to ask one question too many, Younger seemed to be saying that the clever cross-examiner scores points against the witness on an internal scoreboard that the witness and opposing counsel are too dumb to comprehend and fix until it's too late, and that the cross-examiner then finally explains these points to the jury with a great flourish in a triumphant closing argument. Only then it's too late. Anyone who tries this method of deliberate obscurity draws yawns and looks of puzzlement from the jury in closing.

No, the time to impress on the jury that this is a witness whom they should discredit is while the witness is still in the courtroom. Otherwise, the point will be lost in the tidal wave of facts that wash over any but the briefest of jury trials.

> The Rewrite: *Save the ultimate point for closing* becomes *Make sure the jury understands every important point before the witness leaves the stand.*

A fictitious but very "truthy" illustration of this point was made in the famous grits scene in *My Cousin Vinny*. The setup by cross-examiner Vinny Gambini is also classic for showing how a good cross-examiner closes escape hatches before springing the trap on the witness. Recall that the witness on direct placed the defendants' car at the scene of the crime, all in the five minutes that it took him to prepare his breakfast. The cross is priceless on video but pretty good on cold transcript (just put in your ear Vinny's Brooklyn twang contrasted with the witness's soft Southern drawl):

VINNY: Is it possible that two defendants enter the store, pick twenty-two specific items off of the shelves, hand the clerk money, make change, then leave, then, two different men drive up in a similar—don't shake your head yet, I'm not done, wait till you hear the whole thing so you can understand—two different men drive up in a similar looking car, go in, shoot the clerk, rob him, and then leave?

MR. TIPTON: No. They didn't have enough time.

Q: Well how much time was they in the store?

A: Five minutes.

Q: Five minutes? Are you sure? Did you look at your watch?

A: No.

Q: Oh, oh, I'm sorry, you testified earlier that the boys went into the store, and you had just begun to make breakfast, you were just ready to eat, you heard a gunshot, that's right, I'm sorry. So obviously it takes you five minutes to make breakfast?

A: That's right.

[The examiner has just locked the witness into his account requiring that everything happened in five minutes while he was fixing his breakfast. The attorney proceeds to close a couple of other escape routes on the story's plausibility.]

Q: You knew that. Uh, do you remember what you had?

A: Eggs and grits.

Q: Eggs and grits. I like grits too. How do you cook your grits? Do you like 'em regular, creamy or al dente?

A: Uh, regular, I guess.

Q: Regular. Instant grits?

A: No self-respecting Southerner uses instant grits. I take pride in my grits.

[All doors closed now. The witness has committed to having cooked regular, non-instant grits in five minutes. Time to launch the missile.]

Q: So, Mr. Tipton, how could it take you five minutes to cook your grits, when it takes the entire grit-eating world twenty minutes?

A: Um . . . I don't know. I'm a fast cook, I guess!

[Professor Younger would have left the point there, or even stopped one question sooner, once the witness has committed to regular, non-instant grits. But Vinny, as any good cross-examiner would, makes sure the jury gets the point.]

Q: I'm sorry. I was all the way over here. Did you just say you were a fast cook, that's it?

A: [No answer.]

Q: Are we to believe that boiling water soaks into a grit faster in your kitchen than any place on the face of the earth?

A: I don't know.

Q: Or perhaps the laws of physics cease to exist on your stove? Were these magic grits? I mean, did you buy them from the same guy who sold Jack his beanstalk beans?

PROSECUTOR: Objection.

JUDGE: Objection sustained.

[Okay, the sarcasm is a bit much here—hilarious on screen, not a great idea in real life. But hammering the point home with a series of questions exposing the witness's vulnerability is the commandment-violating point here, and a real-life cross-examiner could have done the same with milder yet still pointed questions. All the same, notice how, as soon as the objection is sustained, the cross-examiner asks a new question, and drills until he gets his answer.]

VINNY: Are you sure about that five minutes?

THE WITNESS: I don't know.

Q: Are you sure about that five minutes?

A: I don't know.

JUDGE: I think you've made your point.

[rapping gavel]

Q: Are you sure about that five minutes?

A: I may have been mistaken.[7]

---

7. *My Cousin Vinny*, Dir. Jonathan Lynn, Prod. Dale Launer, by Dale Launer, Perf. Joe Pesci and Fred Gwynne (Twentieth Century Fox, 1992).

Fiction, yes, but written by someone who knows what good cross-examination looks like.

Let's compare this cross-examination with Younger's list. The only commandment Cousin Vinny followed was short questions with plain words. Vinny violated every other one. All of them! He asked non-leading questions and questions he didn't know the answer to, let the witness repeat direct exam testimony, let the witness explain (in fact, insisted that the witness explain), and most spectacularly, didn't save his killer point for closing argument.

Is it time to bury these ten commandments? I rest my case.

Takeaways: Rewriting the Commandments Is Only a Start

Let's look at our rewritten list of commandments again:

1. Be proportional.

2. Use short questions and plain words.

3. Ask simple, plain questions with narrow answers.

4. Ask only questions whose answers you can deal with.

5. Listen to the entire answer, and follow up.

6. Don't quarrel with the witness, except when it's obvious the witness really deserves it.

7. Stick with narrow, simple questions that deny witnesses a chance to explain or to repeat their core message.

8. Stick with narrow, simple questions that deny witnesses a chance to explain or repeat their core message. If a witness insists on explaining anyway, then join battle.

9. Don't chase cheap points on your cross that the witness or redirecting counsel can easily crush.

10. Make sure the jury understands every important point before the witness leaves the stand.

It's a lot more nuanced than Younger's list, isn't it? I'm afraid that's the nature of this beast; there are no easy, memorable formulas that will turn you into Clarence Darrow.

Just in case you're tempted to photocopy this list and then return the book for a refund—and look, I understand, we're all busy trial lawyers looking for shortcuts—let me issue a big disclaimer: This list doesn't capture what it takes to be a good cross-examiner. It doesn't even come close. Yes, this is good tactical advice (but not a full list of all the important tactical points), and lawyers who follow this list will start doing far more vigorous, effective cross-examinations than those stuck in the Younger hyper-cautious school of cross. But tactics are far less important than the substance of what you choose to cross-examine about, and how you go about it, and how you prepare yourself. That's what the rest of this book is about.

Why spend a full early chapter tearing down the old regime? That's this chapter's final lesson. Learning why the old commandments deserve to be broken is a great beginning step in liberating you, the cross-examiner, to be the courtroom advocate you deserve to be: not slick and cheap, but smart, effective, and honest.

Exercise

Pull out one of your own cross-examination transcripts. Look for a place where you stopped short of making your point, out of fear of "asking one question too many" or wanting to "save it for closing."

- In hindsight, how realistic was your fear of finishing the point?
- Did the witness have some devastating rejoinder in her back pocket, or was your fear one of those monster-under-the-bed things?
- What more could you have done with this line of questions?

3

CHOOSING THE WEAPONS RIGHT FOR YOU

Then Saul dressed David in his own tunic, putting a bronze helmet on his head and arming him with a coat of mail. David . . . walked with difficulty, however, since he had never worn armor before. He said to Saul, "I cannot go in these, because I am not used to them." So he took them off. Then, staff in hand, David selected five smooth stones from the wadi and put them in the pocket of his shepherd's bag. With his sling in hand, he approached the Philistine.

—1 Samuel 17:38–40

We have spent the last two chapters in attitude adjustment: building a better you, with less stress and more courage (chapter 1, "Laying the Mental Foundation"), and shedding the fear-laden baggage of too-tight commandments (chapter 2, "Freeing Yourself from the Ten Commandments of Cross"). Now we finish part 1 with this chapter in which we continue to build a better you by introducing how to become a more strategic, analytical cross-examiner. I will elaborate on this system in the rest of the book, starting here, with the selection of the right weapons. And that's a lesson best introduced from one of the great stories of battle some three thousand years ago.

Learning from David versus Goliath

We lawyers love to cloak ourselves in the mantle of young David who slew the giant Goliath. But this story has a lot more to teach than the familiar set piece of a kid with a slingshot who got off a lucky strike at a bigger opponent. No, this is a story about how preparation wins battles before the first blow is struck.

A brief recap from the first book of Samuel, chapter 17: David has courage but is no fool. He volunteers for the job of fighting Goliath because he has wrestled and conquered wild beasts. He sizes up his adversary and sees a way to win, and he ignores the carping of his jealous brothers. He rejects the armor that King Saul proposes to clad him with, because it's just not David; it's cumbersome and slows him down. Instead he picks the weapon that a shepherd boy would know well—five smooth stones from a streambed. He wisely declines Goliath's invitation to fight with swords at close range, where Goliath would have the advantage. He takes one well-placed shot with his sling, then rushes up to finish the job with the adversary's own sword.

For cross-examiners, these lessons leap off the Bible's pages:

- ◆ Take an honest measure of your own skills and experience, and plunge forward only when you can see a realistic path to victory—the difference between courage and foolhardiness.

- ◆ Reject the way other people do it when it doesn't fit your own style and strengths.

- ◆ Choose the suitable weapon with great care.

- ◆ Rebuff your adversary's invitation to fight on his ground with his chosen weapons.

- Aim your first assault at your adversary's most vulnerable point.
- Make sure to finish the job.

So, what are your five smooth stones? What is the borrowed coat of armor that you need to throw off to fight and win your own battles? Let's assess the range of options for your best weapons for cross-examination. I've divided them into, coincidentally, five strategic weapons. I'll develop each with a full chapter or more. I outline these five strategic weapons below in "Five Core Strategies for Cross-Examination."

In this chapter, I give an overview. First I'll sketch out each strategy and what it aims to accomplish. I'll show the simple goal that all these strategies share, which, once reached, lets you know you've finished the job. Then I will sketch out the method to set up and execute the strike, one that works with any of the strategies. I will also discuss how different strategies blend together and how to use the Rules of the Road system for a highly successful cross-examination. But for now, let's look at our five core strategies.

THE FIVE CORE STRATEGIES FOR CROSS-EXAMINATION

All of cross-examination tries to either build our own case through the adverse witness, or tear down the witness's credibility. We can accomplish this in one of five ways. Each strategy is distinct but readily combines with others. Here they are.

Strategy 1: Build the Case by Seeking Agreement

Unlike David, we cross-examiners aren't necessarily trying to slay the person on the witness stand. Our target must always be the adverse party lurking behind this witness. Sometimes the most effective way to slay the adverse party is to recruit the witness to our side, at least with enough key agreements that we create an impression in the courtroom that the witness has defected to our side. So that's our Strategy 1: building our case by showing that the other side's witness agrees with important parts of our case.

For Strategy 1, the Rule is whatever the specific behavior rule for that case is. We want to show that the defendant violated some accepted behavioral norm that had bad consequences for the plaintiff.

Here are some examples:

- A surgeon should not cut something until he knows what it is.

- An employer must not fire an employee before hearing the employee's side of what happened.

- A trucking company must not put a big-rig driver on the road without first checking the driver's safety history.

These Rules follow this format:

- "A [type of defendant, such as product manufacturer, hospital, government agency] [should or must] [do or not do] [type of behavior]."

Good Rules have four essential attributes: they are clear to the jury, hard for the witness to quarrel with, provably violated by the defendant, and important to the case outcome. You can focus these Rules on the defendant's bad behavior that caused the initial harm, or aim them at the defendant's lawsuit strategy (hiding evidence or falsely minimizing the harm caused to the plaintiff, for example). I will say much more about the basic method for developing case-building Rules in the next chapter.

Why is this Strategy 1 in the arsenal of five? Because every witness comes into a trial with a sponsor: our side, or the other guy's. Jurors naturally expect that each side will bring to court only the strongest witnesses supporting that side, especially with paid experts. When one side's witness wavers under cross and starts to agree with important pieces of the other side's case, the logical conclusion is that the side that sponsored the witness must have a pretty weak case, if this is the strongest witness they could find. So a point for your side counts a lot more if you can make it through an adverse witness in cross-examination than the same point made through a friendly witness on direct.

The next four strategies are all about *tearing down* the witness's credibility. The Rules of the Road approach lets us spell out some witness-focused Rules that help execute these strategies. We announce the Rule, get the witness to agree with it, then show that the witness doesn't measure up to the Rule she has just endorsed. Unlike Strategy 1, where the Rules are all specific to the case, you can formulate your witness-focused Rules in all-purpose language that you can tweak from case to case. Each strategy singles out a specific type of weakness in the witness, and the goal is to create an impression with the jury that the witness has one or more of these four weaknesses and thus should not be believed.

Strategy 2: Show the Witness Doesn't Fit

The impression we seek to create with this strategy is that the witness lacks important qualifications to help the jury understand the case. These qualifications can be credentials, training, day-to-day experience, and other elements of an expert's background. For a nonexpert lay witness, this can be the witness's lack of ability to know what's important in the case. The witness can be *unfit*—not having enough of the right credentials, or they can be a *misfit*—having too much of the wrong credentials. Whichever, they're not right for the jury's trust as an expert guide for this case.

Here is the all-purpose Rule that helps us create that *lack of fit* impression on the jury:

- An expert witness must have deep experience and knowledge about what's important in the case.

What if the witness has a lot of experience and knowledge, but it's dated? For example, the witness is a surgeon who hasn't seen the inside of an operating room for a decade or more? Or her board certification is grandfathered and she has never sat for the recertification test that everyone else in the field takes? Then we can tweak our *lack of fit* Rule like this:

- An expert witness must be current in the expert's field.

Or here is a sharper version, if you can show some fudging in the way the other side has brought out the expert's credentials on direct examination:

- An expert witness must not exaggerate how current his credentials are.

Strategy 3: Show the Witness Is Ignorant or Makes Mistakes

We want to give the jury the impression that here is a witness who doesn't know important things that she should know. The witness claims to have read everything and comes to the witness stand to distill it down to the essentials for the jury. If she cannot get her facts straight, what value does she give the jury?

That makes for a simple Rule that the witness has to agree with:

- An expert witness must know the important facts of the case.

Note the operative language: "important facts," not trivial ones. It won't work for us to obtain the witness's agreement with the "important facts" Rule, then proceed to show a bunch of inconsequential facts that the witness has not committed to memory. Try this, and you'll create an impression with the jury that you don't want them to have: *Here is a cross-examiner who nitpicks silly points. He must have a weak case if that's the best he can do.*

But if you have important facts that the witness doesn't know or has gotten wrong, this can be a courtroom-shaking strategy, as we'll see when I give an example of execution later in this chapter.

Strategy 4: Show the Witness Is Biased

Again, the impression we seek to create is simple: the witness shades the truth or tells out-and-out lies because of ties to the other side, self-interest, or some other lack of objectivity. And the all-purpose Rule is this:

- An expert witness must be objective, fair, and impartial.

You say: Too obvious. Tell me something I don't know. Here's the problem: countless cross-examiners have assailed expert witnesses for bias but come up short for the simple reason that they failed to first get the witness to agree to this Rule of expert witness conduct. The lawyers, the judge, the witness, everybody in the courtroom knows this Rule, except the jury. Jurors could well assume that if one side is paying an expert a lot of money, the expert should drop any pretense of objectivity and become a naked advocate. The Rules method bridges this disconnect by making sure everyone in the courtroom is on the same page when we launch this strategy of cross.

Again, we have a good all-purpose Rule, but there are plenty of tweaks for the right circumstances. Let's say, for example, the expert has a connection to the other side that he or she did not disclose on direct examination. Then the Rule you announce as you begin your cross could be something like this:

- An expert witness must disclose all conflicts of interest.

Can you see it now? Gulp, bobs the witness's Adam's apple, as we launch this weapon.

Strategy 5: Show the Witness Contradicts Himself

The Rule for this strategy can take different forms, depending on what it is the witness is contradicting. The one we usually think of is the witness's own prior testimony. Other fruitful sources of contradiction include the witness versus another key witness on his side, the witness in court versus the way the witness works in the real world, or the witness versus his profession's authoritative literature. If it's the witness versus his or herself, the Rule could be as follows:

- An expert witness should be consistent in his or her opinions.

Or

- An expert witness should give the same opinion in court that he or she would give outside of court.

The impression we look to create: there are so many contradictions between the witness and himself, or between the witness and the key players on the other side, or between the witness and the way the world works, that the witness cannot be believed.

This is a tough hurdle. Every human has little inconsistencies and contradictions, and juries tend to forgive a lot of that. To show someone has too many contradictions to be believed takes persistence, a mastery of detail, and as a cross-examiner, you must know the difference between chaff and wheat. That is why contradictions for the sake of contradictions is the last of our five strategies: it's always difficult, often tedious, and too many times falls flat.

There is an entirely different kind of contradictions cross that has more promise. In this one, we care little about the inconsistency; what we focus on instead is showing that what the witness said or did before coming to court is what the jury should believe is true, because it lines up with our case. This is a branch of Strategy 1, case-building cross.

Launching the Weapon, and Knowing When to Stop

Once we've chosen a weapon from among the five just described, we can use a Rules of the Road method to launch any one of them. The steps are straightforward:

1. Create a good Rule, either one specific to the case, or one of the all-purpose witness Rules from among those we've just sketched. Any good Rule has four essential attributes.

    » The Rule is clear.

    » The defendant or witness can't argue with the Rule.

    » The Rule is important to the outcome of the case or the credibility of the witness.

    » The defendant or witness violated the Rule.

2. Announce the Rule and get the witness to agree.

3. Explain why the Rule is important.

4. Show that the defendant (Strategy 1) or the witness (Strategies 2 through 5) broke the Rule.

To keep a witness from slipping out of your snare, this last critical step sometimes means first locking in the witness's version, then showing how the witness violated the Rule. That especially applies to two of our strategies: Strategy 3, show the witness is ignorant or makes mistakes, where you usually have to lock in the witness's mistake first, and Strategy 5, show the witness contradicts himself, where you also need to lock in the witness's current version before showing the contradiction. Other times, you don't need to first elicit anything from the witness to prove the witness is, say, biased or unfit for the case.

Once launched, then what? How do you know when to keep going? How many different lines of attack do you try? The basic answer: *Keep going until you've created the impression you want to leave with the jurors.*

When to stop? That is the perennial question for each line of questions we unleash. As we learned in chapter 2, "saving the point for closing" is usually a terrible idea, one that will make sure the jury is mystified by your closing argument as you pull out snippets of transcript from here and there and try to explain how you crushed this witness and that. The better tactic is to make sure the jury understands each point while the witness is still on the stand. That doesn't necessarily mean you have to get to the ultimate point of proving a violation of the Rule. But sometimes you do want to go all the way.

Let's look at what impressions mean, why they're important, and how they guide the length of our cross-examinations.

A Battle of Impressions, Not Logic

Throughout this book, you will see me asking this: what *impression* are we trying to create of this witness, at this moment, with this line of cross? That's because cross-examination is a battle of impressions, not logic. Paul Luvera of Seattle, a wise man of the plaintiffs' bar, teaches this critical concept, which is so hard for logic-trained lawyers (me included) to accept. The fact is that all human beings reach judgments about what and whom they believe based on intuitive impressions that shortcut logic. Then, we often use the logical parts of our brains to justify and articulate the judgment we already reached using the inarticulate "my gut tells me" part of the brain.

This is the core lesson of Nobel Prize winner Daniel Kahneman's must-read book, *Thinking, Fast and Slow*.[1] The human brain has two cognitive modes, each with its own style: *fast*—intuitive, emotional, and hot; *slow*—deliberative, logical, and cool. As Kahneman teaches, our deliberative brains are also lazy, and when faced with a deliberative question, we often switch to the intuitive brain without even realizing it.

This means that our intuitive brains toss out hard, deliberative questions in favor of easier, intuitive ones.

- *Logical question*: Is the witness correct about what the standard of care is for engineers, architects, or doctors?
  - » *Substituted, intuitive question*: Does this witness look trustworthy?
- *Logical question*: Was there enough light that night for the witness to see who did it?
  - » *Substituted, intuitive question*: Does the witness sound sure of himself?

For cross-examiners, this means our most important goal is to create a coherent impression for this witness in the jurors' minds—to replace the intuitive impression they may have already formed from the direct exam. That doesn't mean we cross-examiners should toss logic out of our toolboxes. Often the single most persuasive way to knock off the witness's halo is to show his or her testimony doesn't add up logically, or is factually wrong on a key point.

---

1. Daniel Kahneman, *Thinking, Fast and Slow* (New York: Farrar, Straus & Giroux, 2011).

An "Independent" Medical Examiner Self-Destructs

So let's see how this method played out in a real case. Remember, here's the plan:

1. Create a good Rule: clear plus inarguable, important, and the defendant or the witness broke it.
2. Announce the Rule and get the witness to agree.
3. Explain why the Rule is important.
4. Show that the defendant or witness broke the Rule.

We don't have to follow all of these steps with each Rule and each witness, but powerful cross happens when we execute all of them. Here's an example from Colorado attorney Jim Gilbert, which shows a deft execution of Strategy 3: exposing a witness who is ignorant or makes mistakes. In this case, the witness gets important facts wrong.

Gilbert's case concerned his client's serious shoulder injury in a car wreck. The witness, a retired orthopedic surgeon, had done the usual one-two: a quick superficial examination of the patient and a light skimming of the patient's medical records. Not surprisingly, he opined that the accident had nothing to do with the patient's lingering shoulder problem. Gilbert set up the cross neatly by announcing a Rule of the Road about the witness's testimony that the witness had to accept.

MR. GILBERT: Do you think it's—do you believe that an expert coming into court testifying in a case like this has an obligation to get the facts straight?

EXPERT WITNESS SURGEON: I do.

Q: Because otherwise, the ladies and gentlemen of the jury are going to be asked to do something, they have a job to do, and if they don't have all of the facts or there's misstatements, they can't do their job correctly, can they?

A: Correct.

The witness then started to fall apart as Gilbert showed his multiple errors of fact and, as a bonus, his cavalier attitude. Gilbert executed the cross methodically.

Steps one, two, and three: With two quick questions, Gilbert had whipped through the first three steps of the technique. Gilbert got the witness to agree with the Rule that he as an expert must get the facts straight. He showed it was important, not just in some abstract way, but concretely to the jury's job. Note how the jurors' ears will naturally perk up when they hear a question that directly invokes the job they have to do in the jury room.

Step four, lock-in phase: Lock in the witness's version of the facts. In this case, the timing of the complaint of shoulder pain was key to understanding if it related to the accident. (Note there are two phases to step four: lock-in and violation.)

Expert Witness Surgeon: To the best of my memory, I think he started having pain two days afterward.

Mr. Gilbert: Okay. So the day he is taken—he was taken by ambulance, right?

A: Yes.

Q: The day he was taken to the hospital by ambulance after this crash, he had no shoulder pain, and then two days later had shoulder pain at night?

A: Yes.

[*Step four, violation phase:* Show the witness and the jury that the witness is wrong, through documents the witness had easy access to:]

Mr. Gilbert: And why don't you read to the ladies and gentlemen what the doctor, the radiologist, noted as the history [on the day of the accident].

Expert Witness Surgeon: It says left shoulder pain and rib pain, as well as back pain.

Q: Now, that was information that was available to you when you did this report, correct?

A: Correct.

Q: Did anyone call that to your attention when you filed this report with the court?

A: No.

[Gilbert then showed another of the witness's factual errors, based this time on the witness's assumption about what a record he hadn't seen would have shown. And he asked the witness an open-ended, commandment-violating "why" question, that the witness then flunked spectacularly:]

Mr. Gilbert: But if you know there is an evaluation and you characterized the evaluation, why don't you pick the phone up and say, "I want the record; I want to look at what the record says"?

Expert Witness Surgeon: I did not do that.

Q: Okay. Do you think you should have?

A: I don't think I should have, no. It's usually nonproductive, it's a waste of time, and the records are as they are.[2]

There you have a witness taking a pair of scissors to his own nose, through a question—*Do you think you should have?*—that broke two of the usual rules of cross: it was a non-leading question, and the questioner didn't know the answer. It worked because there was no good answer to why the witness hadn't sought out the missing facts. The only better answer the witness could have given for himself would have been to confess error and apologize for the mistake. Few paid expert witnesses want to admit they are wrong, especially the ones with fragile egos, so paradoxically they choose a nonadmission, which is actually worse for them, because they come off as callous and indifferent to the truth. And that is the ultimate impression that Jim Gilbert created of this witness, with a logical, tightly structured cross that shrewdly exploited the witness's sloppy work and overweening pride.

Now, just because there are four steps here doesn't mean it's a rigid lockstep deal, and it definitely doesn't mean you must execute

---

2. *Coburn v. Stevinson Chevrolet West Inc.*, Case No. 10CV9934, Denver County, Colorado District Court, April 25, 2012.

all four steps with each cross. Do not write these steps on your own flesh. Instead, just grasp the basic outline and then appreciate the different ways you can flexibly employ the method.

One key step that you usually should not skip is the setup, the announcement of the Rule. That's what puts everyone in the courtroom—you, witness, jury, judge—on the same page. Let's look at an example.

Setting Up the Rule or Norm as Step One of an Effective Cross

When you want to use an adverse witness to show that the defendant has violated a behavioral norm that hurt your client (Strategy 1, agreement cross), the setup can take a lot of back-and-forth. Or it can be as quick as this example, from Tampa attorney Steve Yerrid, cross-examining a college football coach allegedly responsible for a player's collapse and death at an overly rigorous practice session:

Mr. Yerrid: Would you agree with me that to withhold water from a student athlete engaged in an exercise would be a reckless act? Yes or no.

Defendant Coach: It wouldn't be a very responsible act.

Q: That's not what I asked. If an athlete was in need of hydration, would it be a reckless act to withhold hydration from a student athlete involved in a supervised exercise activity on your watch? Yes or no.

A: Yes, it would be.[3]

Notice that Yerrid phrases his questions in the frame of "recklessness," which was the legal norm he had to hurdle to win the case. Also note that he uses the witness to set up his general Rule but doesn't go on to prove the violation with this witness. The coach's

---

3. *Plancher v. University of Central Florida Board of Trustees*, Case No. 2009-CA-007444-O, 9th Judicial Circuit, Florida, June 23, 2011.

defense was "not my fault" and "I didn't know." This was a situation where the coach, to look like a good responsible person, had to undermine his own side's case by agreeing to the plaintiff's general liability theory.

Blending the Five Weapons

Remember, the question we cross-examiners must always ask ourselves is, what kind of impression are we trying to create of this witness? As we've seen, that applies to how long we hammer a particular strategy, and it applies even more when we start to look at blending more than one strategy with the same witness.

The first thing to notice is the key difference between case-building agreement cross, Strategy 1, and the other four strategies. Strategy 1 sends a clear message to the jury: yes, you can believe this witness; just look at how she agrees with our case! Strategies 2, 3, 4, and 5 all send the opposite message: don't believe this witness! So it can be perilous to try to mix these witness tear-down strategies with Strategy 1, because we risk sending contradictory signals. Do we like this witness or not? If we have good reasons that we can show the jury for finding the witness reliable one way but not others, that's fine, but if not, we risk looking like we're arbitrarily picking and choosing when we try to endorse what the witness is saying in one way but tear down his credibility elsewhere.

Sequencing can be a key consideration here. Let's consider a cross that starts with Strategy 1. The witness gives up some great points for your case, right out of the gate of your cross. Why would we ever then segue to an attack on the witness's credibility? It's like welcoming a defector, who brings valuable intelligence from the other side, with a swift kick in the pants. But what if it's a witness we know will be reluctant to "turn" our way, but whom we also know has some good agreement points with our side? Then we might start with a bias cross (Strategy 4) before turning to the agreement. When the witness fights hard to avoid concessions, then you can say later, "See, even a biased witness had to agree with our case, because it's that strong."

Case-building cross can also harmonize well with the ignorant witness, at least if the mistake is an honest one. Then you can show that but for the witness's error, she would agree with our case.

What if it's a witness who will give up nothing in agreement with our case? Then we have no choice but some combination of the witness tear-down strategies: lack of fit, bias, ignorance, and contradictions. These can work well with one another, depending again on the impression we're looking for.

For example:

- The witness who gets his facts wrong over and over, because of the biased way he looks at the case.
- The witness whose qualifications don't fit this case, and because of that, makes a lot of mistakes.
- The biased witness who will say anything, and thus has lots of contradictions, but only if you catch him.

Both bias and contradictions are hard-core assaults on the witness's truth-telling. Ignorance and lack of fit, on the other hand, don't necessarily attack the witness's integrity, and thus you can deploy them with a softer touch.

Example: Bias and Mistakes Cross

Here's an example of the launching of a "biased witness makes a lot of mistakes" cross I did of an expert witness in a malpractice case. The witness, a specialist in newborn baby care, wanted to opine that something out of the control of the doctor delivering the baby had happened to cause the baby's brain injury.

MR. MALONE: Sir, you agree that your job is to be objective?

EXPERT NEONATOLOGIST: That is correct, yes.

Q: You are not, it wouldn't be appropriate for you to cherry-pick certain little pieces of evidence from the record and ignore other things that just inconveniently don't fit with your opinion. Right?

A: No, I don't think I have done that in this review, no.

Q: It wouldn't be right, would it?

A: It wouldn't be right, no, sir.

Q: It wouldn't be right to misread things in the record and draw inappropriate conclusions from them, would it?

A: That's correct.[4]

With that setup, I then showed how his opinion had violated the Rules he agreed with: he ignored inconvenient facts, took other facts out of context, and was just plain wrong on some of what had happened. I have omitted that follow-up transcript here, because it gets deep into the weeds of the facts of that case. Like many cross-examination examples that I've had to truncate for the book, this one needed to spool out for some distance in real time because to make my point that the witness had broken the Rule, I needed to show a pattern, not just a few instances that could be written off as nitpicks.

TAKEAWAYS

I've now sketched the five basic ways we can build up our own case or tear down the witness. Each technique starts with you, the cross-examiner, studying yourself, the case, and the witness, to see which method or combination best fits the unique circumstances. We use the Rules of the Road method to set up clear impressions we want to create of the witness, and we see how far we need to go to create those impressions. Thus we cut through the fog of war, the thousand lumpy facts that clog any trial, and prove that our client is entitled to win.

---

4. *Simpson v. Roberts*, Case No. CL04-213, City of Roanoke Circuit Court, Virginia, May 16, 2012.

Exercise

Look at one of your own transcripts again. Did you have an overall impression you were trying to create for jurors of this witness? How successful was it? How could you have improved the execution just by first articulating the goal in your own mind? Were there other angles of attack that might have filled out the impression of the witness you wanted to show?

PART II

Building the Case with Cross-Examination

Now it's time to build on the foundation we just laid with a detailed study of our first and most important cross-examination strategy: Building the Case by Seeking Agreement. Part 2 has three chapters:

- Chapter 4, "Cross-Examination with Case-Building Rules," starts with how to construct the case-specific rules that we can force a witness to agree with, that mean our client deserves to win.

- Chapter 5, "Witness Self-Interest and Case-Building Cross," turns to a study of the witness's self-interest and how that can be deployed to better win agreement.

- Chapter 6, "Using Treatises to Get to Yes," applies case-building cross to the important subject of bringing authoritative treatises into evidence, which when done right, adds the treatise author as a witness for our case.

4

CROSS-EXAMINATION WITH CASE-BUILDING RULES

One must know the limitations of force; one must know when to blend force with a maneuver, a blow with an agreement.

—Leon Trotsky

I will focus in this chapter on how we develop case-building Rules of the Road and win the other side's agreement, however reluctant, with them.

Just to be clear, let's add some definitions.

- *Case-building* means focusing on actual events that happened in the case—cars that collided, nerve that was cut, crates of books that landed on a client's foot—and building the liability or damages of our case.

- *Witness-tear-down* means attacking the witness's credibility.

Developing case-building Rules was the focus of the Rules of the Road method first devised by my coauthor Rick Friedman for proving liability in insurance bad-faith lawsuits. The two of us expanded the method to other difficult, complex civil lawsuits. In the first two books,[1] the Rules method mainly centered on establishing agreed Rules that were central to the liability issues of the case—rules like these:

- An insurer must help its policyholders with their claims [for a first-party bad-faith case].

- A surgeon should cut only when he knows what he's cutting [a surgical misadventure case].

- An accountant must stay current with tax rules [accounting malpractice].

- An employer must listen to an employee's side of the story before firing [employment wrongful discharge case].

But Rules also can apply to damages issues, or anything else important to the outcome of your case, as we'll see.

Here the dutiful author cues up the organ grinder and tells readers that they really, really should buy both previous books in the Rules of the Road series, because the author couldn't possibly summarize the method adequately in just a few paragraphs here. I agree with that, but I also want to give readers a single volume to work with, so here goes a nutshell description.

Rules of the Road Overview

A case-building, liability-focused Rule of the Road is generally defined as a should-or-must statement in which the defendant is the actor. Here's an example: "A [type of defendant] should-or-must do [type of conduct]."

---

1. Rick Friedman and Patrick Malone, *Rules of the Road: A Plaintiff Lawyer's Guide to Proving Liability*, 2nd ed. (Portland, OR: Trial Guides, 2010); Patrick Malone with Rick Friedman, *Winning Medical Malpractice Cases: With the Rules of the Road Technique* (Portland, OR: Trial Guides, 2012).

The Rule also needs to meet these four attributes:

1. The Rule is clear.

2. The defendant can't argue with the Rule.

3. The Rule is important to the outcome of the case.

4. The defendant violated the Rule.

If the Rule doesn't meet all four requirements, you need to rewrite it, because otherwise the defendant slips off through one of these four escape hatches that you have failed to close and latch.

Bear in mind that if you're on the other side of the case, all you need is to substitute "plaintiff" for "defendant" in the above description, and you can devise good rules to attack the plaintiff's conduct, when appropriate, or that of some nonparty actor for whom you're trying to prove a share of fault.

Good rules come from jury instructions, professional literature, product instruction manuals, statutes and regulations, case law, company policy and procedure manuals, contracts (such as those between the defendant and whoever hired the defendant to do the job), other sources of standards for proper conduct, and, perhaps most importantly, common sense.

In professional malpractice cases, for example, you seldom see in textbooks plain-English, common-sense rules like, "A surgeon must know what he's cutting," or "A lawyer suing someone must identify the right defendant in the complaint." But these rules are inarguable for any semi-honest defendant. And if they're provably violated and were important enough that the violation led to someone getting hurt, you have a good Rule for the case-building, liability-focused part of the case. These liability rules boil down to a set of norms about how the defendant should have acted to prevent foreseeable harm to people like the plaintiff.

Devising a good, escape-proof Rule of the Road for the liability of a case is not always easy. Many times you need to test-drive Rules at depositions of opposing parties and their experts, then take them back to the shop, tinker with them, and bring them back out with new words. Words matter, a lot. As Mark Twain reminded us, "The difference between the almost right word and the right word is really a large matter—'tis the difference between the lightning-bug and the lightning."

From Principles to Rules, from General to Specific

Rick Friedman and I coach attorneys to start with *principles*, then move to *rules*.

- A *principle* is a description of the world the way people think it is.

- A *rule* is what someone should or must do, given the way the world is.

Rules logically flow out of principles. For the types of cases we typically work on, principles focus on recognizing safety risks, and Rules are the behavior norms that seek to avoid those risks, causing harm to the people we represent. So, principles are descriptive; Rules are prescriptive.

We also coach to start with the general and move to the specific. Both of these directional tactics—from general to specific, and from principles to Rules—apply with special force to cross-examination, because it's much easier to win agreement with ideas at a high level of generality, which then form the foundation for forcing agreement to more case-specific Rules.

Here's an example from a malpractice case where a doctor failed to learn key features of what was wrong from talking with the patient.

Principles:

- The patient's history—"his story"—is key.

- History may have the most important clues of all to what's wrong.

- No technology can ever replace what the patient communicates about what it feels like, how it's different than before, how it's changed over time.

- It's easy to miss important clues when the doctor doesn't listen carefully.

Therefore, the Rule follows:

- A doctor must listen carefully to the patient's history.

In the above case, the Rule works if we know the patient said something and the doctor somehow missed it. Typically, some other provider around the same time got the correct history.

Every case is different, and a slight variation of the case just described shows how wording is so important, and why each case needs its own custom set of Rules. No prefab work, please!

Let's say we have a different issue of doctor-patient miscommunication. The defendant says in deposition, "I agree with your Rule. I did listen carefully. Unfortunately, the patient didn't convey the history that would have changed my whole course of treatment." Unlike the previous case, in this one we don't have another provider's records handy to prove that the patient did tell some other doctor the key facts around the same time. So we write a new set of principles and a new rule, like so:

Principles:

- The patient doesn't know everything that's medically important.
- It's not the patient's fault for the doctor missing something unless the doctor specifically asked.
- It's the doctor's job to ask good questions and listen carefully.

The Rule follows:

- The doctor must ask the right questions and listen carefully to the patient's answers.

The doctor who escapes liability under the first framing of the Rule—*A doctor must listen carefully to the patient's history*—because the plaintiff cannot prove the defendant violated that rule, now loses to the "doctor must ask the right questions" Rule. Now we have a Rule that meets all four of our requirements:

- Clear
- Inarguable
- Important to the case
- Violated by the defendant

So tightly worded, case-specific Rules are critical to success with the Rules method.[2]

Clear Plus *Inarguable* Equals Strong Start

Another place where a lot of lawyers falter when they start to use the Rules method is in not appreciating the difference between a *clear* Rule and an *inarguable* one. Any good Rule of the Road must fit both criteria. The *clear* part focuses on the jury; the Rule must be something any layperson can understand without further translation. The *inarguable* part focuses on the defendant; the Rule must be something the defendant or a defense expert—often with lots of squirming and wiggling—acknowledges to be true. Devising a Rule that is both clear *and* inarguable bridges the chasm between a lay audience and the professional whom the laypeople are judging. We usually counsel to start with an inarguable Rule, and then make it clear, rather than the other way around, because if the Rule is clear but cannot be made inarguable, no amount of clarity will save it. On the other hand, inarguable Rules can usually be honed into clear ones just by writing good English prose.

Here, again in the medical setting, is a Rule that's clear but not inarguable:

> A family doctor must make sure his patient gets follow-up tests recommended by a specialist.

---

2. In chapter 16, "Calling the Adverse Party," you will see that adroit and persistent questioning by Jim Leventhal got the defendant in his case to admit he had violated this Rule by not asking the patient the right questions. (Jim didn't call it a "Rule" in his cross, but got to the same place with old-fashioned "standard of care" language.)

The defendant's response: "No sir, not my job; that's the patient's job." The rewrite that makes it both clear *and* inarguable shifts to a different aspect of the doctor's duty:

- A family doctor must follow his patient's medical issues.

In the case where I devised the correctly phrased rule, the defendant had to admit he had forgotten to follow one key medical issue that ended in his patient's death. His obligation to follow his patient's medical issues was plain from the preprinted cover sheet of his records that had blank spaces for filling in all the patient's medical issues, key lab results, vaccinations, and specialist referrals.

Now let's give another example to show how it's easier to go from inarguable to clear than from clear to inarguable. Another medical case: here's a Rule that's inarguable but not necessarily clear, at least to laypeople on a jury:

- A surgeon must tell the patient the risks and benefits of the proposed procedure and obtain the patient's informed consent.

Sure, that's a correct statement of the law of informed consent, and no doctor can argue against it. Yet a lot of jurors will misunderstand it because they have the incorrect notion that informed consent is all about signing what amounts to a waiver form, and once the patient does so—end of case. Here's the rewrite to make this inarguable Rule clear:

- A surgeon must tell the patient the important facts so the patient can make an intelligent decision.

See the difference? Now the case is framed within the jurors' world, not the world of doctors and lawyers.[3]

So clear plus inarguable Rules are a must for a successful use of the Rules method to win liability.

Now, those are some basics. If you need more on how to write Rules, plus examples of successful Rules of the Road in a

---

3. I'll show an example of using this rule in a real case in the last section of this chapter, "Example Three: Agreeing to the Liability Rule and Its Violation."

variety of liability situations, and how to use Rules in opening statements, direct examinations, and closing arguments, go get the book! Better yet, get both! In this book, we will focus only on using case-building Rules in cross-examining the adverse party and the other side's expert and lay witnesses.

DAMAGES: MORE GOOD RULES FOR AGREEMENT CROSS

Every civil lawsuit has other realms besides figuring out whether the defendant did something wrong and hurt the plaintiff. For example, an important question concerns damages: What is the fair remedy, usually in an amount of dollars?

Creative lawyers will see ample opportunities for developing good Rules in both realms. We shouldn't limit ourselves to liability issues in putting forward good Rules that the other side must agree with.

On damages in a personal injury case, for instance, here are some case-building, agreement-seeking Rules straight out of the standard jury instructions:

- Plaintiff is entitled to be "made whole" to the closest measure that money can achieve—a sum that "balances out" (compensates) for everything plaintiff has experienced because of this injury.

- Plaintiff is entitled to a sum of damages that fully pays for all plaintiff's lifetime care needs caused by this injury.

- Defendant must be assessed a sum of money that fully pays for all of plaintiff's lost time from work, past and future.

Profession-specific standards like those from the International Academy of Life Care Planners can flesh out these general damages Rules.[4] For example (and this is a generous paraphrase, but your own expert should endorse the idea):

---

4. The IALCP's 2009 Standards of Practice was downloaded from: http://www.rehabpro.org/sections/ialcp/focus/standards/ialcpSOP_pdf.

- The plaintiff is entitled to all services needed to restore his or her health and functioning to the same level it was before the injury. The goal is to optimize the plaintiff's outcome—to get as close as possible to never having had this injury.[5]

Using Case-Building Rules in Cross-Examination

We saw in the last chapter, in Steve Yerrid's cross of a football coach, that you can accomplish an agreement cross on liability Rules in as little as one or two questions, depending on how central the Rule is to the case and how tightly you word your questions. Here are three more examples of case-building Rules in cross-examination. In the first two examples, we will see that the questioner uses the witness only to set up and affirm the Rule, then proves the violation through other evidence. In the third example, we will show both Rule setup and Rule violation through the same witness. In each, the witness agrees with Rules very much at odds with the position of the party who called the witness to the stand.

- **Example one** comes from a workplace injury case where attorney Jason Itkin examined a corporate spokesperson. The witness had been called on direct to minimize the plaintiff's damages by claiming he could actually make higher pay with the injury than without. Itkin had the imagination to take the witness to the endpoint of his own argument, and showed the witness agreeing to repudiate his own company's lawsuit tactics.

- **Example two** showcases the work of Tennessee attorney Randy Kinnard, exploring with an adverse medical expert the core meaning of the doctor-patient relationship: a patient's

---

5. Other damages-focused Rules for cross-examination aim straight at the witness's credibility when the witness doesn't follow accepted professional norms in calculating the plaintiff's damages. But since those are witness-centered, we will leave them for chapter 8, "Cross-Examination with Witness Tear-Down Rules," when we lay out the four basic methods of witness tear-down cross.

right to trust in the doctor doing the right thing. The witness agreed with this proposition, which undermined the core of the "doctor knows best" defense in the case.

* **Example three** takes a case of mine, involving an unusual birth injury, and shows the witness reluctantly but unmistakably agreeing that the doctor he was called to defend had violated the Rule requiring a physician to fully disclose care options to the patient.

Example One: The Corporation's Spokesman Knocks His Company's Lawsuit Tactics

Houston lawyer Jason Itkin cross-examined a corporate spokesman who had maintained on direct examination that the injured plaintiff, a diver on a Gulf of Mexico oil-drilling rig, could make more money post-injury with the company because he could qualify for a supervisory job. Itkin first challenged the witness to put his company's money where his mouth was: go ahead and make a firm job offer to the plaintiff in open court on the witness stand. The witness balked at that. Then Itkin wrapped up the cross with this quick segment, coaxing the witness into condemning, albeit indirectly, the sharp-elbowed litigation tactics that the company had used in the trial up to that point:

MR. ITKIN: Now, you want Cal Dive when they are responsible for something to do the right thing. True?

CORPORATE SPOKESPERSON: Yes, sir.

Q: Okay. Now, you would agree it is irresponsible to say—to argue that you did everything right when there is clear showings of error. True?

A: I don't know if—if I understand your question.

Q: Okay. That is kind of a bad question. Let me do it this way: If Cal Dive is responsible, if they do something wrong and we have got some disagreement about that. If they do something wrong, Cal Dive shouldn't stand up and say, "I know we did something wrong but to get out of taking responsibility, to avoid responsibility, we are going to call the person that got hurt a faker." True?

A: True.

Q: If Cal Dive is wrong, they shouldn't try to avoid responsibility by sort of saying we did nothing wrong and by kind of hiding or cleaning up evidence. True?

A: True.

Q: If Cal Dive did something wrong, they shouldn't try to avoid responsibility by making light of a person's injuries and saying he is better off than he is or make arguments of that such. True?

A: True.

MR. ITKIN: Pass the witness, Your Honor.[6]

The Rule:

- A company should not take unfair lawsuit positions to try to avoid responsibility for harm it caused.

Itkin stated the Rule with three particulars, the last of which went straight at the witness's (non-) offer of a higher paying job to the plaintiff. Nobody likes a hypocrite.

Example Two: Exploring the Why Behind Key Liability Rules

Some Rules are self-evidently true, like the rule of fair play in lawsuits that Jason Itkin used in the last example. Other Rules take a little more work to explain, and one effective way to do it is with an adverse expert. This next example shows how a Rules-based agreement strategy can add meat to your Rules by having the adverse witness agree to what's important about a Rule and why. Again, the application is flexible. You can touch all the bases of a good Rule: clear, inarguable, important, and violated, or skip one or more.

---

6. *Bryant v. Cal Dive International Inc.*, Case No. 2011-57457, Harris County, Texas District Court, May 6, 2013.

In this example, the cross-examiner, Randy Kinnard, put the clear plus inarguable Rule in front of the witness and the jury, got agreement, discussed importance, then saved the punch line of proving the rule was broken for another witness. This was a malpractice case in a small town in west Tennessee. The main defendant was the town's one family-practice doctor, the daughter of a revered physician who had also served as the town's sole family doctor for many years. One central issue was how the defendant medical team failed to take seriously the patient's complaints of not being able to breathe when taken off a breathing machine, chalking it up to simple anxiety instead of a physiological issue. The patient ended up with severe brain damage from an episode of stopped breathing not long after the machine was pulled. Here, Kinnard's approach was to establish basic ground rules for the doctor-patient relationship that undermined the entire defense. The principle you will see Kinnard developing from several angles is the patient's right to be taken seriously: to not have symptoms dismissed as "all in the head," and to be treated by a doctor who knows what he's doing or who knows enough to send the patient to someone who does. Kinnard developed this as a rule of basic trust, and the logical consequences of a trusting relationship that works both ways: patient trusting doctor, and doctor trusting patient. The Rule became this: *A doctor must believe his patient.* Kinnard developed this Rule with the defense expert James Farrage, MD.

MR. KINNARD: I want to talk to you a minute about the doctor-patient relationship. It's a special relationship, isn't it?

DR. FARRAGE: Yes, it is.

Q: It's a relationship of great trust.

A: Correct.

Q: The patient comes to the doctor, and we expose ourselves to the doctors, we take our clothes off, we put funny little gowns on, and we wait to see a doctor. And we're going to trust the doctor to look after us right, aren't we?

[These nonessential medical details, which every juror has experienced, make an otherwise abstract discussion concrete.]

A: Yes.

Q: Now, in this relationship, the doctor needs to trust the patient. Fair?

A: Yes.

Q: The doctor needs to believe the patient.

A: Yes.

Q: The people at The MED believed Cody when he said, "I've got a problem," didn't they?

A: Yes.

Q: And that is critical to the doctor-patient relationship. The patient has the right to think, "If I tell my doctor something, my doctor will believe me." Fair?

A: Yes.

Q: The doctor needs to believe the patient, right?

A: Correct.

[These basic propositions became central to the key liability Rules of the Road for the case. Here, the defendant doctor fixated on an "it's all in your head" rationalization that discounted what the patient was trying to tell the doctor about his difficulty breathing with the tube removed.]

Q: A patient has a right to believe that if a situation with his doctor is over the head of the doctor, and the doctor could use some help, he can trust the doctor's going to call somebody. That's why we have specialists, right?

[A powerful theme: the patient's right to trust the doctor to do the right thing and be humble in the face of something the doctor is not used to. Note the echo from the prior questions: "the patient has a right to think . . ."]

A: Yes.

Q: There are all kinds of specialists out there in medicine who can help a family doctor with issues. Fair?

A: Yes, there are.

[This focuses the attack on the family practitioner defendant in the case.]

Q: And a patient has a right to believe, if I'm in a particular place, in a particular type of facility, if I need to be somewhere else, where I will be safer, I can trust that my doctor will send me there.

[Another echo: "patient has a right to believe . . ." Repeating key phrases like this makes it easier for a jury to follow the cross-examiner's logic.]

A: Yes. That's correct.

Q: And that's critical to the doctor-patient relationship.

A: Yes. There's—there's exchange of information and the physician has the clinical training and medical knowledge to assess the situation. And taking all aspects into consideration, decide what the best course of action is for that particular patient.[7]

Note how the last answer strayed beyond the strict confines of the yes-or-no statement question. But it didn't hurt the point the cross-examiner made with the earlier questions. This line of questions also helped undermine the defense of medical judgment. In this case, the patient was at a facility that lacked the personnel to cope with a collapsed airway in the middle of the night in a patient who had recently had his breathing tube removed. The inability to re-intubate the patient had catastrophic consequences for his brain function. Kinnard's question about "the patient's right to believe" that he would be transferred if needed to a safer facility reframed the focus from the subjective "doctor knows best" brand of medical judgment to the objective "what's best for the patient" standard, and one also focused on the patient's rights. Again, carefully framed, Rules-oriented questions have brought the witness around to support a key aspect of the patient's theory of the case.

---

7. *Wade v. Healthsouth Corporation*, Case No. 4253, Weakley County, Tennessee Circuit Court, June 26, 2013.

This examination stopped short of making the ultimate point: that the defendant had violated the rule that the expert has just agreed is true and important. Kinnard could show that violation with a safer witness than this adverse expert. The next example walks that final step.

Example Three: Agreeing to the Liability Rule and Its Violation

In this next example, I chose to make the ultimate point through a hostile adverse expert. My main reason was that the expert had made a grudging admission in his deposition that if the defendant doctor hadn't informed the patient of the medically reasonable options, that would violate the standard of care. (The judge in the trial had ruled out the term "safety rules," but the point comes through loud and clear, as you will see, even with the more sterile "standard of care" language.) The witness's feistiness made getting to the bottom line a true rodeo ride. The collateral benefit from the tussle is the witness helped me dramatize the importance of the point for the jury and thus make it more memorable. (A really clever expert will give up concessions in the blandest possible way so inattentive jurors miss the point.)

The case involved a baby who suffered an unusual but devastating injury just before she was born. Her mother's obstetrician stuck a needle into the womb to draw off fluid to test the baby's lungs to see if they were mature enough for an early delivery. The doctor stuck the needle through the placenta and into one of the baby's blood vessels, causing slow bleeding. Despite several red flags over the next few hours, delivery was not accomplished until eleven hours after the needle stick, by which time the baby had lost a large portion of her blood volume and suffered bad brain damage as a consequence.

We had several contentions about what the doctors had done wrong: performed a dangerous and unnecessary test, walked off the job after causing the bleeding without staying around to look hard for any problem, ignored the results of a test that showed the baby didn't tolerate the needle stick well, and failed to counsel the parents appropriately at two key stages: when the test was recommended in the first place, and after the needle stick, when one option would have been to go ahead and deliver the baby immediately without waiting to see if she got into trouble.

The excerpt below focuses only on the two "informed consent" claims. The expert witness under cross-examination was an obstetrician from Richmond, Virginia, named James Christmas, who specialized in high-risk pregnancies. I had set up the liability Rule with our own expert and printed it on a simple PowerPoint slide:

- If there are reasonable options, the obstetrician must inform the patient so the patient can make an intelligent choice.

Because I knew he wouldn't readily help me, I elected to start the examination with a brushback pitch on his bias.[8] This was my very first question on cross:

Mr. Malone: Did you ever wonder, Dr. Christmas, why your phone never rings from plaintiffs' lawyers?

Dr. Christmas: It never crossed my mind, no.

Q: It didn't possibly cross your mind that you were one of those guys who could always be counted on if there is any issue where there might be a little bit of ambiguity—that you would slice it for the healthcare provider? That didn't ever occur to you?

A: With all due respect, I swore to tell the truth about three hours ago, and I take that very seriously.

[Then I jumped to the informed consent issue:]

Q: What I got from those two quotes [in the witness's deposition], putting them together, and you correct me if I am wrong, is that studying her records there is no clear-cut, "Man, she needs

---

8. If you're not a baseball fan, a *brushback pitch* is when the pitcher comes very close to hitting the batter with the ball, to try to get the batter to step back from the plate. The first question here tries to push the witness out of advocacy mode by directly challenging him as biased.

to go straight to early induction preceded by amnio." At least that is my—

A: Based on that information, that is, I don't know that there is a mandate to do that.

Q: Okay. Options, there are options.

A: Again, but, if a clinician taking care of the patient looks at the patient and makes a clinical assessment that says, I believe—I believe that the risk of stillbirth outweighs the risk of effective management, for a physician to say, "Oh, do whatever you want," is irresponsible.

[Like any expert who testifies exclusively for one side, he is doing his best to obscure and evade the point, which was simple: When there are reasonable options, tell the patient.]

Q: No, no, we are not talking about that. We are talking about having a dialogue with a patient and giving the patient the information so the patient can make an intelligent choice. Isn't that what medical standards require in the Commonwealth of Virginia?

[I first put forward the liability Rule orally, before displaying it. The visual comes next, no matter what he says.]

A: To a certain degree, yes. But I think to—

Q: Only to a certain degree?

A: Yes, only to a certain degree. I think when you, to allow a patient to make a bad decision and to not imply to the patient that that is a bad decision is inappropriate.

[I stumbled a bit with this next question. My bad, because the general rule in most jurisdictions is you cannot quote what one expert says to another. There was a simple way around this roadblock, as readers will see.]

Q: Well, let me show you how I had put it earlier, how one of the other experts had put it earlier.

OPPOSING COUNSEL: Your Honor, he cannot and I object to showing testimony from, we don't know where it is from.

Mr. Malone: This is cross-examination.

Opposing Counsel: You don't get to show testimony.

The Court: You can ask him if agrees with the statement or not.

Mr. Malone: "If there are reasonable options, the obstetrician must inform the patient so the patient can make an intelligent choice."

[The Rule is now on the display monitor. The witness shows he has an insatiable appetite for quibbling.]

A: Define "reasonable."

Q: Reasonable options, you—

A: You just asked me to define a word. I am asking you to define reasonable. That is the—

The Court: Do you agree with that statement or not?

Dr. Christmas: I agree with that statement.

[It never hurts to have a fair-minded judge intervene to move things along—but only when the judge volunteers. Had he not done so, I would have asked the witness to go back to his earlier statement that reasonable doctors could differ on what the treatment options were for the patient at this crossroads. But now that the Rule has been agreed to, the next step is to draw out the importance of the Rule.]

Q: Okay. So, because it is the patient's choice, it is the patient's life, they are the ones that have to live with it. Right?

A: To a degree I agree with that.

[This time I don't take the witness's invitation to split hairs. I just move on to finish the trap. With a more cooperative witness, I would have stretched out the importance of the Rule with a few more questions.]

Q: Okay. And so, you had told us also in your deposition, that if—let me back up a second. You showed us the informed consent form or Mr. Batten did, showed us the informed consent form. She signed it.

A: Okay.

Q: I want you to plug in one additional fact, that the patient read the form and signed it because she had not been presented any options and she thought the amnio was a test that she had to have. Are you willing to assume that?

A: Hypothetically or in this case?

Q: Hypothetically and in this case because she testified to this, and you can't judge credibility one way or the other, can you?

A: If that is what she testified to, then I have no way to contradict that. I can only demonstrate that the form says that she understood.

Q: Right. And plenty of patients—

A: And she signed the form.

Q: Sure. And plenty of patients think they understand because they trust their doctor—

A: Where is that at?

Q: I am asking you a question.

A: You just told me something.

Q: I am trying to ask you a question, sir.

A: Okay.

Q: Isn't it true that plenty of patients trust doctors enough that they assume that the doctor is going to give them the options if there are options?

A: I don't know whether that statement is true or not.

[This went back to our case theme that the doctor's failure to disclose choices was a breach of the patient's trust in him. It doesn't matter if the expert agrees, since this is one of those statements jurors know is true.]

Q: Well, we will let the jury judge that, then. The point is didn't you also tell us in your deposition that if there had been no presentation of options, amnio versus—

A: Right.

Q: —expectant management, and by the way, expectant management, watchful waiting—

A: Right.

Q: —would have been a reasonable option for this patient?

A: It would have been an option for this patient. I think that in [the defendant] Dr. Roberts's testimony that the—

Q: We don't get to quote Dr. Roberts.

[Ordinarily I should not have interrupted the witness. But he was so quarrelsome, and so bent on injecting more information than the question called for, that interruption was called for here. The judge also saw this was a witness who wanted to comment on whether or not a discussion had occurred between doctor and patient.]

A: No, you are asking me if I believe a discussion occurred and in Dr. Roberts's—

THE COURT: He is not asking you that at all. You are not to comment on that.

DR. CHRISTMAS: Okay.

MR. MALONE: So the point is that didn't you also tell us that if the two options of watchful waiting versus straight to amnio, do not pass go, and then we will have an elected induction had not been presented to this patient, that would violate the Virginia standard of care?

A: Correct.

[Okay, stop here, Professor Younger shouts! But since I disagree with "saving the ultimate point for closing," I lock down the point with two more questions.]

Q: You did say that and you stand by that testimony?

A: I agree with that.

Q: Okay. So that is just an issue that the jury is going to have to decide who is right on this. If Dr. Roberts just told her, "This is what we are going to do—I am going to do—I am going to put you to early induction and I am going to test the lungs ahead of time," and he didn't give her options, that would be wrong and that would violate the standard of care if that is what they conclude. True?

A: That is true.[9]

Messy, yes, but effective too: the witness has just agreed three times in a row with the ultimate point of our liability case: if the doctor didn't present the options to the patient, the defendant broke the rules of good patient care, according to his own expert.

So there we have three examples of playing out an agreement strategy in cross-examination with case-building Rules. It's a flexible approach whose core involves finding clear, inarguable Rules about the legal case that the witness must agree with. Case-building agreement cross can focus on any aspect of the case: liability, damages, or even lawsuit conduct. How far we go with the technique depends on the case and the witness. Sometimes we go all the way to proving a violation of agreed Rules by the defendant, as in the last example. Sometimes it's enough to put the agreed Rules on the table without more explanation, as it's already evident the defendant has violated them, as in the Itkin example. And sometimes, a dialogue with the adverse witness helps us show the jury the importance of the agreed Rule, as Kinnard did.

In the next chapter, we will add another important dimension to our strategizing: looking for the witness's self-interest so we can figure out how to win agreements that separate the witness from the side that called her.

TAKEAWAYS

The strategy of case-building cross starts with figuring out the simple rules of accepted behavior that our adversaries violated, either in causing the harm in the first place or in the way they defend

---

9. *Simpson v. Roberts*, Case No. CL04-213, City of Roanoke Circuit Court, Virginia, May 16, 2012.

themselves in court. Once we formulate Rules that are clear, inarguable, important, and provably violated, we take them straight to the other side in cross-examination. We obtain the witness's agreement to our clear plus inarguable Rules. We can stop there, or we can go on and use the same witness to show the importance of the Rule and its violation. How far we go depends on a lot of things, including a close analysis of the witness's self-interest, to which we now turn.

Exercise

Take your next case set for trial and start to write a list of principles and Rules for liability. Try to keep it to a single page. Be specific and concrete. Do not just crib from Rules a friend used in another case.

- What are ways the other side can try to dodge what's on your list?
- How can you hone your Rules to force agreement?

5

WITNESS SELF-INTEREST AND CASE-BUILDING CROSS

Lesson No. 1: Empathize with your enemy.

—Errol Morris, *The Fog of War*

We've now learned the basics of writing the Rules of the Road that build our case, especially when we can recruit witnesses on the other side to agree with our Rules. Case-building cross, as we introduced it in chapter 4, "Cross-Examination with Case-Building Rules," requires the right combination of witness, cross-examiner, and topics. And the most important element is the last: we must carefully select those topics most vulnerable to turn-around and pick the right witness to do it with. To fully neutralize the points the witness has scored on direct examination does *not* require that you attack head-on all or even most of the points the witness made on direct. This is lawyer jujitsu, not heavy earth moving. So let's revisit case-building agreement cross and take it to a deeper level.

Core Insight: Looking Out for Number One

Let's think about the big picture first. Many of us who cross-examine witnesses for a living get frustrated when bested by a witness in the battle of wits. We gnash our teeth at the witness's slipperiness, dishonesty, and clever dodges. How dare he fail to cooperate with our carefully planned takedown!?

But why should we get indignant? We should never be surprised when a cross proves more difficult than our fantasy. Here's a simple insight:

Witnesses are like everybody else: they are looking out for number one—with every question you ask.

When we keep this insight front and center in our minds, we can better anticipate each move the witness is likely to make and better plan our countermoves. Better yet, if you are skilled, you can harness the witness's self-interest to create entire lines of powerful Q&A that bolster your case and undermine the other side. Because the witness will always put a higher priority on protecting self-interest than on protecting the side that called the witness to court, when you can line up the witness's self-interest parallel to an important point you want to make on cross, it can be surprisingly easy to win agreement with your points.

Every Witness's Key Points of Self-Interest

So what are every witness's key points of self-interest as he or she settles into the witness stand? For any honest witness with a healthy ego, they include:

1. I want to be believed.

2. I want to be respected, liked, or loved.

3. I want to tell the truth (as long as it keeps me respected, liked, or loved).

4. I want to look good.

5. I want to stay true to my core values and beliefs.

Some witnesses have character traits that are extreme versions of this core list of five, and thus can be exploited:

6. I want to show that I am the smartest person in the courtroom, or at least smarter than you.

7. (Related to above) I know more facts about the subject at hand than anyone else here.

8. I am a person of great virtue—honest to a fault.

9. I don't want to change my position on anything because that might look weak.

To these points of self-interest, which witnesses will hold to varying degrees, add one more, but usually weaker than the others:

10. I want to help the side that called me.

For most witnesses, we can amend this slightly:

11. I want to help the side that called me—as long as it doesn't conflict with my self-interest.

For an expert witness with any shred of honesty, you can set up a conflict between the witness's desire to be believed and some core principle or Rule that hurts the other side. That's the heart of the Rules of the Road method. If the witness has to look foolish and noncredible to stick with her own side, the witness will usually gravitate in the opposite direction toward her self-interested desire to be believed and to look good. Now, of course, some witnesses are shameless, and say preposterous things, hoping to outsmart you and fool the jury by force of personality. You can deal with those witnesses too, but not in a chapter on agreement cross, because they agree with nothing you say.

Steps for Aligning the Witness's Self-Interest with Your Case

Let's put together the basic steps to make the adverse witness's self-interest work for you in your case.

Step 1: Assess Character

The first step is to assess the witness's character. As we stand to cross-examine, the most urgent character question we want to answer is how hard this witness wants to fight. We can divide witnesses into two camps: the ones who start out wanting to assert control just like we do, and the other camp of meeker souls who have a conflict-avoiding response to most stressful situations. A submissive, passive witness is generally pretty easy to control as long as you are not too ham-fisted and provoke the witness's own threat response. So you do best by figuring out the witness's dominance or submissiveness proclivities early and toning down the aggressiveness of your questions for gentler witnesses. The ones who want to assert control without provocation are, of course, more challenging.

But we need to know a lot more than how the witness scores on a fight-or-flight test of stress. I think the best lens is the witness's self-interest. What are the key aspects of self-interest that energize his personality? How honest, how self-important, how agreeable, how vain—all these will help decide if agreement cross will work with this witness, and if so, whether it needs to be done with a soft touch or a hard hand.

Just as farmers don't look gift horses in the mouth (to count teeth and figure out how old the gift horse is), we don't need to sharply question the good faith of a reasonably neutral witness who readily agrees with our points. We tread differently with a witness who has a notoriously one-sided testimonial history (as I did in the last chapter with Dr. Christmas). So for an agreeable witness, we may start with case-building Rules that we have good reason to believe the witness will agree with, whereas the one-sided witness first needs to be outed for the biased sellout we believe him or her to be (even if we can eventually extract some case-building agreement out of the same witness).

Step 2: Identify Rules

Identify all the principles and Rules that help your side and hurt the side that called this witness. If you cannot think of any, you haven't spent enough time thinking through the issues in your case and reducing them to inarguable and clear propositions.[1] When you create a list of principles and the Rules they spawn, starting with the general and getting more specific to your case, you will inevitably find common ground with the witness.

Step 3: Which Rules Will the Witness Endorse?

Figure out which of your principles and Rules this witness might endorse, based on any commonalities between his self-interest and your case. This key final step requires deep thought and a good instinct for human behavior. By now you have a good list of choices, ranging from general to specific, soft to hard, easy to tough. How far you go is best shown by example, in our next case study.

WITNESS SELF-INTEREST IN ACTION: HOW ONE LAWYER "TURNED" AN EXPERT WITNESS

Here is an agreement cross-examination by Oregon attorney Jan Baisch, a top plaintiff lawyer and member of the Inner Circle of Advocates. He was able to shrewdly peel off the witness from loyalty to the side that paid him, by aligning the witness's own intellectual self-interest and core beliefs with the theme of Baisch's case.

The subject matter is one common to both civil and criminal cases: the defendant's consumption of alcohol. A pathologist or toxicologist takes the stand and spins a scientific-sounding account of how much drinking had to have been involved to have produced the blood alcohol level found in the person and how impaired that would make an average person. The testimony is

---

1. See chapter 4, "Cross-Examination with Case-Building Rules," for more on how to write these Rules.

intended to, and often does, create a vivid picture in jurors' minds of irresponsible behavior.

In Baisch's case, late-night drinking and carousing at two adjacent campsites in a national park led to a dispute that ended in an accidental shooting—a vacationing firefighter shot Baisch's client, a truck driver. The truck driver survived, but with serious long-term injuries, for which he sued the firefighter. The firefighter's attorney, trying to turn the alcohol spotlight away from his client onto the injured trucker, called to the witness stand Dr. William J. Brady, a forensic pathologist and retired chief of death investigations for the state. By the time of trial, Brady had testified in court some one thousand times: ergo, a formidable witness who had seen every lawyer "trick."

On direct examination, Dr. Brady told the jury that, based on the firefighter's account of his drinking that afternoon and evening (no blood had ever been taken for analysis), he would have had a negligible amount of alcohol in his blood at the time his gun accidentally went off, enough booze to have relaxed him a bit but not caused any impairment of judgment. The plaintiff trucker, on the other hand, for whom there was a tested blood alcohol level, would have consumed some thirteen to fourteen beers in the hours leading up to the altercation to reach the blood alcohol level found at the hospital, and so the plaintiff would have been quite impaired.

THE THREE-STEP ANALYSIS AT WORK

Step 1: Assess Character

Assess the witness's character, personality, and core values and beliefs. Baisch had the advantage of having hired this same expert for a police shooting case, so he knew the witness, a prominent figure in Oregon medical and legal circles. Dr. Brady had modernized Oregon's death-investigation system, abolishing the old coroner job and instituting a medical-examiner model, and he served as the state's chief medical examiner for sixteen years, conducting ten thousand autopsies. Then a scandal brought him down. He was fired after a newspaper investigation found that his office had sold pituitary glands harvested from cadavers to a national research program, without the knowledge of the decedents' families, and he had used the small sums paid ($16,000 over nine years) to pay for an office sofa, a staff Christmas party, and other sundry workplace amenities. Dr. Brady sued the state for wrongful discharge and won a big jury verdict.[2] He developed a prosperous expert-witness consulting practice, testifying for both sides in civil cases and for defendants in criminal cases. Dr. Brady authored a book about forensic medicine with a chapter advising other witnesses how to put their best foot forward. Having been the state medical examiner, the witness had done autopsies on many victims of shootings, and although not a toxicologist himself, he well knew how to make the standard calculations moving backward from a blood alcohol level to quantity of drinks consumed.

Even though I never met the man, these character traits seem to me a reasonable takeaway from all the above: an honest, hardworking, ethical witness who tried to help the side that called him but would first want to be true to himself. Here is a perfect candidate for agreement-style, case-building cross, if you could find something to align him with some important aspect of your case.

Step 2: Identify Rules

List the core Rules and principles for your case and any special ones for the witness. Here, we can do both case-related and witness-related principles:

1. Case-related:

    a. Alcohol and guns don't mix well.

    b. The more a person drinks, the more impaired he will be in judgment.

    c. No one should handle a gun unless completely sober. (This is a Rule in our system; the others are principles from which the Rule follows.)

---

2. Taylor Clark, "The Organ Grinder," *Willamette Week*, Nov. 9, 2004, accessed at http://www.wweek.com/portland/article-3811-the_organ_grinder.html

d. When an unarmed victim is shot by an armed shooter, the victim's own drinking matters less in what happened than the shooter's.

2. Witness-related:

   a. An expert's opinion is only as good as the facts behind it.

   b. When an expert has to rely on an interested party's say-so, his opinion is less reliable than if it was backed up by hard, independent data.

Step 3: Which Rules Will the Witness Endorse?

Look for the commonalities between your case and the witness's self-interest and core values and beliefs. This witness had been a public servant for many years. In his thousands of autopsies, he had to have dealt with many victims of the lethal combination of guns and alcohol and their grieving families. So he is likely to agree with a line of questions about our first principle listed above: guns and alcohol don't mix.

As a forensic witness who testifies about alcohol and its impact on a person's impairment, he also has to agree with the second case-related principle above: impairment and number of drinks go hand in hand.

He might be softer on the third principle (no one should handle a gun unless sober) and the fourth (when an unarmed victim is shot by an armed shooter, the victim's drinking matters less than the shooter's) from the case-related list, so we can hold those to one side and see how the "safe" parts of the exam go. Examination on the first two principles will help us gauge how this witness balances his personal integrity with his natural desire to help the side that hired him.

On the two witness-specific principles listed here, both seem to be ones that a witness with his track record and integrity would readily endorse. The first—"An expert's opinion is only as good as the facts behind it"—is one of those classic agree-or-look-foolish Rule of the Road principles. How readily he agrees with it could be a good barometer of how the rest of the cross will go. That was where Jan Baisch elected to start.

Cross-Examination of William Brady, MD, by Jan Baisch

Mr. Baisch: Doctor, good morning.

Dr. Brady: Good morning, Mr. Baisch.

Q: First of all, I would like to establish that during these thirty years that you have been testifying, you have testified for the police, and you have testified in this court for me in a shooting case, and you have testified all across the board. And what you do, is you take the data, without interviewing the people involved, and then give an opinion on what they—how much any person probably had?

A: That's a very precise summary.

Q: And that's a fair characterization?

A: It is, sir.

Q: Okay. And in fact, you have written a book on how to be a witness, and how to testify in court?

A: I have written a book. It contains a chapter on the subject you alluded to.

Q: Okay. And in this particular type of a case, and in any case, for that matter, you have to rely upon the credibility of the data that's being given to you concerning how much an individual has had, if there is no blood alcohol reading?

[Baisch first asked the general question, not about *this defendant*, but about *any* defendant. It's usually best to start from the general before moving to the specific.]

A: Correct, sir.

Q: Okay. And I believe that you call that—there is a term for that. It's called garbage in, garbage out. Is that what you—how you characterize that?

[The extra question restates the same point and underlines it with a catchy phrase.]

A: I think that's a fair statement. The opinion is no more solid than the basis, factual basis on which the opinion is based.

Q: And in this case, the shooter and his blood alcohol are not capable of any precise scientific computation, because he never had his blood tested at any material time?

A: I have no blood alcohol level, no, sir.

Q: All you have got is his word for it. Is that right?

A: The information that Mr. Templeton gave me, I believe, is based on his—on the information he received from his client, yes.

Q: Okay. And so, therefore, without going into any math whatsoever, would you agree that if the information that he gave to the police and his lawyer concerning the amount of booze that he had that afternoon and that evening is inaccurate, then your computations would be totally worthless here?

A: They would be inaccurate.

[If Baisch had been less skilled or confident, he might have demanded a more precise answer to the provocatively phrased question "totally worthless." You can hear the barking now: "Answer my question! It would have been totally worthless! True?" But that would be argumentative and unnecessary, because the witness agreed with Baisch—he just used a little more subdued wording—and the easier and more productive path is to continue to explain the core point, as Baisch does here.]

Q: Yes. And along those same lines, if he had more beer and more wine than what he said he did, the blood alcohol reading and the judgment, coordination, self-control, care, and normal sense of care and caution—I believe you termed those?

A: Yes, sir.

Q: Would be correspondingly impaired, vis a vis the amount of extra alcohol he had?

A: Correct, sir.

[Now on to the next logical point of agreement, first general, later specific.]

Q: Okay. And what does alcohol do to a person who has got a gun, who is upset and is ingesting alcohol? Does it have an effect upon one's ability to use care, caution, and self-control?

A: It does, sir.

Q: A loaded gun?

A: Well, the normal sense of care and caution, Mr. Baisch, whether it relates to traffic situations, or to situations involving weapons, all depends on the person's normal sense of care, caution, and self-restraint, which is impaired to a greater or lesser extent by the alcohol that they have consumed.

[Baisch brings the impairment point down to this case, with a quick summary of what the defendant did.]

Q: And would you agree, Dr. Brady, that a person who is kind of upset, or kind of unfriendly, that has a loaded .357 Magnum strapped in a fanny pack on his person, who goes over to a campground, where there are people that he doesn't know, that he thinks are drinking, but he can't confirm that, if that person has any alcohol whatsoever, the situation is more volatile than if he didn't have any alcohol?

A: Fair.

Q: And each drink of alcohol that the gunman has ingested would correspondingly impair his ability to behave in a reasonable, normal manner the way that normal people in our society behave?

A: It would.

Q: Do you agree with that?

A: It would change depending on the amount of alcohol that he had. The more alcohol, the more it would change, sir.

[Rephrasing the question just a hair allows the good point to be underlined for the jury.]

Q: And would you agree that any alcohol in a person who I have described would be worse than no alcohol?

A: It would. He would have loss of his normal abilities to a greater or lesser extent.

Q: And as the Oregon state medical examiner over the past thirty years, you have seen a lot of shootings, have you not?

[Baisch pulls back to highlight the witness's experience. No need for precision here: a good plain term like "a lot of shootings" works fine.]

A: Yes, sir.

Q: A lot of dead people?

A: Yes, sir.

Q: A lot of gunshots?

A: Yes, sir.

Q: And in what percentage of those was alcohol involved?

[Baisch breaks the "commandments" by asking a non-leading question and, what's more, one he didn't know the answer to. It works because as long as the percentage is nontrivial, it helps the questioner's point. And the facts are more impressive coming from the witness's mouth.]

A: Oh, I couldn't give a precise number, but it's high, certainly well over half, perhaps more.

Q: It's a huge problem in our community. Isn't it, Dr. Brady?

A: Alcohol is a problem in the community, sir, yes.

[Baisch gently steers the witness to the precise point. Note how he makes the back-and-forth sound like a normal conversation.]

Q: I was referring to alcohol and guns.

A: It's a mixture that oftentimes produces tragedies.

Q: It's a lethal combination?

A: It's a serious problem.

Q: And you would agree that any shooter who has a gun that is loaded, who is upset and has ingested alcohol is a dangerous problem?

A: Well, an intoxicated person with a loaded gun represents a problem, sir.

Q: Okay.

A: Potential problem.

Q: And a person who gets shot by such a person who has ingested alcohol, whether he's intoxicated, 0.10, 0.15, whatever, a person who gets shot, it doesn't really matter what his blood alcohol is, does it, Doctor, when the shooter pulls the trigger?

[This was a very delicately phrased question. Baisch doesn't get quite the answer he wants, but doesn't overreact, and with his next question, rebalances the point.]

A: Well, I don't know how to respond to that, Mr. Baisch. Obviously, the incident, whether it be here or in many cases, escalates because of intoxication on the part of more than one person. I just don't know how to respond to your question.

Q: That's fair. That's a fair answer. Would you agree that, in this case, both parties were drinking, the victim and the shooter?

A: That's my understanding, sir.

Q: Okay. And that's the evidence. And that your conclusion would be that the victim had more alcohol than the shooter had. Do you have an opinion on the number of drinks that the victim had, an estimate, but you don't have any scientific data on how much the shooter had, other than his word for it?

[This is a safe question because the witness has already made this concession. Having him make it again helps bring home the point of the preceding line of questioning.]

A: Correct, sir.

Q: All right. And no matter how much he had, with the gun in his hand, his self-control and his normal sense of care and caution would be impaired to some degree?

A: Depending on how much he had, it would be impaired minimally or perhaps more.

Q: It's a sliding scale depending on how much he had?

A: That's correct, sir.

MR. BAISCH: Okay. Thanks very much, Dr. Brady. That's all.[3]

FINDING THE CORE WEAKNESS AND STRUCTURING AN EFFECTIVE CROSS

Baisch's cross-examination worked well because he focused first on the biggest vulnerability in the expert's testimony: his core opinion was based entirely on the defendant firefighter's say-so of how much drinking he had done and when. Baisch also recognized a critical tension between what Dr. Brady was called to testify to and his central beliefs from his years of work as a medical examiner. Here was a scientist being asked to take sides in a contest between two drinkers that had ended with one of them badly wounded by a firearm. And the man who fired the gun was the one Dr. Brady was trying to exculpate. Having seen the carnage wrought by guns and alcohol throughout his career, Dr. Brady no doubt felt uncomfortable taking sides with the shooter and felt better about himself when Baisch gently nudged him to retreat to a position of neutrality.

Baisch then tailored a limited set of points within that frame, drove home each nicely, avoided difficult but tempting topics (such as taking on the expert's calculations of Baisch's own client's blood alcohol level), all of this while steering the witness into safe territory where Baisch could drive his case home: guns and alcohol never mix safely.

And speaking of two things that don't mix safely: case-building cross and witness takedown cross with the witness's prior "bad acts" of thin relevance. Note what Baisch did *not* do. He could have done a cheap-shot impeachment cross-examination with two points:

- "You were fired! You sold body parts from dead people without their families' permission!"

---

3. *Pullen v. Millhouse*, Case No. 94-148-JO, United States District Court, District of Oregon, March 19, 1995.

- "Now because you lost that job, you make a lot of money testifying as a hired gun for the first lawyer to hire you in a case!"

Of course, if Baisch had done that, there would have been plenty of blowback: Dr. Brady would have been allowed to explain on redirect how he had been vindicated in his lawsuit against the state, how he had spent all the money on amenities for his staff and hadn't pocketed any for himself, and he would add that, yes, he has worked for a number of lawyers, including Mr. Baisch, and if he thinks the lawyer has a bad case, he tells the lawyer. He then would have walked off the stand with his head held high. What would be the ultimate point of a cross that left both witness and cross-examiner spattered? Not much, especially in comparison with what Baisch got instead with a gentle agreement cross. His questioning followed this basic outline:

1. Dr. Brady's testimony about how impaired or not the defendant would have been relied entirely on the defendant's uncorroborated account of his drinking that day.

2. A different description of the amount of drinking could well have led to a different conclusion about how impaired he was at the time of the shooting.

3. Alcohol does cause people to misuse guns, a topic in which Dr. Brady had vast experience.

Each of the key points could have come and gone in an instant, but Baisch did a nice job of stretching them out without getting tedious from too much repetition.

Phoenix lawyer David Wenner, famed for his jury-bias instruction of plaintiffs' lawyers with Alabama attorney Greg Cusimano, ties this focus on witness self-interest to the Rules of the Road method. Says Wenner,

> I think this is one reason why cross-examining around rules is so valuable. Every witness is subject to normative influence and wants to perceive himself in the best light. Most of the time that means complying with the

prevailing norms. The rules are framed around social norms that promote personal and community welfare and to disagree would create cognitive dissonance in most people, especially physicians who need to see themselves as being concerned for patient welfare. It is thus self-serving to agree with the rule because it enhances self-esteem.[4]

The Lesson of Sponsorship and Case-Building Cross

A final observation on this example: Never forget the power of sponsorship in the perception of whose side a witness has helped or hurt. Either side could have hired this witness and made valid points through him. Imagine if Baisch had been the sponsor and had called Dr. Brady to the stand to make the same points brought out in his cross. The impact would have vanished, because the jury would have expected much stronger points from one's own expert. But when the same points are made through a witness the other side has sponsored, they take on much more power. This is why case-building cross-examination is so important, because it lets you turn the tables of witness sponsorship.

Oregon, where Baisch practices, does not usually allow for experts to be deposed. That can work well if you are willing to spend some quiet time analyzing the witness's self-interest and looking for pressure points. Of course, in states with expert depositions, you can lay much of this groundwork in discovery. The only risk is that the witness will be prepared to push back as much as possible, after woodshedding by the sponsoring lawyer, when the time arrives to seek agreement in front of the jury.

---

4. Personal communication from David Wenner.

SIZING UP THE WITNESS: HOW NOT TO

Flaming disasters of cross-examination can be just as instructive as those that go smoothly. The disasters certainly are more entertaining. Here, in one question, Arthur Liman, counsel for the Senate committee investigating the Iran-Contra affair, ruined his cross-examination of Colonel Oliver North, the ringleader of the plot:

MR. LIMAN: Colonel North, was the day Iran-Contra unraveled the worst day of your life?

[Let's pause the video for a second. From a witness self-interest perspective, what is the questioner asking the witness to admit? That he is selfish and self-absorbed and thinks only of the trouble he's in? No witness at all cognizant of his self-image would want to agree with the question. Here, a clever and articulate witness knows that the image he wants to project on national television is the selfless public servant, and he comes up with an answer that fits his true self-interest. Now, we hit *play*.]

COLONEL NORTH: No, Mr. Liman, the worst day was in Vietnam when I was in a foxhole with my best friend, and the Viet Cong threw a grenade into the foxhole, and my friend threw himself on top of it and saved my life. My best friend died. That was the worst day of my life.[5]

The question was ill-advised on multiple grounds. Even if the witness had meekly said, "Yes," what's the point? How does it advance the inquiry? But the real lesson here is to scope out where the witness's self-interest lies and avoid questions that feed the witness's interest but hurt yours.

If you win the witness's agreement with key portions of your case, you're entitled to bask in a Perry Mason moment. There is no better cross-examination. You are not picking nits with alleged contradictions between what the witness said in a deposition and

---

5. Jim Zirin, "Getting at the Truth? Cross-Examination Is the Crowning Glory of Our Legal System," *Forbes*, Feb. 11, 2014, http://www.forbes.com/sites/jameszirin/2014/02/11/getting-at-the-truth-cross-examination-is-the-crowning-glory-of-our-legal-system/.

what she says now, which often seem inconsequential to bystanders. Nor are you slinging mud at the witness for alleged bias, always a messy affair. No, this kind of cross is a full-on Hollywood clinch, where the witness seemingly snuggles up and you coo at each other.

This can happen to you, more often than you might think, if you follow the prescriptions in these last two chapters.

Takeaways

Building an effective agreement cross-examination strategy requires asking yourself for every witness that old question: *What's in it for this witness?* Only when you've done that will you be able to tailor your questions to fit the sweet spot where the witness's self-interest aligns with your case. This is a core part of the approach this book teaches: know yourself, know your case, know the witness.

Exercise

Go back to "Every Witness's Key Points of Self-Interest" at the beginning of this chapter.

1. I want to be believed.

2. I want to be respected, liked, or loved.

3. I want to tell the truth (as long as it keeps me respected, liked, or loved).

4. I want to look good.

5. I want to stay true to my core values and beliefs.

Notice how this list fits with the Rules-development technique we've advocated. Once you create a set of inarguable, clear, important Rules for your case, the witnesses who want to be believed, respected, and true to their own values can hardly help but agree with important aspects of your case, because you've made it in their self-interest to do so. Try it now with a key witness whose cross you are planning.

6

Using Treatises to Get to Yes

A book lying idle on a shelf is wasted ammunition.

—Henry Miller

We now finish part 2, "Building the Case with Cross-Examination," with one more powerful weapon to get to yes with the witness: how to use treatises to build your case. In chapter 4, "Cross-Examination with Case-Building Rules," we went over how to construct case-building Rules of the Road for your case. In the last chapter, we looked at how an analysis of the witness's self-interest can help you pick the right witnesses for your case-building cross. Now, we look at a way to build your case with less cooperative witnesses who are trying to do everything they can to hurt your case.

This chapter focuses on another kind of rule, a Rule of Evidence. This Rule on learned treatises gets its own chapter because treatises are an important way to build your case through cross-examination, yet many lawyers lose the opportunity because they don't know how to use authoritative literature with an adverse witness.

When each side has its own experts yammering at the jury with opposite conclusions, treatises and other professional literature can be the tiebreaker for jurors looking for objective authority. So it's an attractive field to plow. Yet three basic problems come up over and over:

- First, the lawyer doesn't lay the foundation properly with precise questions.

- Second, the witness gets to escape by confusing the foundation issue—by saying in effect, "I don't agree that the statement in this document you want to ask me about is authoritative," when that isn't the foundational issue at all.

- Third, the lawyer cuts short the line of questions too abruptly to leave any impression on the jury.

I've put two samples in this chapter that show the right way to use authoritative literature to good effect. The first, from Denver attorney Jim Leventhal, is a superb overall illustration of how to go beyond the bare-bones foundation to show how important the treatise really is and how it bears on a key issue in the case. In the sample below, you will see that Leventhal obtains with the treatise so much dominance over his witness, the defendant in a malpractice case, that he can even venture a "why" question at the end of his segment with the treatise.

The second example, from my *Rules of the Road* co-author Rick Friedman, shows a different way of getting into the quoted treatise, and also shows how a good cross-examiner deals with a witness's efforts to play dodgeball over the meaning of *authoritative*.

Before we study the examples, it's worth lingering over the text of this critical rule:

> The following are not excluded by the rule against hearsay, regardless of whether the declarant is available as a witness: . . . (18) A statement contained in a treatise, periodical, or pamphlet if: (A) the statement is called to the attention of an expert witness on cross-examination or relied on by the expert on direct examination; and

(B) the publication is established as a reliable authority by the expert's admission or testimony, by another expert's testimony, or by judicial notice. If admitted, the statement may be read into evidence but not received as an exhibit.[1]

Here are the key takeaways from the rule's text:

- First, you cannot just start quoting to the witness what some writer said in a publication somewhere. That's classic hearsay, when you quote someone not in the courtroom for "the truth of the matter asserted."[2] This rule gives you the tools to get past the hearsay objection.

- Second, the publication you want to quote from must be blessed as a "reliable authority," by either this witness, another expert (easiest is to use your own expert in direct testimony to rubber-stamp what you want to later use in cross with another witness), or the judge.

- Third, it's the *publication* itself, that is, what the rule refers to as the "treatise, periodical, or pamphlet," which must be acknowledged as a reliable authority. You do *not* have to establish that the particular statement within the publication that you want to quote to the witness is reliable authority. A lot of lawyers and judges misunderstand this fundamental point. If you had to get the witness to agree that a particular statement within a publication was reliable authority, then no cross-examiner could ask a witness about any statement in a publication with which the witness disagreed. That's why the rule says you can cross-examine about a particular statement

---

1. Fed. R. Evid. 803(18).

2. Fed. R. Evid. 801(c): "'Hearsay' means a statement that:

(1) the declarant does not make while testifying at the current trial or hearing; and

(2) a party offers in evidence to prove the truth of the matter asserted in the statement.

if "*the publication* is established as a reliable authority."³ See the Friedman example for how a clever expert tries to avoid being confronted with a quotation he doesn't like, and how Friedman foils the ploy.

- Fourth, the rule says you can read the statement into evidence, but it doesn't go back to the jury room as an exhibit. This creates a couple of problems you need to anticipate. One is that for jurors who are visual learners, you will want to show the statement in black and white. Typically we make a poster board with the cover of the book or journal on the left side and the quotation (usually retyped to make it easier on the eyes) on the right side, and then show it to the witness and jury at the same time. Now, some literal-minded opposing counsel may object that the rule says only that the statement "may be read into evidence," but most judges will let you show an accurate rendition of the quotation.

The other problem with the authoritative statement not being received as an exhibit is that the jury doesn't know this rule. So a very common request from the jury room in deliberations is, "We want to see that treatise the attorney was quoting from." And when the judge declines, usually with some note that says the treatise is "not in evidence" or is "not an exhibit," that can deflate your case dramatically, because the jury can misunderstand that to mean that your entire cross on that topic should be disregarded since they cannot now read the treatise. Here are two ways to head this off at the pass:

1. Try to get the other side to stipulate that literature quoted can be received as an exhibit. (More likely than not they will refuse, but it's worth a try.)

2. Tell the jury in your closing argument that the quotation is evidence but that the technical rules don't let it go back to the jury room, then show them the quote again, and invite them to copy it into their notepads if they want. If the quotation is important enough to your case, you will definitely want to do this.

---

3. *See* Fed. R. Evid. 803(18), section (B). (emphasis added)

Example 1: Model Use of Authoritative Literature

Now watch a skilled use of professional literature by Denver lawyer Jim Leventhal. Too many lawyers go through the groundwork abruptly, asking only the "magic words" question without dwelling on what it means to be a *reliable authority*. This was brought home to me once when, during a focus group, I was quoting the *New England Journal of Medicine* as the be-all and end-all medical authority. Then one of the focus group members snorted, "I don't care what some damned magazine says!" I deserved it, since I assumed everybody knew what this journal was and had never explained anything about medical journals in general or why this particular journal and the randomized clinical trial reported in it was so important. In Jim's case, he had a neat way to establish the authority of the textbook he wanted to quote.

Let's listen in.

Mr. Leventhal: I, throughout this case, have used a textbook of medicine called *Harrison's Principles of Medicine*. And I represented that this was a textbook you had on your desk in your office?

Defendant Doctor: I have that in my office.

Q: Not always on your desk.

A: It fluctuates.

Q: This is a textbook that [is] a reliable authority; in fact, it is one of the basic textbooks of medicine that almost everybody has who practices medicine, family medicine at least?

A: It was one of the primary books, yes.

Q: You had it in there, because you used it as a reference book?

A: I will rely on it at times, yes. I don't do that on a daily basis; but yes, I have used it as a resource, if I need to use it.

[A less skilled lawyer using one or two questions might have won the technical point but failed to convey the authoritativeness of the book;

Leventhal used five questions to make plain how important the book was, and then published the key quotation. This is usually best done by showing the quotation on a screen or poster board at the same time you read the text aloud. Inviting the witness to read the text aloud is often a prelude to a garbled, unintelligible recitation.]

Q: And you admit this is the textbook in effect at the time—and this is the Fifteenth Edition, 2001.

[This was a 2003 case.]

Q: It included the statement that

> If a patient's history or examination is consistent with aortic dissection, imaging studies to evaluate the aorta must be pursued promptly, because of the high risk of catastrophic complications with this diagnosis. A chest X-ray is not sufficient to exclude this diagnosis. Appropriate tests include a chest computed tomography—that's a CT scan—with contrast, or an MRI—magnetic resonant imaging scan—in patients who are hemodynamically stable; or a transesophageal echocardiogram in patients who are less stable. Aortic angiography is no longer the first test of most institutions.

You admit that you have that textbook, and that that statement, that rule, is in the textbook, don't you?

A: That is correct.

Q: Would you tell the jury why a chest X-ray is insufficient, a chest X-ray is not sufficient to exclude the diagnosis of an aortic dissection?

[Asking a "why" question at this point posed a risk, but not a large one. The witness has just agreed that the authoritative textbook that he keeps in his office and uses from time to time taught that a chest X-ray is not enough to find an aortic dissection. The witness could now respond that he disagrees with the textbook, but instead gives a valuable admission that is all the more strong for being put in his words, not Leventhal's.]

A: It doesn't have the appropriate sensitivity, meaning, you could have a normal chest X-ray, and miss an aortic dissection.

[Leventhal now brings the literature quotation down to this case.]

Q: You knew that when you saw Mr. Epperly and you ordered the chest X-ray, that that was not the test to run, if you were going to exclude or rule out aortic dissection. Didn't you?

A: If I was going to be looking for aortic dissection, I would have ordered a CAT Scan.[4]

Many cross-examiners might have used this treatise with many fewer questions and much less impact. They would have incanted the magic words establishing it was an authority, then read the quote, then moved on elsewhere and "saved the ultimate point for closing," as the old commandments counseled. Leventhal instead showed why the book was important, how it was available to the defendant, and how if it had been followed, it might have saved a life.

Example 2: The *Publication* Has to Be Authoritative (Not the Statement within It)

Here's another very good use of a treatise, which also illustrates a common dodge of experts trying to avoid being crossed on a piece of literature they're uncomfortable with. This is taken from Rick Friedman's "polarizing" cross of a forensic psychiatrist in a case where the doctor was accusing Friedman's client of faking his chronic fatigue syndrome.[5]

---

4. *Epperly v. Perez*, Case No. 08CV165, 13th Judicial District, Colorado, January 15, 2009.

5. *Polarizing* is a technique that Rick Friedman explains in his book *Polarizing the Case: Exposing and Defeating the Malingering Myth* (Portland, OR: Trial Guides, 2007). The basic method is to push the witness to the logical extreme of his or her position; for example, a witness who says that "there is no objective evidence" for the plaintiff's complaints of pain is really saying that the plaintiff is a fraud and a cheat.

Mr. Friedman: All right, and it's the forensic psychiatrist's responsibility to highlight and emphasize facts favorable to the side that hired them and to de-emphasize or ignore facts that don't help the side that hired them. Is that fair to say?

Dr. Rosenberg: No, I would say that's a gross mischaracterization.

[The statement actually comes from a treatise that the witness had already cited to the court for a defense motion. The witness had written another, unrelated chapter in the same book. One effective way to use treatises is to first put the statement forward that the attorney wants to use, elicit the witness's comment, then reveal the source of the statement. That's an especially good way to see if a witness will disagree with something the witness has written or is closely associated with, as this treatise is.]

Q: Isn't that what most forensic psychiatrists believe?

A: Your assertion is what most of them believe?

Q: Yes, yes.

A: I wouldn't say so, no.

Q: You filed an affidavit for the judge in this case. Do you recall that, actually, a declaration?

A: Yes.

Q: All right, and a declaration is a statement under oath upon which a party offers and asks the Court to rely upon. Is that right?

A: I'm not an attorney, but that sounds about right.

Q: Yes, and you're very familiar with declarations and how the court systems work, aren't you?

A: Yes.

Q: All right, and in your declaration you cited to Judge Mahan a book called *Principles and Practices—Principles and Practice of Forensic Psychiatry*, Second Edition, are you familiar with that book?

A: I'm familiar with the book. I don't recall whether or not I had cited that in my declaration.

Q: If you'd turn to page five, lines seven and eight.

A: Okay.

Q: Did you cite that text to the judge?

[Reading.]

A: Yes.

Q: And you cited it to the judge because you considered it a reliable resource regarding forensic psychiatry. Is that right?

A: No, I cited it as one reasonable basis for this particular assertion about malingering, not as a blanket reliable source in forensic psychiatry.

[Here the seasoned witness begins to fence with the lawyer over whether the text he has cited meets the magic-words criterion of *reliable authority* so the lawyer can quote from it to the witness. A "blanket reliable source" presumably means all statements in the publication are gospel, but that's not what the rule requires.]

Q: Well, you wouldn't be citing the Court to an unreliable source in forensic psychiatry, would you?

A: Well, certainly I didn't pick out something that I thought was unreliable, but again the premise that I, therefore, accept the entire text or chapter as necessarily reliable or authoritative doesn't follow in my mind.

[This is a common expert dodge for a treatise. The expert mixes two different concepts: the publication's overall reliability and authoritativeness versus whether the witness agrees with the treatise's entire contents. Read carefully and correctly; the treatise rule, Fed. R. Evid. 803(18), requires only that the *publication* be established as authoritative before you can call a quotation in that publication to an expert's attention on cross.]

Q: So you're kind of picking and choosing amongst the portions of the book that will support your case and the portions that don't?

A: No, it's that I'm not willing to fall into agreeing that everything in the chapter or the book that you could find is necessarily authoritative. I gave what is a scholarly and appropriate quote in support of my declaration.

Q: I wasn't asking you to admit it was authoritative, but you thought the book was a reliable resource, didn't you? That's why you own it; that's why you cited it to the judge?

A: I wrote one of the chapters on PTSD in the book, so I certainly think it's a good book, but again I'm not willing to accept that the entire book or even the entire chapter is reliable. Things change over time, things—those are all summary chapters. Yeah, things change over time; evaluations are more sophisticated, so I don't know how else to put it.

Q: All right. Well, let me ask you about a section in your book—

[The witness has come close to acknowledging the reliability of the treatise, but to make sure, the lawyer asks the judge for permission to display it.]

Mr. Friedman: Your Honor, may I show this to the witness on the screen?

The Court: Yes, sir.

Q: This is from page eleven in the book, Dr. Rosenberg, and it reads, "both attorneys and forensic psychiatrists—most attorneys and forensic psychiatrists consider it the responsibility of the forensic psychiatrist to put a spin on the data and highlight and emphasize facts favorable to their side and de-emphasize or even ignore data that are not." Do you agree with that statement?

A: No, I don't. For attorneys, yes, not psychiatrists.

[Friedman's next question links the statement in the treatise to his theme, which he announces directly to the witness.]

Q: Well, that's what you did in this case, isn't it, Dr. Rosenberg? You highlighted the facts that support your malingering theory and de-emphasized or ignored the facts that don't support that theory?[6]

Of course, the psychiatrist will deny that, but Friedman made the point that the book the psychiatrist had quoted to the judge for one purpose has a revealing statement about how at least some forensic psychiatrists go about their courtroom work.

Takeaways

As we end part 2, "Building the Case with Cross-Examination," we have added one more essential skill to our toolbox for effective case-building agreement cross. Learning how to use authoritative literature in cross-examination has both technical elements and nontechnical ones. The quotation gets in front of the jury only when we master the magic words of *reliable authority* and the difference between a *publication* and a *statement*. But that's only the start. Then we have to show why it matters. When we do, we have effectively added another witness to our side of the courtroom drama.

---

6. [*Mead*] *v. Paul Revere Life Ins. Co.*, CV-S-00731-JCM-RJJ, U.S. District Court, District of Nevada, Dec. 10, 2004. (Note that the plaintiff's name in this case is changed to protect privacy.)

PART III

Tearing Down the Witness

The first two parts of this book focused on building: part 1, "You, the Cross-Examiner," focused on building a better you. Part 2, "Building the Case with Cross-Examination," showed us how to build our case with agreement cross.

Now, the demolition derby begins. Witness tear-down cross requires some length to lay out, because there are multiple, distinct ways to do it and because there are lots of opportunities with each of them, and fixable problems too. Here is our plan for part 3, "Tearing Down the Witness."

- Chapter 7, "Planning: The Essential Weapon for Speed," shows how to plan each witness's cross: organizing our material, sorting and ranking it, then working out a full set of good cross questions for each of the best lines. This is the essential nitty-gritty that lets us turn half-baked mush into the art of verbal warfare.

- Chapter 8, "Cross-Examination with Witness Tear-Down Rules," reintroduces the four basic weapons for witness tear-down cross, which we first saw in chapter 3: lack of fit, ignorance, bias, and contradictions. As we look at them again, we see how each works with, and sometimes clashes with, the others, and how sequence can be important in creating the coherent impression of the witness that we strive for. We also discuss how we can sometimes pair case-building cross that was our focus in part 2 with a witness tear-down.

After chapter 8, we drill down with a full chapter on each of the four tear-down strategies introduced in chapter 3.

- **Show the Witness Contradicts Himself:** Chapter 9, "Fixing Contradictions Cross," examines where this type of cross so often fails by first focusing on the two very different goals of a contradictions cross. We could be trying to build our case, and thus we want the jury to decide that what the witness said on some other occasion was the real truth. Or we could be trying to prove that this witness says so many different things that he or she cannot be believed. Failure to think through our goals, as we'll see, is the root of most failed forays into contradictions cross. I will also cover the technical elements of a contradictions impeachment and how we can vary them to good effect, how to anticipate the witness's dodges and excuses, and other ways to improve on this often-launched, often-fizzled cross weapon.

- **Show the Witness Is Ignorant or Makes Mistakes:** Chapter 10, "Exposing the Ignorant Witness," shows why merely exposing errors isn't enough. It's vital to take a witness's error or ignorance about important facts to the next logical step. If we push hard enough, one of two things should happen: we recruit the witness to our side on this important fact, and score a big point for our case-building effort, or we show the witness as hopelessly biased and unworthy of belief.

- **Show the Witness Is Biased** takes two chapters: chapter 11, "Shooting It Out with the Hired-Gun Witness," and chapter 12, "Polarizing the Extreme Witness." Chapter 11 starts with the two most common types of cross-examination of these witnesses, what I call "money cross" and "one-sided cross." They're often combined into a single take. You know the drill: here is a witness who always shows up on the same side of the case and gets paid a lot for it. I explore why these twin bullets often miss the mark and how to improve our aim. Then in chapter 12, I introduce another important weapon in deflating the hired gun: the polarizing cross that pushes the witness to the logical extreme of her position, to show how absurd it really is.

- **Show the Witness Doesn't Fit:** Chapter 13, "Fundamental Attribution," takes the lack-of-fit analysis to the next level. We lawyers often see only one side of *lack of fit*: What's missing from this witness's résumé? The other side of the coin is all the facts about this witness's background (none of which the sponsoring lawyer will ever bring out) that have nothing to do with this case, and that if we play them right, make the witness seem wrong in a weirdly creepy kind of way. I call this the *misfit* facts about the witness, whereas the usual approach is for only the witness's *unfit* attributes. It's powerful stuff.

So how do you find these juicy misfit facts in advance of your cross?

- Chapter 14, "Mining for Dirt," adds to the usual two methods of depositions and email queries to friends and colleagues. In this chapter, I advocate a third way to discover misfit facts.

It's a lot, these eight chapters in part 3. But once you're done, you'll be in the home stretch.

7

Planning: The Essential Weapon for Speed

Speed is the essence of war. Take advantage of the enemy's unpreparedness; travel by unexpected routes and strike him where he has taken no precautions.

—Sun Tzu, *The Art of War*

In part 3 of this book, we will dive deep into the four main ways that we can tear down a witness's credibility with cross-examination:

- Lack of fit
- Mistakes or ignorance
- Bias
- Contradictions

First, in this chapter, we will step back and look at the Achilles' heel that mars more cross-examinations than perhaps any other: disorganization. The issue goes beyond tidiness. This is about thinking through your material and deciding what to do with each line of

cross, then striking quickly and decisively. As in war, so too in cross-examination: speed is essential, and no cross-examiner ever attains the necessary speed without meticulous organization. Dead time is not just embarrassing during a cross, it's counterproductive, because prolonged silence in the courtroom:

- lets jurors' minds wander.
- helps the witness think up a good response.
- allows the adversary time to set up roadblocks.
- counts against you in the judge's internal calculator of time and leeway she will allow for your cross.
- and, maybe most importantly, kills the suspense that keeps your cross riveting and memorable.

So let's put together a system to sideline silence, our unnecessary enemy.

All methods of organization are better than no organization. The only test is whether the method gives you instant access to your chosen weapons. What follows is what works for me. You will notice a fair amount of tree-cutting and redundancy in my method. A hot document I might squirrel away into two or three topic folders, each behind a separate memo, and witness statements similarly take several spins around the photocopier merry-go-round. That's because painful experience has taught me that as soon as something is stored away for safekeeping, it's all downhill from there, as the law of entropy teaches. Things tend to get lost and misplaced. Having backups for critical stuff, both hard copies and on computer, prevents insanity and grouchiness.

Remember that we're working to develop strong cross-examinations that follow one or more of five strategies:

- *Case-building agreement cross,* as we just learned about in part 2, in which we seek agreement from the witness with important principles and Rules that apply to liability and damages or rules of lawsuit conduct.
- *Lack of fit* between the witness's qualifications and the case.

- *Mistakes or ignorance* by the witness about important matters.
- *Bias* of the witness.
- *Contradictions* between the witness and herself, the witness and outside authority (such as the norms of the witness's professional society), the witness and others on her side, or between the witness and common sense.

When we organize our material, therefore, we're looking ultimately to drop each nugget into one of those five buckets. But that comes near the end of the process, as we brainstorm our various lines of questions. First, we analyze all our material, then compile it into a notebook, then do a scoring or ranking of the best, the very best, and the "meh." Finally, we will be ready to write powerful lines of questions.

Organizing for the Case

Before you hone in tightly on organizing for any individual witness, develop a master list of all the principles and rules relevant to the case. The key ones will go on a poster board to display at trial with your witnesses and select adverse witnesses. Sort these with liability on one board, damages on another, and fair-play rules on still another. If your liability case seems too complex to fit all the principles and Rules onto a single poster board—with a maximum of four to six tight sentences—you may be over-thinking the case. On your internal copy of these lists, annotate with the names of all witnesses who might agree with any principle or Rule (and for adverse witnesses, the deposition page or exhibit by which you expect to force agreement). On the public copy of the list, as you win a witness's endorsement of any particular statement, add the witness's name to that item. You could do this on a screen, with a PowerPoint slide, but writing it on a physical object, your poster board or artist's pad, has the squeak of the marker and the smell of the ink to add reality to your work. Plus, at the end you have your whole case neatly summarized on a single board you can use in closing.

Here's an example from a case in which the plaintiff was fired a few weeks after she complained to management about a coworker's sexual harassment. The employer contended she was fired for skipping a key meeting and other unrelated reasons. The employee alleged these reasons were "pretextual" and barred by federal law.

PRINCIPLES BEHIND FAIR AND LEGAL TREATMENT OF EMPLOYEES

Employers want to attract and retain good workers.

Companies do better when they have a reputation as a good place to work.

Evenhanded treatment of employees shows the employer is fair.

Employers can show evenhandedness by following written policies with all employee discipline.

Sexual harassment is illegal and wrong, and complaining of harassment is no reason to fire an employee.

RULES FOR LEGAL TREATMENT OF EMPLOYEES

Employers must not fire employees for making good-faith complaints about sexual harassment.

When firing happens soon after an employee's complaint, employers must show legitimate reason for firing.

Before firing an employee who complained about harassment or discrimination, employers must do the following:

- Tell the employee what she or he did wrong.
- Listen to the employee's side of the story.
- Fit the "punishment" to the "crime."
- Give a long-term valuable employee a chance to fix the issue.
- Fire the employee as a last resort.

Of course, the specific items we listed as Rules to measure the legitimacy of the employer's stated reasons were all violated by this employer and so made for good Rules of the Road.

Look back at the two lists of principles and Rules in chapter 4 for medical miscommunication cases, and see how easily we can adapt the lists to a poster display for cross-examination.[1]

Organizing for the Witness

Now we turn to each witness, with a five-step process:
1. Analyze and sort.
2. Compile.
3. Make a scoring system.
4. Brainstorm your questions.
5. Listen to the direct and adjust your plan, but don't toss it.

Step 1: Analyze and Sort

The first step: analyze the witness's statements and sort each piece by subject matter. Anything in the witness's own words qualifies here. Some are, of course, easier to use than others because they are pre-authenticated, like a deposition transcript compared to an unsigned statement. Yet deposition transcripts have a problem of bulk. Except for short, perfunctory depositions, it's easy to get lost in the forest of words.

Do you dictate deposition digests? I stopped years ago when I realized the digests weren't much good to me, except as a training device to force me to read the transcript line by line and think it through. The finished product, page after page of dense text starting at page one of the transcript and plowing through to the end, is just not a helpful tool for finding things. The organization is completely artificial: by page number and order of questioning in a deposition.

---

1. See chapter 4, "Cross-Examination with Case-Building Rules," and go to the section called "From Principles to Rules, from General to Specific."

What works instead, at least for me, are these:

- an alphabetical topic index
- a more focused subject matter summary and analysis
- a "contradiction" memo
- a "hot quotes" document

An Alphabetical Topic Index

An alphabetical index lists all the subjects discussed in a deposition, with a tight summary of what the witness said on each subject, with page and line references on the side. I pull this together from an old-style deposition digest, then rearrange it by topic. This becomes my master guide to the entire deposition. Here's an excerpt for the defendant in a case about a severe stroke a patient experienced from a radiologist's attempt to "coil" an aneurysm in her brain:

ALPHABETICAL TOPIC INDEX

Backup Neurosurgeon:
  Lined up none for emergency 67–68

Blockage A-Comm:
  Increased stroke risk 24
  "Only time will tell" 24
  Is "complication" unless original plan is to block parent artery 133
  No cause for immediate concern 29

Cross flow:
  Needed 13–14, 60, 65, 114, 116
  Not needed 148–49, 168–69

CT scan at 3 p.m.:
  What it showed 108, 109, 129
  Why ordered, for perforation risk 109

A More Focused Subject Matter Summary and Analysis

I create a summary and analysis for each of the key topics the witness testified about. I typically do a cut-and-paste from the digitized transcript, with the witness's actual words on one side of the paper and my comments on the other side, or one on top of the other (we're not sticklers for uniform page layouts in my office), like this:

> **PAGE 66—SURGEON HANGS HIMSELF— PAIN UNRELIEVED BY MEDS**
>
> Q: But sometimes narcotics can mislead you in a patient with abdominal pain. They can mask the seriousness of the problem?
>
> A: I don't think so. If a patient truly has peritoneal signs, no amount of pain medicine is going to cover it.
>
> [show nurses notes of unrelieved pain]

A "Contradiction" Memo

This document compares what the witness said on a key topic with other witnesses, documents, literature, and so on. The easiest way to do this is to line up the witness's key statements on the left side of the page, and on the right side, list all the corresponding contradictions with sources and record citations. Creating these cross-referenced lists will help you readily see promising lines of cross.

A "Hot Quotes" Document

This document puts the best "dirty dozen" or so statements of the witness onto a sheet or two of paper, cross-referenced to whatever digital file I've created to put the quotation in front of the witness and jury on a display screen.

Showing "Hot Quotes" During Cross

When I have particular hot quotes that I want to show to the jury during cross, I usually do some combination of the following:

- **Text clips**
  A digital text clip shows the deposition transcript with page and line numbers.[2] Or if it's a written report by the witness, a text clip could be an excerpt showing where it came from in the report.

- **Large poster boards**
  Poster boards should show the same text, dressed up with the witness's full name, deposition date (or report date), and any other authenticating details. This could include the witness's signature on the errata sheet noting no changes to the transcript or the witness's photo if it seems *really* important, or if I think I can use this same board in closing argument. I try to always use posters because their hard, tangible reality beats a soft screen display every time.

- **Video clips**
  When showing video clips, I show the full question and answer, or at least the answer. Video clips work best when you ruthlessly cut them to the core essential quotation, but watch out for the rule of completeness, discussed in chapter 15, "Evidence Rules Every Cross-Examiner Must Know." I try to name these video files in some logical way that makes them easy to find. For example, a file named Smith0722 is a video clip for witness Smith's deposition starting on page 7, line 22. I usually mark my copy of the transcript itself with the names of each video clip and their start and end points. That helps remind me I did a clip on a subject even if I don't have the master hot-quotes document in front of me.

---

2. Both text clips and video clips are easy to create in a program like Sanction or Trial Director. The big trick is, once made, finding them again. That's why I create index documents and special digital trial presentation folders for each witness and each topic.

Practice Tip: Video Clips

When you use video clips, the confrontation with the deposition quotation moves much more crisply than when you have to hand up a copy of the transcript to the witness and read it aloud. The impact on jurors' eyes and ears of seeing the same witness say something quite different than what he just said in the courtroom is also hard to beat.

Give the same treatment to any other witness statements worth special attention, such as a piece of professional literature the witness wrote. Create both a digitized version to display on screen and maybe also a hard copy to set up on an easel.

Practice Tip: Rule of Completeness

In all this digesting and analyzing, watch out for the "rule of completeness," an evidence rule intended to prevent sneak attacks with out-of-context material. Make sure you're not missing something that changes the meaning of what you want to quote with this witness.

Step 2: Compile

The next step is to compile in one place all the material you want to use with the same witness. I set up a three-ring binder for each witness.

Obvious stuff for inclusion:

- the witness's deposition
- any other statements
- interrogatory answers if this is a party

- the witness's résumé or CV (which after all is a "statement" itself, written by the witness)
- emails to and from this witness
- any other relevant tidbits I've learned about this person

All my memos analyzing the witness go in this binder too. This becomes my working notebook for the witness. I use highlighter, sticky tabs, and other ways to mark the good stuff.

I duplicate most of this material in a digital folder on my laptop. I use Dropbox to synchronize everything in this folder between my office PC, my laptop, and other members of the trial team. That way, if I get an idea that I want to add to a certain strategy memo or witness Q&A outline, I can do it anywhere and it's automatically synced everywhere it's needed. (Bear in mind this doesn't work in a courtroom with no Internet connection.)

Now, back in the world of paper: Anything I might want to use while the witness is on the stand, I will make an extra copy to hand to the witness. This always includes a complete, clean copy of the deposition, plus any other documents I might want to use with this witness. If there are more than just a handful of these, I sort them by topic with old-fashioned manila folders. At the end of this process, I have a stack of documents for each Q&A topic sorted into a single folder. Then at the top of that folder, I write my outline of facts I want to bring out in this line of questions.[3]

STEP 3: MAKE A SCORING SYSTEM

The next step is to make a simple scoring system to sort the wheat from the chaff. Here is a way to prioritize the contradictions, factual errors, bias, and miscellaneous dirt you may want to pursue with this witness:

---

3. We'll get to that outline later in this chapter, in the section called "Sample Chapter and Page Outline: Lack-of-Fit Cross-Examination of a Life-Care Planner."

WITNESS INFORMATION SCORING SYSTEM

Which version? (underline)	Underline the version that helps. For any contradictory statement, ask, Which version helps your case? Ordinarily any changes to a witness's story or new elements will hurt your side, and you want the fact-finder to accept the old version. But not always: sometimes a new fact helps you, and the most you need to do with it is underline it so everyone remembers it.
Matters a lot (***)	Give three asterisks if the fact matters to the case outcome. Put another way, if the *opposite* of Fact A were proven to be true, would it matter? This also works for witness-centered facts. Does the fact directly and obviously undermine the witness's credibility?
Helpful (*)	Give one asterisk if the fact is helpful but not decisive. These single-star items I will usually drop eventually, unless I can pull together some pattern that makes their combination a three-star play.
Doesn't matter (-)	Give a minus sign to facts that don't matter, unless there are a lot and they show a pattern.
Prepared to handle (+/-)	Add a plus for items you are pretty sure the witness isn't ready to deal with, a minus for items where the witness will be well rehearsed.

So, what matters? Lots of facts that seem like tasty morsels at first really don't count when you try to finally wedge them into the relevance box.

For example, is the fact embarrassing to the witness but not related to credibility? Such as in these cases:

- Is the witness on his sixth marriage? (But if the witness purports to be an expert in sexual harassment, that fact might matter to credibility if played right.)
- Did the witness declare bankruptcy a few years ago? (But bankruptcy could be relevant to credibility if it fits with an attack on money motivating the witness's testimonial work.)

These miscellaneous items of dirt are often "minus" facts that you don't want to touch directly, unless you can develop specific further facts within them that go straight to truth-telling. Without the direct link to truthfulness, these dirt items soil your hands and smack of desperation.

Our last scoring item ("Prepared to handle") focuses on how well prepared the witness will be to withstand the cross on any particular point.

Some things to think about:

- Does the witness know the inconsistency you are digging into or have a way to anticipate your line of cross before getting up to testify? For example, if the witness changed a fact, did the old version of the fact appear in a report the witness signed, and does the adverse attorney know about it? If the witness knows about the inconsistency, be aware that the witness may have thought up some clever way to discount the inconsistency's importance. But that may not dissuade you from pursuing it, especially if you can establish that at the time of the prior statement, the witness had every opportunity and motive to get the facts right.[4]

- Has the direct examination brought out the witness's error and tried to neutralize it? This can either add or subtract from how you rate this error. If your opponent handled the correction smoothly and persuasively, it may eliminate the item from your list of potential cross. But if there's any awkwardness or defensiveness in how the witness explains the error in the direct exam, consider marking the item with a + to indicate you should ask about it.

- Did the witness make this a new error on direct examination for the first time (and your opponent did not correct it)? If so, add an asterisk. The witness will likely be unprepared for you to expose the error and will be more ripe for you to win a

---

4. See the checklist in chapter 9, "Fixing Contradictions Cross," on prior inconsistent statements.

clean concession or to show as completely biased. Remember, exaggerations can count as errors too, and even worse since they're usually not innocent like a simple mistake would be.[5]

- Do you have original research on the witness that you did not obtain through formal discovery? This pushes up the priority of the item, as long as it's relevant to credibility.[6]

This scoring system gives you a quick way to select the points you want to make on cross.

For example:

- **Any decisive fact.** If the witness has gotten the fact wrong on direct, it will be worth marking with a + to definitely ask, even if you suspect the witness has been informed of the error. *However*, if the witness explains the error so persuasively on direct examination that you are completely deflated, then leave this fact off your list.

- **Helpful but not decisive facts.** Mark these with a + to definitely ask if you believe the witness is unprepared to deal with them.

- **Facts that don't matter.** These are hardly ever worth raising, even if you're convinced the witness is unprepared for your thrust. *However*, if you have a lot of these facts that form a pattern supporting whatever overall impression you are trying to create of this witness in jurors' minds, it might be worth raising these facts. But be prepared for a lengthy cross as you go through all these separate items trying to create a coherent picture.

Once you have a set of facts to examine the witness about, you're ready to brainstorm your questions, topic by topic.

---

5. Randy Kinnard provided a great example of how to pounce on an exaggeration that first came up in direct exam, in his "Easter Sunday" cross featured in chapter 17, "Technique Problems and Their Cures."

6. See chapter 13, "Fundamental Attribution," for a beautiful case study of a cross-examination of an expert composed almost entirely from stranger-than-fiction facts gleaned by cross-examiner Jim Lees from public documents.

Step 4: Brainstorm Your Questions

The next step is to brainstorm each of your cross topics and figure out how you want their sequence to flow. Your most important organizing tool for cross-examination starts with a single sheet of blank paper. If you follow this simple system, your cross-examinations will become more creative and effective, you will win more cases, and your teeth will remain forever bright. (Perhaps an exaggeration, but only slight.)

Do this:

1. Start with what you've tentatively decided is the most promising line of questions for this witness.

2. Write at the top of your blank sheet the *goal* for what you want the jury to conclude after you've finished this line, for example:

    » What the witness said earlier is more likely to be the truth than what he said on direct.

    » This expert doesn't have as impressive a background as the other side's expert.
    Or whatever impression you are trying to create on that specific topic. Of course, any good Rule of the Road qualifies for a top-of-the-sheet headline.

3. On the same sheet, write all the facts that you can prove that lead to this conclusion. Go down the page, one fact to a line.

4. Beside each fact, list the source of the fact. Be specific. For a deposition, use the page and line numbers. For a document, use the exhibit number and page. Instant retrieval is your goal.

5. Consider attaching an extra copy of the key excerpts from these source documents to the back of your single sheet. (Remember what NASA taught: redundant systems don't fail.)

6. Add a third column on the page for your notes to yourself about any particular fact or the source material.

7. Finish up with a single sheet that has your goal at the top and three columns below, listing each fact, its source, and any comments that go with the fact. Each single sheet becomes a chapter in your story.[7]

8. If you go longer than a single sheet, consider breaking your goal statement into sub-parts, and do a sheet for each part.

9. Do this single-page method for each line of cross.

As you start working through your facts and goals, you will realize this is a dynamic (and fun!) process. You will see that some goals are too broad and you need to narrow them. You will develop more facts that lead you to persuasively establish a particular goal. Or you will see that your facts for a particular goal are so sparse you're never going to persuasively establish it. So you do more fact work or drop that line of cross. It just gets better and better the longer you work with this method.

This method is not merely an antidote to disorganization. It helps you think about each issue in depth, clarify your achievable goals, and develop good lines of questions with more persuasive depth than you ordinarily would have. An example will show the power: an outline of a lack-of-fit cross on an expert witness's qualifications.

Before the example, an important word on muscle memory: I don't expect you to use the chapter and page method for each witness, each topic, and each trial for the rest of your career. You won't need to. The process of thinking through the material and writing it down will eventually free you up from a script. It will become like muscle memory. As we will see on prior inconsistent statements, there is a list of facts to run through that show why the old statement is more reliable than the new contradictory one. When you write that out a few times, you will learn how to do it without notes. Then you will have hit your peak as a cross-examiner.

---

7. In their terrific book *Cross-Examination: Science and Techniques*, 2nd ed. (LexisNexis, 2004), Larry S. Pozner and Roger J. Dodd first called this the "chapter method" of cross. See especially their chapters 9 and 10 for more examples and further elucidation of the technique.

Sample Chapter and Page Outline: Lack-of-Fit Cross-Examination of a Life-Care Planner

In a recent trial, I represented a young woman who lost her left leg above the knee when a wall of improperly built concrete blocks crashed down onto her. To prognosticate about her future medical and caretaking needs, we hired a doctor who specialized in physical medicine and rehabilitation (PM&R). PM&R doctors see these patients regularly over the many years that they live without a limb. The defense hired a nurse who did full-time life-care planning for legal cases, and 99 percent of that for defense lawyers. Her plan costed out about one-tenth of my guy's plan. We also had on our side a *prosthetist*, not a doctor but a highly trained technician employed by a prosthetic device company, who regularly fits and adjusts prosthetic limbs and who had seen our client many times for adjustments and fittings.

I like to take advantage of the two-phase cross that we are allowed with expert witnesses and nearly always ask a carefully developed line of questions about the witness's qualifications. Even if I have zero chance of winning a motion to knock out the witness as unqualified, if I can deflate the witness's credentials in front of the jury before any opinions ooze from said expert's orifice, I've won a substantial victory in the contest of impressions.

So for this witness, here is the first top-of-the-page headline I wrote:

> *This witness doesn't have nearly the experience of the plaintiff's expert in working with above-knee-amputation patients* (AKA in amputee jargon).

Below that I started writing facts, like this (with a few comments in parentheses):

- Not a PM&R doctor.
- Not a doctor of any kind. (Spin this out: no medical school, no residency, no power to write prescriptions for drugs or therapies.)
- Never supervised amputee or prosthetic clinic.

Planning: The Essential Weapon for Speed

- Never worked in amputee or prosthetic clinic (none listed in credentials in CV).

My facts list transitioned into questions for the witness about what she knew:

- Is she aware there are such things as amputee clinics?
- Where are such clinics in the D.C. area? (Likely to make lucky guess that local military hospital has one, so may not ask.)
- Ever volunteered at an amputee clinic? Or prosthetic clinic?
- Ever even *been to* one such clinic? (Ask if shows vulnerability with prior questions.)

That fills a page right there, and once I started cogitating, I realized there was much more to do with this witness's qualifications. So I started a new sheet with a slightly narrower headline goal:

Doesn't work with AKA patients. Just writes care plans for lawsuits.

- Outside of lawsuits, works with no amputees on regular basis.
- Works with no doctors who see amputees regularly.
- Works with no prosthetists who regularly refit patients with new devices.
- Never met our client's prosthetist.
- Never talked to our prosthetist.
- Never asked prosthetist to comment on her care plan.
- Doesn't work with any physical therapists re: amputees.

Again, my facts list transitioned into questions for the witness:

- When was the last time measured any stump to refit prosthesis? (Constant issue for our client due to tissue changes, injuries to stump, and so on.)

- When was the last time did home visit of AKA patient, not for a lawsuit?
- As a nurse, have you ever treated patient with skin breakdown in leg stump?
- Have you ever *examined* a patient's stump in any ongoing patient-nurse relationship?
- Have you ever examined our client's stump? (Client says no. Report doesn't mention.)

And then I started another sheet, with this headline: *Just writes care plans for lawsuits.* (I pulled this from the last sheet, since I filled that sheet with clinical facts and didn't have room to get around to the related but different point about being a lawsuit nurse.)

And more questions on this new sheet:

- So your *only* experience with amputees is in litigation?
- You've generally been on side adverse to them?
- And you see them once or twice at most?
- For something they will live with for rest of their lives?

Remember, since you have a right to challenge the qualifications of any expert before that expert is allowed to give opinions, that effectively means that any expert cross can be divided into two phases: qualifications (sometimes called voir dire) and substance. Here, I'm still on the qualifications phase of the cross. I haven't even started puncturing her knowledge of the facts of our client's prosthesis, where I have other lines of questions set up to show how little she knows.

Step 5: Listen to the Direct and Adjust Your Plan, but Don't Toss It

When we stand up to start our cross-examination, we need to be careful not to let our vivid new courtroom impressions trump our careful pretrial plans. This is a classic error for the warrior going into battle. In 1812, the Prussian strategist Clausewitz put the point this way in his *Principles of War:*

> Visual impressions gained during actual combat are more vivid than those gained beforehand by mature reflection. But they give us only the outward appearance of things, which, as we know, rarely corresponds to their essence. We therefore run the risk of sacrificing mature reflection for first impression.
>
> The natural timidity of humans, which sees only one side to everything, makes this first impression incline toward fear and exaggerated caution.
>
> Therefore we must fortify ourselves against this impression and have blind faith in the results of our own earlier reflections, in order to strengthen ourselves against the weakening impressions of the moment.[8]

We need to take Clausewitz's admonition to heart. Of course, the witness might look a little more polished than she did in a deposition many months earlier. But don't falter. At the core, this is the same witness as before. You have read and organized the transcripts. You have catalogued all the inconsistent statements and the hot documents that the witness will want to run from. You have a well-thought-out set of goals for building your case through this witness and, if necessary, tearing down the witness's credibility. So take heart: good planning and organization will see you through.

Not that you get to coast half-listening through the witness's direct examination. Intent focus on the actual words that your opponent and the witness use, and appreciating what they have

---

8. Carl von Clausewitz, *Principles of War*, translated by Hans Gatzke (Washington, DC: Military Services Publishing Co., 1942).

left out, will help decide your top priorities for the cross. Any misstated or exaggerated fact can make a spectacular springboard to start an effective cross. Pay attention to the witness's tone, demeanor, choice of words, hesitations: all that provides fodder for last-minute adjustments of your outline. Eleventh-hour fear and doubt should not be part of this equation, except for realistic fear that goes with an honest assessment of what this witness has to say and your own capacities to work with it.

Takeaway: The Thrill of Thoroughly Thinking It Through

Organization of your material is a lot more than shuffling and arranging paper. The real goal is tough analysis and development of a game plan, any element of which you can instantly pull the trigger on.

Once you start the creative process of brainstorming your questions, you see how exhilarating it can be. You are using your own brainpower and wits to uncover treasure troves of cross-examination that otherwise you might have skimmed with a quick drive-by to little effect.

The rejoinder to this is, "Well, you've got great facts going for you. My cases are tougher." My response is, no. We cross-examiners create our own opportunities with hard work. We imagine what the facts might be, and then discover they've been laying there all along, just waiting for us to notice.

Further Reading

Be sure to read chapter 14, "Mining for Dirt," which will help you find a lot better material for cross than any deposition. A spectacular example of what a lawyer did with a simple Internet search of an opposing expert's history of setting up corporations is found in chapter 13, "Fundamental Attribution."

Exercise

Do not leave this chapter before you look back over your notes for the next big witness you have to cross examine and develop a better organization of your material, followed by a close analysis. By the end, you should have a set of chapters of cross, with nice clean goals on the top of each page and annotated lists of all facts that get you to each goal. Formidable, yes!

8

Cross-Examination with Witness Tear-Down Rules

In preparing for battle I have always found that plans are useless, but planning is indispensable.

—Dwight D. Eisenhower

Now that we've organized our material for the witness, it's time to consider in more depth the four basic strategies of witness tear-down cross-examination, which we first introduced in chapter 3, "Choosing the Weapons Right for You." In this chapter, I will sketch out the four methods in more detail and show how each works or doesn't work with each other and with agreement cross that we learned about in part 2, "Building the Case with Cross-Examination."

This is another step in planning effective cross-examination. As Eisenhower recognized, the *process* of planning can be more important than the eventual plan itself. Planning helps you think through the possibilities and prepare for the unforeseen events that happen in any battle, when the enemy does not respond exactly as forecast.

Remember, with case-building Rules, we enlist the witness's help in undermining the other side's case, by showing that the witness has to agree with key elements of our case. But when the witness cannot or will not help our cause, then it is time to undermine the witness's credibility with witness tear-down Rules. At the same time, we must keep our focus on building our case, not merely taking down the witness.

The four strategies of witness tear-down cross follow:

- *Lack of Fit* (show that the witness's background and knowledge don't fit the case)
- *Ignorance or Mistakes* (show what the witness doesn't know)
- *Bias* (show the witness is biased)
- *Contradictions* (show the witness's contradictions):
    » between the witness's current testimony and the witness's prior statements
    » between the witness and other witnesses
    » between the witness and published authorities
    » between the witness and common sense

Keeping in mind the goals for each of these will help us construct good Rules in each category. That's the first step. Remember, as set out in part 2, "Building the Case with Cross-Examination," on case-building Rules, the method for executing any Rules-focused cross-examination is:

1. Create a good Rule: clear, inarguable, important, and violated. (And make sure you can show, either with this witness or another, that the Rule is important and was broken here.)
2. Announce the Rule and get the witness to agree.
3. Explain why the Rule is important.
4. Show the Rule has been violated.

A special note on lay witnesses: The same categories of cross-examination apply to lay witnesses just as much as experts. We also go through the same analysis to set up Rules and show their violation. *But* one thing we might do differently with a lay witness is to skip announcing the Rule and having the witness agree with it. That is, after all, eliciting an opinion from a lay witness, who is ordinarily present in court only to give facts he or she observed.

When we think about each category of witness-centered cross-examination, some clear plus inarguable Rules become, well, clear. That will also help us to start to see ways we can mix and match these four different types of witness-centered cross in the appropriate case.

LACK OF FIT

The point of a lack-of-fit cross of an expert is to get the fact-finder to conclude: "This witness is not really an expert on what seems important in this case." Lack of fit focuses on the witness's background and ability to perceive things, and how that *fits* for this case. With an expert witness, the expert is always going to be an expert in *something*; the issue is whether it's the kind of expertise that the jury needs. Or in the case of a lay witness, there's something about the witness's ability to perceive events—memory, vision, hearing, whatever—that makes the witness's observations unreliable.

The lack-of-fit cross-examination goes hand in hand with an ignorance-or-mistakes cross-examination. The latter focuses on the witness's errors about case-specific facts. But it ought to be clear that people who lack the background to really know a field will make more mistakes when they're asked to opine about something they have no business dabbling in.

So here's our all-purpose lack-of-fit Rule for experts:

- An expert witness must have deep experience and knowledge about what's important in the case.

That rule is best tweaked for the particulars of the case, and in the final chapter of this book, you will see how I adjusted the rule for an expert who had deep experience, but in the distant past, and lacked current credentials.

I showed an outline of a lack-of-fit cross of a life-care planner in the last chapter on organization. Here's some actual Q&A of the same kind of witness by San Francisco lawyer Mike Kelly. We don't want to pick on life-care planners too much, but sometimes they offer fat targets. Kelly's case concerned a man who fell down a stairwell and was paralyzed. As Kelly shows, the lack-of-fit issue not only concerns what the expert lacks, but what the expert does have that doesn't fit the case, sometimes in weird ways.

MR. KELLY: Do you recognize these pages as some of the pages off of your website?

EXPERT LIFE-CARE PLANNER: Yes.

Q: You would never want to put anything up that was untruthful, would you?

A: No.

Q: And, in fact, on this particular site you advertise that you do hair removal. Correct?

A: Correct.

Q: Botox injections?

A: Yes.

Q: Is photo rejuvenation a skin care?

A: It is.

Q: Is that something you do?

A: Yes.

Q: You do collagen injections?

A: I do filler injections.

Q: What is filler?

A: Collagen.

Q: Laser skin care?

A: Yes.

Q: And do you have a health plan for women that for $150 a month they get their medical care plus all their hair removal?

A: They have a choice of services. If they don't have insurance, yeah, they can join that.

Q: And there is no advertising on here that you have a specialization in spinal cord injury?

A: No.

Q: There is no advertising on here that you welcome people paralyzed or in wheelchairs, is there?

A: No.[1]

Nice. Now you may wonder, why do such innocuous details grip our attention? And why can these details in the right combination devastate the witness's credibility? It's a cognitive bias we all share called *fundamental attribution*: our tendency to look inside others, to their fundamental attributes, to explain their behavior, rather than looking at how external circumstances might have brought about the same behavior.

We will come back to how good cross-examiners exploit fundamental attribution in chapter 13, "Fundamental Attribution," where Jim Lees uses it to execute a lack-of-fit cross that shows how an expert who professes to be a jack-of-all-trades is indeed a master of none.

Ignorance or Mistakes

At the end of a cross focused on established facts in the case that the witness doesn't know or is mistaken about, we want the fact-finder

---

1. Testimony of Kelly Lance, in *Sherman v. Hotel St. Francis*, LLC, Cause No. D-101-CV-2012-00920, First Judicial District Court, County Of Santa Fe, NM, June 17, 2014.

to conclude: "The witness doesn't know important stuff that he should know."

An ignorance-or-mistakes Rule for experts:

- An expert witness must know the important facts of the case.

We saw a spectacular ignorance-or-mistakes cross by Jim Gilbert in chapter 3, "Choosing the Weapons Right for You." Remember how he announced the Rule as he started the cross: *Do you believe that an expert coming into court testifying in a case like this has an obligation to get his facts straight?* Plain English is good English. We will also show later in this chapter how an ignorance-or-mistakes cross blends well with a lack-of-fit cross.

BIAS

A *bias* cross should have jurors reaching this conclusion: "I cannot rely on this witness as an objective truth-teller because he's got an ax to grind." But it's almost never enough to point out the simple fact of bias or self-interest. If it was, our cross-examination of the adverse party in a case would start and end with, "So you're the [defendant or plaintiff] in this case, is that right? Nothing further." We usually have to put bias examinations together with something else to prove the witness's unreliability. Often that becomes the witness's evasions, exaggerations, contradictions, or inconsistencies.

A bias Rule for experts:

- An expert witness must be objective, fair, and impartial.

A bias Rule for all other witnesses:

- It's okay to have an interest in the outcome of a case, but you have to acknowledge your bias and recognize it might color your testimony.

This Rule for nonexperts is one you likely will deploy in court infrequently, at least out loud. It's clear and inarguable, but remember, we challenge witnesses with Rules only when we think we can show that the witness violated the Rule. And most lay witnesses who violate this bias rule will admit it only by their demeanor on the witness stand. Their words most likely will deny any coloration to their testimony from their interest in the case. Paradoxically, a witness who quietly acknowledges the truth of the Rule may gain credibility, not lose it. So deploying this Rule explicitly only makes sense if you think the witness will "protest too much," and thus convict himself of bias by refusing to admit the obvious.

One important feature of bias cross is your tone of voice and sharpness of questions. For a hired-gun professional witness, you are okay with a challenging tone and sharp questions. For a novice witness, use a gentler approach. And sometimes the goal of starting a cross with questions about fairness and objectivity is not to prove bias, but to remind an honest witness of the ground rules so as to win concessions more easily on substantive issues.

In a case about a teenager who experienced a brain injury in an accident, Rick Friedman faced a neuropsychologist who had testified only once before. The defense counsel who hired this doctor also had plenty to work with: the plaintiff had had some cognitive functioning issues before the accident, and he had made a seemingly good recovery for the most part.

So a softer tone was required:

MR. FRIEDMAN: Doing an IME, an independent medical exam, like you did in this case is a big responsibility, isn't it?

EXPERT NEUROPSYCHOLOGIST: Yes.

Q: It's a really serious thing?

A: Yes.

Q: Before you come into court and tell the jury that someone doesn't need a particular support or a particular type of care, you want to be really careful that you've got it right, don't you?

A: Yes.

Q: Because you understand that if the jury accepts your view of things, someone might not get care they otherwise need?

A: Yes.

Q: So you want to be thorough?

A: Yes.

Q: You want to be unbiased?

A: Yes.

Q: You want to be careful?

A: Yes.

Q: Fair?

A: Yes.

Q: You don't want to speculate?

A: Well, often we—you put us into the position of having to speculate, so I do need to speculate sometimes on whether something is going to work or not, so—my understanding of the word, "speculate," this is what I don't like about legal work, is that I am put into the position of having to speculate about the future for a particular client, and I—that's a very difficult decision for us to be put in, let me tell you.

Q: Well, you weren't put in the position; you had a choice, didn't you?

A: Exactly, yes.

Q: You're not saying anybody forced you to be here, are you?

A: Correct.[2]

When the witness's track record justifies a firmer approach, there are many sources of bias worth exploring in the right case. For experts,

---

2. *Stewart v. Martin*, Case No. 07-2-36853-1, King County, Superior Court of the State of Washington, May 20, 2009.

anything that puts the witness into the hired-gun box—annual testimonial income, money on this case, testimonial patterns favoring one side—can be worth doing, because jurors heavily discount professional witnesses.[3]

Contradictions

A successful *contradictions* cross seeks to create one of two impressions with the jury:

- What was said previously is closer to the truth than what the witness just said on direct examination.

Or

- We cannot trust this witness as a truth-teller because she keeps contradicting herself

    » about what she said or did before.

    » about what others say.

    » about what we know is true.

Those two impressions are more different than they might at first look. The first one is about building your case. The second is about tearing down the witness.

Case-building contradiction, looking to establish the *truth* of the prior statement, is often a lot more productive than witness tear-down contradictions cross. If the prior statement helps your case, the witness's fight to renounce the point helps you enhance its importance, as long as you can clearly bring out that these are two very different statements and not "oh, you misunderstand what I was trying to say back then." Also, when you're trying to show the reliability of the previous out-of-court statement, time is on your side. Most humans remember things better closer to the original event. The more recent version is automatically more suspect. Plus

---

[3]. We'll treat this in more depth in chapter 11, "Shooting It Out with the Hired-Gun Witness."

there are a bunch of other ways besides the passage of time to show the reliability of the original statement.[4]

On the other hand, if the purpose of the contradictions cross is witness tear-down, it's usually not enough to point out one contradiction, especially on a trivial matter. (And if the witness's previous statement doesn't help the merits of your case, you are trending toward the trivial when you make a big deal about differences between then and now that ultimately don't add up to much except that they are different.)

If you're really serious about using contradictions to attack the witness's overall credibility, then you need to expose a pattern of contradictions that, in the end, has the bystander saying, "This testimony just doesn't add up."

So here are two contradictions Rules for experts that we can try:

- Expert witnesses should be consistent and reliable in their opinions.

Or,

- Expert witnesses should give the same opinion in court as they would give outside of court.

You can try variations of the above, depending on the case. For example, in a case where the witness had a routine practice outside of court inconsistent with his in-court opinion, the advice comes to mind that Richard Nixon's first attorney general, John Mitchell, gave to the press corps at the start of his presidency: *"Watch what we do, not what we say."*

When she has a contradiction like that in her pocket, New Mexico attorney Randi McGinn likes to open an expert cross-examination like this: "Dr. _____, have you heard this saying: 'Actions speak louder than words'? What does it mean to you? Do you agree with it?"

---

4. See my checklist on inconsistent statements in chapter 9, "Fixing Contradictions Cross."

All those questions are safe and, better yet, fun, for a number of reasons:

- This is a clear plus inarguable Rule, one the witness will look foolish trying to argue with.

- People understand it's an anti-hypocrite Rule. Nobody likes a hypocrite.

- The witness is likely to have no good answer prepared. Witnesses say dumb things when they're unprepared.

- Alert jurors will sense this is the setup for a tear-down and will perk up. Nobody can avoid gawking at a car wreck when one appears ahead.

Of course, you have to execute on the follow-through and show that the witness's words in court differ from what she did or said outside of court.

Contradictions with Professional Norms

Contradictions between the witness's lawsuit work and the norms of his or her profession can be a potent source of cross-examination. Of course, the same contradictions can make for a good *Daubert* motion[5] to knock out the witness entirely, but shrewd cross-examiners recognize that this weapon can sometimes be better left sheathed until trial.

Defense medical examiners are often vulnerable to attack for issuing courtroom opinions that violate the usual rules of medical diagnosis. For instance, listen carefully to the patient's history (a good rule for the examiner who does only a paper review without

---

5. The core idea was captured in Justice Breyer's opinion for the Supreme Court in *Kumho Tire Co. v. Carmichael*, 526 U.S. 137 (1999), when he wrote of the *Daubert* doctrine's gatekeeping requirement: "The objective of that requirement is to ensure the reliability and relevancy of expert testimony. It is to make certain that an expert, whether basing testimony upon professional studies or personal experience, *employs in the courtroom the same level of intellectual rigor that characterizes the practice of an expert in the relevant field.*" (emphasis added)

ever laying hands on the patient). Or, look at all the patient's X-rays (or whatever relevant tests the expert has overlooked).

An overall Rule that often works for these experts:

- A doctor's courtroom diagnosis should be at least as careful and thorough as a diagnosis made in the clinic.

All professional societies that have published norms for their members' testimonial work condemn the cherry-picking expert who grabs facts here and there but ignores other data that don't fit the story the expert wants to sell.[6]

So a simple Rule to cross-examine such a witness could be as follows:

- A doctor who examines a plaintiff at the request of the defense must consider all relevant facts about the injury.

For other damages experts, you can try Rules like these:

- A witness developing a life-care plan must consider what might happen if assumptions turn out to be too optimistic and the patient needs more resources than planned for.[7]

---

6. For example, the American Academy of Orthopedic Surgeons asks its members who testify to sign an oath pledging, among other things: "I will conduct a thorough, fair, and impartial review of the facts and the medical care provided, *not excluding any relevant information*." http://www3.aaos.org/member/expwit/statement.cfm (emphasis added). Our firm has compiled a good set of these expert ethics statements from several dozen medical societies, here: http://www.patrickmalonelaw.com/useful-information/legal-resources/attorneys/legal-resources-attorneys-injured-clients/medical-society-statements-expert-witness-testimony/.

7. David Ball suggests more potential rules along these lines, such as, "To protect the patient, the life-care planner must create a plan based solely on what's best for the patient, not on the financial interests of the defendant." And, "To protect the patient, the life-care planner must specify all possible harmful consequences of each item you leave out of your life-care plan." (personal communication)

- An economist figuring lifetime costs must not force the plaintiff into risky investments to be able to pay for needed care.

We saw in chapter 4, "Cross-Examination with Case-Building Rules," that damages issues can make for case-building agreement cross, where we're not so much trying to pull down the witness's credibility, but to build up the core of our case. The Rules sketched out above straddle the line between agreement cross and witness-tear-down cross, because they set out norms that the witness should, but usually won't, agree to.

Impressions from Contradictions Cross

Always with contradictions cross, ask yourself this: Where am I going with this? What is my point? When we're cross-examining with professional norms, it's those norms we want to hold up as signposts for the jury to adopt. When we're doing a self-contradiction cross, we have to decide which version of the witness's story we want the jury to accept. Always we are looking to create an impression of the witness. Where self-contradiction cross-examinations often fail is in having too few contradictions or contradictions on trivial points. That adds up to a quibbling, ineffectual cross, if the purpose is merely to discredit the witness and not prove that what he or she said before is what counts.

Jurors have a much higher tolerance for inconsistencies than lawyers do. The contradictions cross that we finish with seeming triumph, wanting to high-five everyone at the counsel table, can leave jurors unmoved. That was the lesson a team of jury consultants found when they surveyed 810 mock jurors on how their impression of a witness would change with the introduction of an inconsistent statement. The answer: surprisingly little. Jurors tend to want to cut witnesses a lot of slack and assume an honest mistake is the reason for variations between pretrial and trial statements.

The consultants concluded:

> The lesson for lawyers here is that they should not be so quick to assume that catching a witness in an

inconsistency destroys his or her credibility. Jurors will look at how the witness comports himself or herself on the stand in determining how much weight to ascribe to the inconsistency. Chances are better than not that, even if the inconsistency causes the witness to lose that point, he or she can still carry the day on other issues.[8]

How do you know what is enough for a cross whose goal is to create the impression that the witness's story just doesn't add up? Here's an analogy that works for me. Consider two hanging baskets filled with what seem to be live plants. One is fake, the other genuine. How do we tell the difference? The fake plants are too perfect. The real ones have some leaves starting to droop, flowers starting to fade, insect bite marks here and there. So too with witness stories. The fake ones are just too convenient, too tidy. When we point out only one or two blemishes in an account, that can backfire on the cross-examiner, because, just like the basket of real plants with real untidiness, no human is perfect. So once we start pointing out blemishes and contradictions, we generally have to take the cross quite some distance to avoid the impression that these are just ordinary human foibles in a genuinely honest witness. Again, that's if we're trying to tear down the witness's overall credibility. If we're trying to build up our own case and establish that what the witness said before is what should count, we have a different task.

I've now laid out the four kinds of witness-centered cross. Let's look at the ways that all the different types of cross fit together—and sometimes clash—as well as the sequence with which we combine the different types of cross for best effect.

---

8. Richard Stuhan, Melissa Gomez and Daniel Wolfe, "Impeaching with Prior Inconsistent Statements: It's Not as Devastating as You Might Think," DRI (Defense Research Institute) (2007). Reproduced at http://mmgjury.com/publications/mmg/Impeaching_with_Prior_Inconsistent_Statements.pdf.

Agreement Cross Meets Witness-Centered Cross

Let's first see how agreement cross—the case-building method that uses Rules of the Road to win agreement with the merits of some important piece of our case—blends, or not, with the four witness-centered types of cross:

- Lack of Fit
- Bias
- Ignorance or Mistakes
- Contradictions

Harmony is our watchword. We are looking to create an overall impression of the witness.

Lack of Fit and Agreement

This is a good instance of how the sequence in which we do things in a cross-examination can be important. Let's say we first establish that this witness *agrees* with a key aspect of our case. Why would we then circle back to try to establish that the same witness doesn't "fit"—doesn't have important credentials? After all, if he lacks "cred," who cares if he agrees with any aspect of our case? Hitting the witness's credentials or the witness's ability to perceive key facts seems counterproductive and undermines our hard-earned point that this witness agrees with our case. The very act of asking a witness to endorse some important aspect of your case tells everyone that you respect the witness enough to ask that line of questions. So we would never go from "look how this expert agrees with us" to "this guy doesn't even belong here."

If we reverse the sequence and attack lack of fit first, then we can hold the agreement item in our pocket and bring it out only if the fit attack fizzles and the witness's credentials hold up. Then an endorsement of a substantive piece of our case has some value, coming from a witness who knows a thing or two. But if we start with lack of fit and carry it off successfully, it's pointless to then seek the tarnished witness's agreement with our case.

Bias and Agreement

Showing that the witness is biased against our side *but still* has to begrudgingly admit the truth of some central aspect of our case—that can work well. The strategies harmonize nicely, especially when presented in the right order: bias first, then agreement.[9]

The flip side of that coin is when the witness has easily defected to our case and agreed with important aspects; it doesn't seem right to then launch a bias cross of the same witness. Why bite the open and honest hand that has just fed you a tasty morsel?[10]

So bias plus agreement makes a decent combo for the difficult, truly biased witness, but not for the cooperative one who lacks any real bias except that she had the temerity to sign up with your adversary.

Ignorance and Case-Building

Case-building cross can also fit with ignorance cross, especially if we can show that but for the witness's mistake, he would have to agree with the merits of our position.

Here is Houston attorney Jason Itkin starting a cross of a surprise witness whom Itkin had never deposed, an accident inspector on a Gulf oil-drilling rig. Itkin started with agreement points about how the inspection needed to be done according to the company's manual, then moved to show that the witness hadn't followed the book, then proved that the witness really couldn't say after all that the company's version of the accident was correct. We've already seen the finish of this cross in chapter 2, "Freeing Yourself from

---

9. That's the way I structured the cross in chapter 4, "Cross-Examination with Case-Building Rules," of the doctor who agreed with feisty reluctance that the obstetrician for whom he was testifying had violated my client's informed consent rights. First we showed that he never testified for patients, then we pried the agreement point from him.

10. We saw that with Jan Baisch's cross of the forensic pathologist in chapter 5, "Witness Self-Interest and Case-Building Cross." It would have been jarring and pointless to bring out the minor scandal in the witness's prior career once the witness had testified from personal authority that he had seen too many instances of guns and alcohol mixing tragically, exactly the theme of Baisch's case.

the Ten Commandments of Cross," in which the witness first asserts he's 100 percent sure that no one cleaned the deck before the investigator arrived, then backs off that and admits the accident site could have been cleaned up just like the plaintiff maintained. Watch what happens as Itkin probes the holes in the official investigation.

Itkin starts with some safety principles that help lull the witness into agreement mode.

MR. ITKIN: Your focus is safety 100 percent?

ACCIDENT INVESTIGATOR: [nodding head]

Q: And because safety is very important of the vessel. Is that right?

A: For sure.

Q: It can be very dangerous working offshore, true?

A: Yeah.

Q: And because of that, there's all sorts of safety rules that Cal Dive has that are important. Is that right?

A: They are, sir.

Q: And Cal Dive has a pretty lengthy safety rule book. Is that right?

A: Yeah. They have a—like a Safety Management System that—that is quite extensive.

Q: And the reason is—if you go to page 286—Cal Dive has a vision of people going home safely. And I think you and I can agree not only people going home safely but people going home healthy. Fair?

A: Couldn't agree with you more.

* * *

Q: And there is a section on conducting the formal investigation. And it says kind of in the middle of that first paragraph: "A formal investigation shall be thorough and conscientious." Do you see that?

A: Yeah.

Q: And you agree—I mean, put aside you are not a paperwork guy. Even though you are in court with your suit on and everything, I hear you. You agree with that just in general principle?

A: Yeah. That is the guideline, yeah.

Q: Do it thorough as you can?

A: Okay.

Q: Be as accurate as you can?

A: [nodding head]

Q: Is that right?

A: Yes, sir.

Q: One of the things that Cal Dive wants you to do as part of your job is to interview the people involved, right?

A: Yeah.

Q: And what they want you to do is take complete notes of what each person says. Do you agree, right?

A: Uh-huh.

Q: Okay. That's what it says right there in Part B. I am not making this up.

A: Right.

• • •

Q: So, where it says here take complete notes of what each person says, you didn't do that?

A: By the book, no.

[Itkin then established that the lack of interview notes in the report meant that the safety investigator hadn't interviewed anyone. Itkin made sure the jury got the bottom-line point: that there was no way the witness could support the official company line about what had happened and, worse for the company, a photograph of a power washer snapped by the investigator at the scene strongly suggested someone had cleaned the oily mess right before the investigator arrived. Then, to finish the cross in agreement mode, he shifted to some questions on the defendant's responsibility.]

Q: Okay. Sir, if someone gets hurt on a Cal Dive vessel—

A: Yes.

Q: —and it is Cal Dive's fault, you think that Cal Dive should take responsibility?

A: Yes, I do. Yeah.

Q: And I want to know what "responsibility" means to you because you have got—you have got people's safety in your hands. Okay. Someone gets hurt on a Cal Dive vessel and it is Cal Dive's fault—should they take care of the man's wages while he—if he can't go back to work?

A: I mean, lots of things that are applicable. If he got hurt on a vessel, yeah.

Q: They should?

A: Yeah.

Q: If he got medical costs and he got hurt on a vessel, Cal Dive—part of taking responsibility takes care of those medical costs, true?

A: It is not something I get involved in, but I would like to think so—

Q: Okay.

A: —under the right circumstances.

Q: Someone gets hurt on a Cal Dive vessel, Cal Dive should generally try to make it right, fair?

A: Yeah. Agree with all of that.

MR. ITKIN: Pass the witness, Your Honor.[11]

---

11. *Bryant v. Cal Dive International Inc.*, Case No. 2011-57457, Harris County, Texas District Court, May 6, 2013.

By the end of the cross, the attorney has painted a clear picture: this safety investigator took a casual approach to his job, interviewed no one who could have corroborated or undercut the company's party line, had no good excuses for his performance, and then, perhaps to salvage his own self-esteem, readily agreed with the cross-examiner's assertions about the company's responsibility. He has come very close to a complete defection to the other side. This is what an adroit cross-examiner can do with an ignorant witness who has no excuses for the self-inflicted holes in his head.

Contradictions and Agreement

Similarly, an agreement cross can match well with a contradictions cross if, for example, what the witness does outside the courtroom agrees with our position on the case—an "actions speak louder than words" point. Randi McGinn was trying a case for a young woman whose chest pain in an emergency room had been dismissed, without testing, as having nothing to do with her heart. She was too young, opined the defense expert, who said that sometimes you don't need to have any worry that chest pain might mean heart attack. Turned out the same doctor had given a television news interview making the opposite point, that all chest pain in any adult needs to be taken seriously as a sign of potential heart attack, exactly the theme of McGinn's case. Once McGinn rolled the video in her cross, two points were made with the one item:

- "You agreed with our case before you were hired as an expert witness."
- "Yes, chest pain must always be taken seriously."

Again, we need harmony. Trying to blend a few agreement points with a few unrelated self-contradictions that don't fit together creates a soupy mess. We always have to ask ourselves, what is the point of showing the witness has contradicted herself? If it's just for the sake of the contradiction itself, that often fails to get anywhere with forgiving jurors who know people make minor changes in what they say all the time.

So case-building agreement cross can work in the right set of circumstances with three of the four types of witness-centered cross. The only one it doesn't seem to readily work with is "fit" or credentials cross, because it doesn't make sense to tear down someone with one hand and build up their importance with the other.

What about blending the witness-centered cross techniques? That's up next.

BLENDING THE TYPES OF WITNESS-CENTERED CROSS-EXAMINATIONS

When the goal is simply to tear down the witness and not obtain any agreements with our case, any of the four types of witness-centered cross can work together—bias, ignorance, lack of fit, contradictions—or not, depending on your analysis of the witness's character and what she says on direct. Remember, we are trying to harmonize a coherent impression of the witness in jurors' minds: a one-sentence takeaway.

A few general thoughts:

- **Bias:** Bias is an all-purpose seasoning, too much of which can ruin the dish. Trial lawyers naturally believe that any witness who signed up to testify for the opposite side must have some hideous hidden bias. But unless you have the goods on the witness, an attempted bias cross may only lock in the impression of a decent, honest, caring witness. So beware, and use that saltshaker judiciously. On the other hand, for a true say-anything hired gun, you must go all out to show that this delectable morsel offered up by the adversary is actually a poisoned dish.

- **Ignorance:** An easier hill to climb is ignorance and mistakes. Here, you're not attacking the witnesses' character, and you're not saying they have deliberately slanted their testimony. You're just shrugging off their testimony by pointing out that they don't know much, and so what can we expect?

- **Lack of Fit:** Lack of fit goes perfectly with ignorance, as the example below shows. A witness who doesn't have the background knowledge suitable for the case is also going to make a lot of mistakes and miss a lot of important stuff.

- **Contradictions:** Bias and contradictions go pretty well together, as we will see in the next chapter. Contradictions can work with ignorance and lack of fit too, depending. It's hard to generalize.

We will have more good examples in later chapters of blending the different types of witness-centered cross, but let's finish this chapter with a lack-of-fit-plus-ignorance cross, topics that harmonize so well together.

CROSS OF AN EXPERT GOING TO LACK OF FIT PLUS IGNORANCE

Super lawyer David Boies cross-examined a political scientist and college professor. The defense in *Perry v. Schwarzenegger*, the lawsuit challenging California's Proposition 8 ban on gay marriage, called this professor to testify to the ability of gays and lesbians to participate in the political process. His view was that gays as a minority were not discriminated against to the point that they had no political voice.

The case was tried in 2010 before U.S. District Judge Vaughn Walker in San Francisco, without a jury.

Boies did an extensive cross over two days, the main thrust of which was to undercut the professor's claims to be an expert in gay and lesbian participation in the political process and to show that he was ignorant about a lot of things that an expert should know of that subject. Here is a short excerpt, just long enough to show that an accumulation of small bits of ignorance can eventually create a strong impression of the witness, where any one of these particular lines of questions could be written off as nitpicking.

MR. BOIES: Now, with respect to the question of political power of gays and lesbians, is your expertise on that limited to the present time?

EXPERT POLITICAL SCIENCE PROFESSOR: I wouldn't say that it's—I'm not holding myself out as an expert on the full history of the gay and lesbian rights movement. I have read about it and so I—I think I have a view of the trajectory of the movement, based on what I have read. But I would say that—it's fair to say that my—the deeper knowledge is on the more contemporary period, say, from the 1970s forward.

[The witness gives a fuller response than yes or no and claims expertise in the gay rights movement from the 1970s forward. Boies is ready for this and proceeds to undermine the claim.]

Q: For example, at your deposition you were not aware of what the Mattachine Society was, were you?

A: I could not recall what that was at that time.

[Sometimes hyper-vigilant lawyers object to any reference to a deposition not used to contradict the witness's trial testimony. Here there is nothing wrong with using it to remind the witness that he didn't know something that he should have known when he gave the deposition.]

Q: Have you researched that since?

A: I did take a look and did some further investigation and learned the Mattachine Society, yes, as being founded by Harry Hay around 1950 and being an important early gay rights organization.

Q: And did it play a particular role in the 1970s, the area that you said that you were an expert in?

A: Well, yeah. The—there are different iterations of this society. It was founded first in Los Angeles and then had other organizations, and—

Q: All I was asking is whether it played a particular important role in the 1970s, which was a period that you said you were—you had expertise in. Answer that question "yes" or "no."

A: I believe that did, yes.

Q: And at the time of your deposition you didn't know who Allan Spear was, did you?

A: That's correct.

Q: And you didn't know who Elaine Noble was, correct?

A: That's correct.

Q: Now, since your deposition, have you discovered who those people were?

A: No, I haven't done further investigation on those.

Q: You don't know that Allan Spear was the first openly gay man elected to state office?

A: I—I did not know that, no.

Q: And you didn't know that Elaine Noble was the first openly gay woman elected to state office?

A: I did not know that, no.

Q: And that they were so elected in 1976 [and] 1975 respectively?

A: Again, I didn't know their names, no. I knew that openly gay people were first elected to office in the mid-1970s.[12]

A fair enough rejoinder for the witness; the problem is that he set himself up as an expert on a historical era where it turns out he didn't know the names of key players. I'm omitting a dozen more back-and-forth exchanges that added up to a lot of "I didn't know that at my deposition."

Lessons for Ignorance plus Lack-of-Fit Cross-Examinations

Lessons I draw from the Boies excerpt:

- Once Boies shows the witness has a superficial grasp of the history of the gay rights movement, it's a lot easier to paint a picture consistent with a theme of spotty knowledge. The

---

12. *Perry v. Schwarzenegger*, Case No. C 09-2292-VRW, Northern District of California, United States District Court, January 25, 2010.

listener starts paying more attention to the witness's answers of "don't know" and less to the answers he does know.

- Each individual fact queried about has little significance. Their accumulation matters.

- A careful fact-driven deposition was key to the success at trial. The deposition locked in everything the witness didn't know; at trial he was in a lose-lose situation: he could admit to having looked up something after deposition that he should have known already, or if he didn't look it up, it suggests a careless attitude.

- Asking a witness a narrow relevant fact that the cross-examiner knows, and knows that the witness doesn't know, is a strong tactic. I stress *relevant*. The cross-examiner should be ready with a one-sentence response for each such fact if challenged on why it matters.

Next, we look more in depth at an important branch of contradictions cross, the impeachment with prior inconsistent statements. We will see how the Rules of the Road method improves the execution and how to write good all-purpose setups for this important type of impeachment.

Takeaways

We build our case and we tear down the adverse witness, but not usually at the same time. We now see that case-building agreement cross can work, in the right sequence, with tear-down cross about the witness's bias, mistakes, and contradictions. Tearing down the witness for lack of fit stands out as the one method we don't want to try with an adverse witness who has agreed with an important piece of our case. For the other techniques, we have the chance to create strong impressions of the witness, like this:

- This expert is biased, but our case is so strong he has to agree with it.

- This witness did agree with our case, before they paid him a lot of money to come in and contradict what he said before.
- This witness would agree with our case, if he hadn't gotten his facts all wrong.

And lack of fit is no orphan that only works by itself. It combines nicely with an ignorance-or-mistakes cross, to create this impression: *What would you expect from an expert who isn't really qualified? Lots of mistakes and holes in his knowledge.*

9

FIXING CONTRADICTIONS CROSS

Do I contradict myself? Very well, then, I contradict myself.
(I am large, I contain multitudes.)

—Walt Whitman

Every day, in hundreds of courtrooms across America, cross-examiners confront witnesses with changes in their stories. Too often, the confrontation falls flat.

We can fix that.

Impeachments[1] with prior inconsistent statements, one important branch of what we've called contradictions cross-examination, fail for one or all of these reasons:

---

1. The word *impeach* has an interesting backstory. It comes from a late Latin word *impedicare*, meaning to catch or entangle, and usually involved snaring the foot (the *pedi* part of the word), and also comes from a Middle English word *empechen*, which meant to cause to get stuck fast or to interfere with or to accuse. The word now means to bring charges against an official for improper conduct in office, or to otherwise try to discredit someone, as lawyers do when we impeach witnesses.

1. We haven't adequately thought through the goal.

2. We nitpick tiny inconsistencies that bore and irritate everyone but us.

3. We make technical errors in execution.

4. The witness escapes with a clever story (or a shrug like Whitman's).

Let's consider each of these and how we can cure them.

This discussion applies not only to the witness who says two opposite things on different occasions, but also to the common problem of witnesses who have new facts they want to dole out whereas before they had said nothing. That's a special branch of inconsistent statement, which I will also discuss on its own.

One: Thinking through the Goal

The first reason that impeachments fail is that the goal seems so obvious it's hardly worth discussing. And so we don't really think it through. The goal is to show the witness has said two opposite things, right? Wrong. That's a partial goal, and if it's the only goal, it's a setup to fail. Human beings change what they say all the time, so varying the details is no big deal, unless you carefully show it's a big deal and why. That starts with a clear goal.

The real goal with any prior inconsistent statement is one of two things:

- What the witness said in the prior statement is the truth, and we want the jury to adopt the prior statement as the correct version. (And, we care because it's an important fact.)

- This witness is so tangled up in contradictions that we cannot rely on anything she says.

Notice how different these are. The first one is case-building, and the goal is case-building. The second is witness-centered and witness-destroying. Most of the time, we should elect the case-building goal, because our enterprise is to win cases, not merely to tear down witnesses.

So, if we're trying to win the case, and the witness has just handed us a helpful fact that contradicts some unhelpful statement said earlier in a deposition, do we bring out that inconsistency? Of course not, because all we will accomplish is to either undermine the witness's credibility (and the reliability of this new helpful fact he has spilled) or leave the jury hopelessly confused as they watch us fighting with a witness over a fact that helps our case. No, we look this gift horse in the mouth only when it serves some clear goal. When we lack a clear goal, we can destroy our own case by misguided impeachment.

Moreover, these two goals of case-building versus witness-destroying call for different questions, as we will see when we outline the cross for each. Not having a clear goal also messes up the technical execution.

Two: Getting Past Nitpicking

The second reason that many impeachments with prior inconsistent statements fail is that they're boring because they don't add up to anything. Worse, they make you look bad. What is the jury supposed to conclude when you waste time bringing out an inconsistency, when neither version matters to the case outcome? That you like to waste time? That you have no sense for the relevant? That you vindictively punish opposing witnesses for no clear aim? None of the options are attractive.

Inconsistency is part of the human condition. As Aldous Huxley once said, "The only completely consistent people are the dead." That means that any witness who still has a pulse will have plenty of inconsistencies, and if you are looking to expose them, you will have no shortage of ore to mine. But what does inconsistency mean? If it doesn't concern a fact intrinsically important to the case outcome, then the only reason to bring out the inconsistency is as part of a witness-destroying cross. That is a difficult, sometimes necessary mission, but one that you should venture into only if you have the goods to make it stick. In other words, you have to make a mature judgment at the outset of the cross that you have enough important material to render this witness so self-contradictory as to be unworthy of belief.

If you have a clear goal and can avoid nitpicking minor things, you're halfway to a successful inconsistent-statement cross. We have two more traps to consider: failures in technical execution and the witness's excuses for her inconsistencies.

Three: Executing the Inconsistent-Statement Impeachment

Error in technical execution is the third reason that impeachment fails. Let's first lay out the standard, tried-and-true method for impeachment with a prior inconsistent statement. Then we'll look at ways to improve it.

Impeachment the Tried-and-True Way

The standard method has six steps:

1. *Listen closely* to the direct exam and identify any statements that differ substantially from what the witness said before. These can be whole new facts or just different facts from what was said before.

2. *Lock in* the new version. Without repeating too much of the new version, make sure the witness is committed to it as the truth.

3. Establish that the witness has *spoken before* on the same subject.

4. *Reinforce* the truth-encouraging circumstances of the prior statement. If it was a deposition, this is the who-when-where of the deposition as case event. If it was some other situation, like the witness composing an email on his own computer at work or giving a statement to police at an accident scene, bring out those circumstances.

5. *Publish* the prior inconsistent statement to the witness and jury.

6. *Stop* and do not ask the witness to explain the contradiction. (This is the conventional wisdom, which you can sometimes violate to good effect with the right witness.)

Execution: Improving on the Tried-and-True Method

The first thing to note about the tried-and-true method is that you do not need to apply the steps rigidly in a particular sequence. You can play with the order of some of this. You can easily flip four and five around. Then the order goes like this:

1. *Listen.*

2. *Lock in:* "Here's what you're saying now: ___. Did I get that right, not the whole thing, but the essence?"

3. *Establish what was spoken before:* "You gave a statement on the same subject before?"

4. *Publish prior statement:* "Here's what you said then: ___. Did I get that right?"

5. *Reinforce prior circumstances:* "Here's the who-when-where of what you said before."

6. *Stop.*

This leads much more naturally to what I call *the forbidden question*, when we invite the witness to adopt the truth of the previous statement.

In the right circumstances, if you are fairly confident the witness will backtrack to adopt the prior statement, you can even skip the lock-in of the current statement. The only purpose of the lock-in is to highlight the contradiction, so you don't need it, and it can be counterproductive to highlight the difference, because you will be undercutting the witness's reliability when all you want to do is get to yes on adopting the prior statement.

Set Up Your Cross Questions

The next step in improving technical execution is to outline the line of questions, keeping in mind the purpose.[2] First, we write the goal at the top of the page. As noted, most of the time the goal for a case-building cross will be simply this:

What the witness said before is the most reliable.

Then we write our checklist of reliability-reinforcing facts about the previous statement, as outlined in the next section.

Set up this chapter and page in advance, before the witness testifies. You might protest: *But how do we know the witness is going to contradict the prior statement?* You don't know, but you can prepare in two ways:

- You can make an excellent educated guess. Anything the witness said before that really, really helps you and really, really hurts the side the witness is loyal to—that is a strong candidate for attempted historical revisionism.

- You can set up your line of questions on helpful admissions as if the witness is going to stick to what she said before. Then you use the impeachment checklist about the prior statement only as a backup.

Checklist of Reliability Facts for Prior Statements

If your goal is case-building, and you want to show that the prior statement is the right one, then you need to carefully teach the jury why. Skipping this step is a big failure in correct execution, because you leave the jury wondering which version of reality they should accept.

To reinforce the reliability of the witness's prior statement, I like to use the five Ws and an H: Who, What, When, Where, Why, How. Here is a standard set of questions for the witness that you can adapt to most circumstances. We never use all of these, only enough to set up the impression we want to create, without being tedious.

---

2. For more about outlining and organizing your questions, see chapter 7, "Planning: The Essential Weapon for Speed."

Who

These questions surround *who* might have been present when the witness made the statement.

Q: Who are you?

If the statements took place in a deposition or court hearing:

Q: Who is your attorney?

Q: Who was the court reporter?

Q: Who was the judge?

Q: Who were the [family members, friends, colleagues, bystanders, if the statement took place at, say, an accident scene] nearby when you made this statement?

What

These questions are about *what* is in the witness's statement.

Q: Was this statement under oath to tell the truth under penalty of perjury?

Q: Was this statement voluntary—no coercion?

Q: Did you spend enough time to recount everything you knew on this subject?

Q: Is this your signature [at end of statement or deposition errata sheet]?

Q: Did you review this statement and have a chance to look it over and fix errors?

When

These questions confirm that the statement was much closer in time to the events reported than now.

Q: When was the event, and when did you make your statement?

Q: How much time has elapsed from the date of your prior statement to the date of your new statement?

Where

These questions confirm *where* the statement took place, to help confirm that this statement was reliable. Include details if they will help establish reliability.

Q: Where did you make this statement?

Q: Did you make this statement in a lawyer's office with full opportunity to take breaks, consult with your lawyer, and think about your answers?

Why

These questions concern the statement's purpose. *Why* did the witness make it? If the statement's purpose was to help others, ask more specific questions:

Q: The statement's purpose was to tell the truth. Is that correct?

Q: To help police investigate the accident?

Q: To help doctors care for the patient? [statement in medical records]

Q: To help coworkers do their jobs? [statement in ordinary course of business]

Q: To teach young doctors how to practice medicine safely? [treatise written by witness]

Q: To give the other side fair notice of your opinions? [expert witness in deposition]

How

These questions surround *how* the witness expected that the statement would be used.

Q: Did you know people would rely on your statement?

Q: Did you know that your statement would be evidence?

Q: Did you know that contradictions between your previous statement and your testimony in court could be brought out?

Remember: this list is a menu. Only a glutton orders everything on a menu. Stop before you bore or annoy your audience, or worse, they forget about the contradiction you're trying to highlight. Be selective, and tailor your points to the reason for the contradiction. For example, if the witness flatly contradicts something said in a deposition, you may need only to do some *what* and *why* points. The witness:

1. Gave a deposition.

2. Answered under oath to tell the truth.

3. Had a chance to look at all relevant documents before and during the deposition.

4. Was given the right to change the transcript but made no changes.

If instead the witness is claiming a new memory different from the prior statement, then focus more closely on *when*: the date and circumstances of the prior statement compared to the underlying event.

One more point on this five-Ws-and-an-H checklist: You can certainly photocopy the page, shrink it down and laminate it, then pull it out of your wallet in the middle of your next tough cross. But I don't advise it. It's much more effective to write out the list for yourself, in your own words. You won't need to do it for each trial. But if you want to create habits that will serve you well in heated mid-trial moments, writing a practice outline is the next best thing to performing the cross-examination itself. This creates the lasting muscle memory that lets you perform at your highest level, locking eyeballs not with your notepad but with the witness.

Getting to Yes with the "Forbidden" Next Question

The natural—but forbidden (under the old commandments)—question at the end of these five-Ws-and-an-H statement-reliability questions has always been this:

Q: So this really is the truth, what you said before?

I say this is a "forbidden" question, because we hardly ever ask it. Our forefathers (and they were all men back then) taught us not to. Why not? Because it violates the commandment that says, Don't ask a question you don't know the answer to. And they argue that the question invites an explanation—although it really doesn't—and any such explanation would break the commandment that says, Never let the witness explain.

Remember, though, in chapter 2, "Freeing Yourself from the Ten Commandments of Cross," we exposed these old commandments as feeble, scaredy-cat, impossible to follow, and not even helpful. Our rewritten commandment:

- Ask only questions whose answers you can deal with.

So here we are. You've asked the witness a string of questions all intended to bolster the reliability of what the witness said previously. Do you pull the trigger on the next question? I submit you will have a good feel for that on your feet, based on the cues the witness gives you. Some witnesses, especially the truthful kind and the go-along-get-along kind, will give it up to you, if and when you ask that ultimate question, to confirm that the prior statement was true.

"Yes," they will say (as you suppress a smile).

And you can encourage surrender with some variation on these:

Q: You had just forgotten what you'd said before?

Q: When I reminded you about it just now, that refreshed your memory?

Q: You just misspoke earlier on direct examination?

We talked about the fundamental rule of witness self-interest in chapter 5, "Witness Self-Interest and Case-Building Cross." That rule states that every witness wants to look good *and* look truthful, when he or she can. So offering witnesses an easy out to adopt a prior statement as what they currently believe is a graceful way to save face. And you have now closed the circle on getting the witness to adopt as true the prior statement that helped your side. Congratulations!

But as I take my bow, the skeptical reader says, Not so fast! What about the witness who won't adopt his previous statement? My answer—just like I said in our rewritten commandment—let's deal with it.

Four: Closing the Escape Routes

Some witnesses, of course, will never surrender. They have a series of predictable excuses. Conventional wisdom calls for not allowing witnesses to explain their discrepancies, but nine times out of ten, they will anyway, whether we ask or not. So we have to be prepared to deal with it, whether in our cross or in our response to redirect.

Favorite Excuses

The excuses tend to follow predictable scripts. I will put some ideas for comeback below each excuse. Anticipate hearing one or more of these excuses and plan for them.

"I Was Mistaken"

A: I was mistaken at my deposition. I've now seen some more documents that remind me of what is correct.

Comeback: This is dangerous because it's superficially plausible. If it's an important point, you must jump right in:

Q: Oh, which documents?

Q: Who wrote them?

Q: And what did they say exactly?

Q: And how is it that you saw them only after your deposition?

Q: Did the defense lawyer point them out to you?

Or, better, when you line up supporting sources in advance, you can show the witness a document consistent with the point you want to make, and say,

Q: This one supports your prior statement, doesn't it?

Q: So did you see this one after your deposition?

The point is this: if the witness pulls this excuse, you cannot let the witness get away with vagueness. It may turn out that the only document the witness has seen that "refreshes" the witness is some memo written by the witness's attorney. You, as cross-examiner, get to inspect all that refreshing-recollection stuff.[3]

"I Wasn't Thinking"

A: I just wasn't thinking clearly that day.

Comeback: This is another excuse jurors might want to credit, but you can undermine it with our five-Ws-and-an-H statement-reliability checklist, especially if the following have occurred:

1. The witness took no steps before climbing onto the witness stand to correct the prior "misstatement."

2. The witness said nothing on the day of the prior statement about any foggy thinking.

3. The witness cannot point to anything else he wants to change, except this one vital point that really hurt his own position back then and that he now wants to retract.

Belated Corrections and New Facts

If these corrections and new facts come from a party in a civil lawsuit, remember the no-surprises rule that is supposed to govern. You as the adverse party ordinarily have a right under the discovery rules to be told about these in a supplemental interrogatory answer.

> A party who has made a disclosure under Rule 26(a)— or who has responded to an interrogatory, request for production, or request for admission—must supplement or correct its disclosure or response: (A) in a timely manner if the party learns that in some material respect the disclosure or response is incomplete or incorrect, and if the additional or corrective information has not

---

3. *See* Fed. R. Evid. 612.

otherwise been made known to the other parties during the discovery process or in writing[.][4]

Rather than whine at the bench, the better approach is to confront the witness or party on the stand:

Q: You didn't say anything about this [changed or new] fact at your deposition?

Q: When you signed interrogatory answers responding to our question about important facts you relied on, you didn't mention it then either?

Q: You knew about your duty to give us a supplemental interrogatory answer as soon as you realized your old answer was incomplete or wrong, right?

Q: You didn't give us a supplemental answer either?

"I've Been Thinking"

A: I've thought a lot more about this since then.

Comebacks: (there are several)

Q: You've had many [months or years] to study the statements you previously made that didn't help your position. But you waited until today to tell anyone (except your lawyer) that you wanted to change them?

Q: Can you point me to specific facts that you didn't have access to when you gave the statement, which you do have now?

Or a more pointed comeback:

Q: What you've thought a lot about is the consequences of losing this case, not about how you can be more accurate in your testimony.

---

4. *See* Fed. R. Civ. P. 26(e)(1).

"This Is Stressful"

A: It's very stressful testifying here in court. I've never done it before, and I'm doing the best I can.

Comeback: This is a confused response that suggests the witness is playing for sympathy (and could well get oodles). But it also suggests that if anything is mistaken, it's the current testimony, not what the witness said before under calmer circumstances. Again, go back to our statement reliability checklist for sample uses of the five-Ws-and-an-H questions in determining reliability, and point out the items that should have made the prior statement less stressful. For example,

Q: You testified in your own lawyer's office?

Q: You could take a break whenever you wanted?

Q: The lawyer was sitting right next to you, not halfway across a courtroom like this one?

Q: There wasn't a whole roomful of strangers watching you?

"I Forgot"

A: I forgot, but I remember now, because my memory was refreshed by ____.

Comeback: This is similar to the first excuse above, "I was mistaken." Bear down on what exactly the witness forgot and what exactly filled the gap. Often the two don't match. See also the discussion of "new facts" below.

"I'm Being Consistent"

A: What I'm saying then and saying now are totally consistent.

Comeback: Careful parsing of the two statements side by side will let everyone see if this passes muster. You have to slow down and really get everyone to see exactly the differences. This is probably the most common excuse from an expert, especially one who has worked with the opposing counsel to massage the contradiction.

"This Is Out of Context"

A: You're taking what I said out of context.

Comeback: This is a variant of the "I'm being consistent" excuse. You must always be ready to show that the two inconsistent statements mean what you say they mean, fairly considered, in context.

You have to be knowledgeable enough about your material to know whether this is a giant bluff on the witness's part and, if so, to call it with your next question:

Q: Oh, what was the context?

If you're right, the witness will flounder when challenged to point out some "context" that really isn't there in the prior statement.

The Witness with New Facts That Don't Directly Contradict the Old

Now let's deal with one other excuse that may be no excuse at all: the witness with a brand-new fact. This is a treacherous but solvable problem. The witness wants to offer new information that doesn't exactly contradict what she said before; it's just fishy that it would be coming out for the first time in the middle of trial. In cross-examination taxonomy, what we want to do is called *impeachment with silence or omission*.

These witnesses have what sounds like a pretty good excuse:

A: Nobody asked me this before.

A: I just now thought of it.

Let's deal with each on its own.

"No One Asked Me Before"

A: Nobody asked me this before.

Comeback: The best preventive medicine for this one is a competent deposition or recorded statement, either of which should include "exhausting" and "door-closing" types of questions at the end, such as:

Q: Anything else you can recall about the event?

Q: You understand we're here today to try to obtain your complete recollection about the event?

Q: Will you let your lawyer know and he will let us know if you think of anything new?

Q: Is there anything [documents, photos, etc.] you have not seen that might bring more details of this to mind? [This is a vaccination shot against a later appearance by the refreshed-recollection witness.]

Another approach to sealing this door closed is seen in this deposition example from Kansas City attorney Jim Bartimus, asking a defendant about his recollection of treating a patient.

MR. BARTIMUS: Anything specifically after that you are pretty vague on?

DEFENDANT DOCTOR: Two and a half years ago.

Q: Absolutely, and I'm not fussing with you about it.

A: Okay.

Q: I just don't want to be surprised later on that you all of a sudden have a vivid memory of a conversation where you are telling me today under oath that you don't remember. Do you see what I mean?

A: I agree.

Q: Because this is my only time before trial to find out what you are going to say, what you did and why. Fair enough?

A: I agree.

Q: In other words, I don't want to be sandbagged.

A: I agree.

Q: And I won't sandbag you with my questions. Fair enough?

A: Thank you.[5]

---

5. Deposition of Daniel Farrell, *Kirkeminde v. Midwest Division-OPRMC, LLC*, Case No. 14CV04745, Johnson County, Kansas District Court, December 9, 2014.

If it's a party witness, interrogatory questions asking for the facts behind all defenses or allegations will also be useful. Any such Q&A in your saddlebag for this witness will turn the impeachment into a straight inconsistent-statement cross, because your next question after the witness says, "I was never asked," is this:

Q: But actually, we did ask you. We asked you for everything you could recall. Did you hold back this fact?

The chapter and page method for the "new facts" witness looks like this:

Headline: *Any ordinary person without a bias would have already said all they know.*

Facts on the page would include:

- All opportunities the witness had in the ordinary course of work to state this fact, such as emails with colleagues, official statements like a discharge summary in a hospital record, and so on.
- All opportunities the witness had to cooperate with investigators (police, supervisors, and so on) and give these facts.
- All times the witness was asked in deposition to say everything she knew.
- All times the witness was asked in interrogatory to summarize all key facts.
- A statement that the witness knew we wanted all her facts.
- A statement that the witness had no reason to withhold facts—unless trying to get unfair advantage.

A related chapter and page could then build on the last one:

Headline: *New fact is dubious.*

Facts on the page would include:

- No good reason new fact was held back.
- No specific document or conversation with other witnesses "refreshed" memory here.

- "Refreshed" memory came from talking to lawyer and no one else. (In fact, most party witnesses operate under a strict admonition from their lawyer to discuss the case with no one else.)
- New fact is self-serving.
- New fact doesn't fit with other reliable evidence.
- Witness has no other new facts, only ones that help her side.

You won't necessarily ask questions of the new-fact witness on all these issues. But this will give you a good summary to argue why the "fact" should get the other side nowhere with the jury.

"I Just Thought of It"

A: I just now thought of it.

Here we have an utterly innocent explanation, if it comes from the witness with no dog in the fight. So if the witness is truly disinterested, we need to turn down the heat on the cross and develop questions that gently suggest the earlier memory was more accurate. (See the five-Ws-and-an-H statement-reliability checklist above.) And if we cannot do that, a graceful retreat is in order.

But if this is a party or someone else linked to the party, we turn back up the heat and use the questions in our chapter: *New fact is dubious.*[6] And we do another chapter.

Headline: *Witness is biased or interested in outcome.*

That one lists facts like these:

- witness's connections to the other side
- witness's loyalty to the other side
- witness's meetings with the other side's lawyers
- witness's interest, financial or emotional, in the other side winning
- witness's hostility or dislike of cross-examiner's side

---

6. See "Headline: New fact is dubious" in the previous section, "'No One Asked Me Before.'"

The Liar Liar Witness

We'll close with the ultimate excuse, which is a gift to you: the witness who says,

A: My prior statement was wrong because I lied.

Very occasionally in a criminal case, and rarely in a civil case, a "liar liar pants on fire" witness will take the stand. They have no well-massaged excuse for why their prior statement was wrong. No mistake, no memory lapse, nothing. When confronted with the old statement, this witness says, *My prior statement was wrong because I lied.*

When this bomb goes off in the courtroom, you might be tempted to sit down, because the witness made the impact you want. But you shouldn't, because you need to remember that this witness wants the jury to buy the current testimony as truthful and to forgive the prior moral lapse. (Forgiveness and redemption are powerful themes that can work against you with the wrong witness.)

Again, using the chapter and headline method:
Headline: *Here is someone who will say anything, even a deliberate lie, to get out of a jam.*

You can use questions like these to make that impression soak in with the jury:

Q: So what you said before was untrue?

Q: You knew it was untrue when you said it?

Q: It wasn't a mistake?

Q: It was a choice to tell a lie?

Q: The oath that you swore to tell the truth on that prior occasion—that didn't matter to you?

Q: The reason you told a lie was you wanted to mislead the person you were talking to?

Q: You wanted that person to believe it was true, even though you knew it wasn't true?

Q: You thought it would help you to tell a lie?

Q: Now today, you want the jury to believe what you're saying is true?

Q: It would help your position if the jury decides what you're saying today is true?

You can wallow around in those kinds of questions as long as you want. Just be sure to wash your hands after.

Final Thoughts on Witness Excuses

I don't have the final word on what your snappy comeback should be to each of the predictable excuses for new and different testimony from witnesses. Every case has its own warp and woof, and the appropriate questions will depend on the specifics of your case. I do know this: If you plan through your case-building cross, looking for all the ways the other side concedes important elements of your case, you can certainly expect blowback when you then recruit the other side's witnesses to make your points through evidence that you thought you'd nailed down before trial. It's never enough to show the new statement is inconsistent. We have to anticipate that one way or another, the witness will be allowed to explain the change-up. But we know the universe of explanations is limited, and so we can plan our comebacks and expose the ultimate truth.

Remember, this approach focuses on winning our case, and there are a few bumps along that road that old-style ten commandments cross-examiners may not face. The commandments cross-examiner is focused instead on not screwing up and not hearing any surprises from the witness stand. I would rather win the case! And that means using the witness's prior helpful statements to prove my case rather than using them solely for a demolition job on the witness. It's pretty predictable that our witnesses will help our case, and the other side's witnesses will help their case, but if we can make their witnesses help our case, we ought to win over some jurors in the process.

Case Study: A Contradiction Finish to a Bias Cross-Examination

Of course, there are some witnesses whom neither Perry Mason nor Atticus Finch nor any real-life cross-examiner could ever win over to their side on anything helping their case. In those instances, we have no choice but to discredit them with any weapon at hand. By the end, we want the jurors to see and smell how unbelievable this witness is. With this type of witness, a contradictions cross doesn't seek to establish the truth of what was said before. Instead, the contradiction becomes part of a larger pattern. The cross-examiner's goal to achieve an impactful contradictions cross is made a lot easier if the witness's credibility can first be softened up with a good bias cross, as Gary Fox does with a money and testimonial history cross that we will see in chapter 11, "Shooting It Out with the Hired-Gun Witness." Here, I'm jumping to the end of that cross to show how Fox finished the cross by veering from the witness's bias to a single but central contradiction point. Bias and contradictions fit hand in glove when our goal is to cause the jury to reject the witness's credibility.

The impression we want to leave with a combined bias-contradictions cross is that the witness has big holes, contradictions, and inconsistencies in his testimony because he has a self-interest or bias in the case. With a party opponent, the self-interest is obvious and you don't need to belabor it. But with a smooth expert witness, especially one who mildly asserts his objectivity at every turn, you need to tease out the bias with a careful line of questions. Then, once you establish bias, showing contradictions on one or more key points of substance can have a strong impact. Otherwise, if you focus the cross solely on contradictions, it can backfire. When the jury sees a witness they like, who seems to have no dog in the fight, being raked over for an alleged contradiction, they are more likely to discount the importance of the contradiction and conclude that you are being unfair to the witness.

In the excerpt below, Fox has just established that the witness doesn't want to answer simple questions about money and prior testimony. Then Fox pivots to the merits of the case, and he has only one topic: Was the baby sick before he stopped breathing and died? At deposition, the witness had said yes, in hindsight, the autopsy showed the child must have had a pneumonia in his lungs but without any "clinical manifestation" before he stopped breathing and his heart stopped. At trial, the witness gave a little different answer: in fact, no, the child had no illness before his heart stopped. At first, it's puzzling why the cross-examiner repeatedly uses the term *illness* and seeks the witness's agreement with the simple proposition that the child had no illness before he died, but it then becomes clear when the deposition is brought out and the witness had given a completely different answer to the similarly phrased question.

This also has a nice setup explaining the importance of a deposition.

Mr. Fox: Let's visit, if we could, a little bit about Levi Slayton. And I listened carefully to your testimony. And I wrote down some notes. And correct me if I'm wrong, but your testimony is based upon the assumption that Levi Slayton was not sick before the illness occurred, and the illness being the time that he stopped breathing. Is that correct?

Dr. Radetsky: It's based on the medical records, that the child did not have an illness prior to the time his heart stopped.

Q: That's an assumption of yours in this case?

A: It's not an assumption, sir. It's based on the records as they actually exist.

Q: It's based upon your belief that that represents the true state of facts. Can we at least agree to that?

A: Well, I mean, that's the—that's the information that's available. So based on the information that's available, I interpret the information.

Q: In any event, your understanding is Levi had no illnesses prior to his instantaneous death, correct?

A: He was not a sick child prior to his heart stopping. He—

Q: Is that a yes?

A: I'm sorry, sir. The reason—words are so tricky. He had problems as a newborn. He was a little bit premature. He had some feeding problems. Evidently, he had a bout or two of irregular breathing, but he wasn't a sick child prior to his heart stopping.

Q: As far as you know, he had no illnesses prior to the time he stopped breathing. Is that fair or not?

A: It's fair as I use the word *illness*, but he had newborn problems. Feeding problems, he had the jaundice problem, but those aren't illnesses in the way that can explain why his heart stopped. That's why I'm trying to answer it my own way, sir.

Q: Well, Doctor, using your definition of illness, can we at least agree that you believe that Levi had no illnesses until he stopped breathing?

A: As I understand that word, sir, that is correct.

[I count seven questions before the cross-examiner obtains a clean, simple answer to the no-illness question.]

Q: You've read the deposition of Julie Slayton?

[Julie Slayton was Levi Slayton's mother.]

A: Yes.

Q: You don't question her truthfulness or her memory, do you?

A: I'm sure she testified based on her best memory of the time.

[The concession implicitly made here is that the mother's testimony about her son's symptoms in his last day of life was truthful, which contradicts the witness's assertion that the child had a silent disease without any detectable signs.]

Q: Let me ask you this. You—you understood why we went out, or why we took your deposition that was taken in Albuquerque?

A: It was taken in Albuquerque.

[Here's a rare example of a professional witness being asked a "why" question on cross, and the witness not taking up the offer to give an extensive answer. That was likely because the witness knew he was about to be impeached with his deposition, and the "why" question was intended to set up the importance of the deposition.]

Q: And from the four hundred plus depositions you've given, you understand that the reason we do that is so we can find out what opinions you have and what thoughts you have and so we can prepare ourselves for a trial like this. You understand that's the purpose of the deposition.

A: That was even said at the time of the deposition, sir.

Q: Yes. Because folks like us, we're lawyers, we're not doctors, so we want to try to be thorough and get out all your opinions at the time of the deposition. And you understand that's the process?

A: It was told to me at the time.

Q: But you knew it long before that, didn't you?

A: You know, sir, I'm there to answer the questions that are put to me and to answer them honestly. My understanding is that's the purpose of the deposition is so the person who's asking the questions can get those answers.

[This witness has a habit of gratuitously inserting into his answers that his job is to answer questions "honestly." You can either let it go, as here, and save for closing argument a comment on the curiosity of a witness asserting his own honesty without being asked, or you could confront the witness along these lines:

Q: Isn't this now the third or fourth time you've volunteered today that your job is to answer questions honestly?

Q: Doesn't that go without saying, when you get on the witness stand and you've taken an oath, that you're going to answer the questions honestly?

Q: When you volunteered to us these several times that your job was to answer questions honestly, were you worried that someone might think you were dishonest?

[Here Fox probes the honesty issue a little differently, by bringing out the witness's attendance at law school. He drops it after a couple of questions and returns to impeaching with the deposition. Here his approach is to ask the witness to contradict what he has just said, that the child had no illness before his lungs and heart stopped working, and to agree instead with the plaintiff's contention that the baby had a lung infection for a day before his death. When the witness disagrees with the plaintiff's contention, only then does he spring out the deposition transcript.]

Q: Yes, sir. And you probably know that from law school, right? You went to law school, didn't you?

A: Well, I went to one year of law school, many years ago, sir.

Q: And did you learn about depositions at law school?

A: No, I didn't.

Q: In any event, Doctor, while you and I may disagree about some things about Levi Slayton, one of the things we can agree on is that, for at least a day or so leading up to the time that Levi Slayton stopped breathing, for at least a day or so, maybe more, Levi Slayton had pneumonia?

A: No.

Q: Do you have your deposition there, Doctor?

A: I do, sir.

Q: Page sixty?

A: Six-oh?

Q: Six-oh, yes, sir.

A: All right.

Q: See if you remember this question being asked and you giving this answer.

> Question: So now, if I understand correctly, Doctor, you don't believe Levi had any illness up until the time that he stopped breathing?
>
> Answer: In retrospect, he must have had the pneumonia for a day or so based on what I understand to be the histology of the lungs at the time of autopsy, but there were no clinical manifestations of it.

A: That's correct, sir.

Q: Do you remember giving that answer to that question?

A: I do. I thought I gave exactly the same answer moments ago.

Q: No, sir, you didn't. Now, if in fact, as you testified under oath, Levi had pneumonia at least a day or so before he stopped breathing, Levi would have had pneumonia at the time that Dr. Penrod examined him. Is that true, sir?

A: No.

MR. FOX: Those are all the questions I have, Your Honor.[7]

The examination ends with the witness having contradicted himself:

1. No, the child had no illness before he stopped breathing.
2. Yes, the child had pneumonia for a day before he stopped breathing.
3. But no, the child didn't have the pneumonia when the doctor examined him a day before he stopped breathing.

While it's usually better to bring out a multitude of contradictions when doing a contradictions cross-examination, it worked here to focus on a single subject for these reasons:

- The focus was central to the case.
- The witness had a three-way contradiction.
- All this followed a bias impeachment, which we'll see in chapter 11, where the witness evaded giving any straight answers to simple questions about money and testimonial history.

---

[7]. *Slayton v. Professional Park Pediatrics, P.A.*, Case No. 03CA1622, 2nd Judicial Circuit, Florida, June 22, 2007.

Takeaways

Before launching any cross-examination about a prior inconsistent statement, you must fix your goal in mind.

- Do you want the jury to credit the prior statement? If so, you need to reinforce why the old statement is objectively more reliable.

- Do you like the new statement and want the jury to credit it? If so, you probably don't want to mention the old contradictory statement at all; you just want to lock in the new statement.

- Do you not care which of the contradictory statements is true? If so, then you need to carefully weigh whether you have enough material to crush the witness's overall credibility and whether this is a witness you want to destroy. Because there is no other good reason to bring up inconsistencies that don't matter in themselves. And if you fall short on a witness-destroying mission, you may instead be the one hurt.

Once your goal is clear for each and every piece of inconsistent cross you want to execute, you will be able to carry off the cross so that your goal and success are both clear to the jury.

The last word here: Courage!

Exercise

Look back over your notes for your next big cross-examination. Highlight the best points supporting your case in this witness's prior statement or deposition. Now anticipate what the witness might do to

1. Change the testimony to make it unhelpful to your side, without necessarily changing black to white and yes to no.

2. Finesse, minimize, or otherwise deal with the impeachment cross the witness knows you will mount.

Then figure out how you can respond. This exercise often works best not on paper but in a playacting session with colleagues in your office. When you get to trial, the witness may behave, and you won't need to unleash the impeachment cross. But if the witness changes up, you'll be ready.

10

Exposing the Ignorant Witness

Everyone is entitled to his own opinion, but not to his own facts.

—Daniel Patrick Moynihan

Ignorance is a state of beauty for an adverse expert witness, at least for us as cross-examiners. Proving that the other side's witness has gotten something important completely wrong satisfies our own blood lust and leaves the witness dazed and confused. The weakened witness then teeters on the brink of complete collapse, all set up to become our best witness of all, the one who defects from his side and agrees with some important piece of our case.

That, at least, is the promise when we face a witness who is tangled up in provably wrong facts. If you can demonstrate that—

1. the witness doesn't know a fact (or has the fact wrong)

2. the fact is important to the case

3. the fact is one that this witness really *should* know

—then the next logical question is: Why does the witness not know this fact? The possibilities are limited. Either the witness didn't spend the time to study the facts, or the witness did a sloppy job. Either is good for you.

If the fact is one that can turn the case in your direction, then proving the witness's mistake or ignorance about the fact leads you to one of two places, both good:

- The witness changes his view and agrees with this part of your case (and thus becomes the witness who agrees with important elements of your case).

Or

- The witness continues to fight and argue, and establishes himself as so hopelessly prejudiced that his opinions cannot be trusted. After all, a prejudiced witness is one who has pre-judged the case and has decided that the facts don't matter to him, because he has chosen his side. His motto: *Don't confuse me with the facts.*

One or the other of these outcomes will happen, and our job as cross-examiners is to make sure to push hard enough to tip the witness over the edge to surrender or foolishly argue. We don't want to merely establish the witness's error or ignorance, but to show why it matters: the witness agrees with our case or shows himself as biased and untrustworthy. Yet reaching this tipping point is not always easy.

OUTING THE BIG ERRORS AND DECIDING WHICH TO CHASE

Every witness makes mistakes. Especially when a case is factually dense, it's hard for a witness to hold everything in the brain that may be important. So you can always expect a witness to slip up in ways large or small. Your job as a cross-examiner is to capitalize on the important errors and let the other ones go. If you go after every little inconsequential error, you will brand yourself as a nitpicker and risk the jurors siding with the witness. But a big exception is when you can develop a pattern of small errors or "don't knows" that together add up to something.

We will see that in the next section, "A Pricey Expert Proves How Little He Is Worth," in a cross by Denver lawyer Jim Leventhal, working over an expert who charged five figures for his case review but had no idea who the key doctors and nurses were who treated Leventhal's client. Before we jump into the Q&A, let's first go back to the basic setup for an ignorance cross.

The Rules Setup for Cross-Examining the Ignorant Witness

The first thing in cross-examining a witness whom you can show is ignorant is to establish the important premise: *facts matter*. Let's put that concept into our Rules of the Road framework:

A Rule worth talking about at trial and, in this instance, on cross-examination, is a *should* or *must* statement that has these four attributes:

- The Rule is clear.
- The witness can't argue with the Rule (or will look foolish).
- The witness violated the Rule.
- The violation is important. (Usually we say important to the outcome of the case, but in cross-examination, the violation must at least be important to determining if this is a credible witness.)

So the Rule that we want to establish, at the beginning of the section of cross where we intend to expose the witness's ignorance or error on a key fact, is as follows:

- An expert witness like you must know the important facts of this case.

It's usually not hard to get an expert witness to agree with this kind of statement.[1] We tinker with the Rule slightly, thus:

- A witness like you whose job it is to know important things needs to get those facts right.

And we can underscore the importance of this Rule by getting the witness to agree with the principles underlying it, using these sample questions:

Q: The jury has to decide this case based on an accurate understanding of what happened, true?

Q: If the jurors get a wrong impression from a witness like you, that can make it harder for them to do their job?

Example: A Pricey Expert Proves How Little He Is Worth

After establishing that an expert witness, a neurosurgeon, was charging upwards of $16,000 for his court appearance, Denver attorney Jim Leventhal went straight to what the witness had failed to learn in his supposedly thorough review. This case concerned an emergency room's failure to realize that a patient (Ms. Gasteazoro) with a sudden bad headache, nausea, dizziness, and trouble speaking might be having a stroke.

Mr. Leventhal: And we were told what you reviewed. Do you remember that?

Expert Neurosurgeon: Yes.

[Leventhal announces a witness-centered Rule that ties in what the jury needs to hear.]

---

1. We saw a setup like this by Colorado lawyer Jim Gilbert with an "independent medical examiner" expert in chapter 3, "Choosing the Weapons Right for You," when the expert quickly agreed he had an obligation to "get the facts straight." A similar setup works when the witness is not an expert *per se*, but is someone tasked with knowing stuff—like the safety investigator cross-examined by Jason Itkin in chapter 8, "Cross-Examination with Witness Tear-Down Rules."

Q: It's important, like it is for this jury, that you, as an expert witness, consider the evidence because you know that they're going to rely on what you say, right?

A: In general, that I consider at least the relevant evidence, yes.

Q: I mean, just like we're asking this jury to look at every piece of evidence carefully, it's important, if you're going to express an opinion, that you do the same?

A: Every piece of evidence, I would agree, that's relevant to my opinion. I would think that I would not need to look at all the evidence that this jury is going to need to look at.

[Leventhal pounces on this standard that the witness has set up. The expert just said twice that he needs only to look at evidence "relevant to my opinion." Fair enough, but Leventhal next points out the witness read, and billed for reading, depositions that had nothing to do with his opinion. Later Leventhal will show the witness missed evidence that should have been relevant to his opinion.]

Q: For instance, you actually decided to read the deposition of the guardian, didn't you?

A: That's correct, yes.

Q: But the guardian wasn't in the emergency room?

A: That's correct.

Q: You decided to read and you made notes of how many hours to the minute that you spent reading the deposition, didn't you?

[Good use of the witness's billing invoice.]

A: Yes, I did.

Q: And you decided to read the deposition of the conservator, Ms. Eder, even though she wasn't in the emergency room, right?

A: That's correct, yes.

Q: And—but then you made the decision not to read the deposition of Nurse Diamond, right?

A: That's correct.

Q: Or to look at her records.

A: On that, I don't think it's the case. I believe I've reviewed her records, yes.

Q: But Nurse Diamond is a nurse who saw Ms. Gasteazoro just a couple of days after she left the emergency room, right?

A: Correct, yes.

Q: When I asked you who Mr. Scolardi was, you weren't even sure?

A: I had said it had been quite a while since I reviewed the records and I would need to refresh my memory. That's correct, yes.

• • •

Q: Do you know who he is?

A: I believe that he is a nurse.

Q: Where does he work?

A: I believe in the hospital where Ms. Gasteazoro was seen in the emergency room.

Q: What hospital?

A: I'm not sure the exact name of the hospital without reviewing this. It's a hospital here in the Springs.

Q: So you carefully read the records in this case—the records have the name of the hospital on every page—but you don't know the name of the hospital?

[Does the name of the hospital really matter? Not by itself. But with a $2,000/hour witness, who has just been shown to have an uneven pattern of looking at irrelevant depositions and ignoring others that sound more important, that small fact starts to paint a picture.]

A: It would be—it's not the kind of thing that I necessarily would want to take a look and memorize. In that I have all the records in front of me, I can certainly obtain that at any time.

Q: What role, if any, did Mr. Scolardi play?

A: Well, as I said, I believe he was a nurse in the emergency room.

Q: What role did he play with regard to the care of Ms. Gasteazoro, if any?

A: He was one of the people who had treated her in the emergency room, at least had cared for her.

Q: Was he the triage nurse?

A: I don't believe so.

Q: What treatment did he provide?

[Open-ended questions let the witness sink himself. This shows the power of quizzing a witness on facts the witness should know. Think how much less effective a leading question would have been here:

> Q: You don't know anything about the treatment he provided, do you?
>
> A: Not true, I know he was one of the nurses, and so on and so forth.]

A: I can't specifically tell you what treatment he provided. He was one of the nurses who was caring for her, and there were several notes that were—there were notes within the medical records that he had authored.

[The questioner asks a more specific question that shows the relevance of the nurse witness whom this expert knows little about.]

Q: Dr. [name], did Mr. Scolardi testify that, in his deposition, that he realized that one explanation for Ms. Gasteazoro's presentation was a stroke or a brain bleed?

A: I don't specifically recall, but I would—I would need to review his deposition, but I believe I have some recollection of that, that he might have mentioned that, but I would have to specifically review his deposition.

Q: Do you know who Bonnie May is?

A: No, I don't.

Q: Were you given the records of the chiropractor in the case?

A: Yes, I was.

Q: And do you—did you read them?

A: Yes, I did.

Q: Did the chiropractor identify that Ms. Gasteazoro may have a focal deficit?

A: Not to my best understanding, no.

Q: You didn't see anything in the chiropractor's records that indicated that she noticed a limp?

A: Not that I can recall.

Q: Did the chiropractor in her records say that this patient needs more evaluation?

A: Again, not that I can recall, no.

Q: So you don't remember anything in the chiropractor's records that said that she thinks that Ms. Gasteazoro needs a full spine X-ray or anything of that sort?

A: Again, not that I can specifically recall, but I would be happy to review that, if you'd like to point that out to me.[2]

Note how tight organization makes this line of questions effective. Over and over, Leventhal quickly establishes that the witness doesn't know who a player in the case was or what that person did, then with more questions makes the relevance of the missing knowledge plain.

---

2. *Gasteazoro v. Catholic Health Initiatives*, Case No. 2011CV2036, El Paso County, Colorado District Court, November 9, 2012.

Example: Ignorance of a Corporate Defendant

Now let's look at an ignorance cross of a corporate defendant's spokesperson, the hiring manager for a trucking company whose truck was involved in a deadly accident. The cross-examiner is Larry Grassini, a top southern California trial lawyer, whose theme is that the company's hiring showed lethal apathy about people it employed to drive its trucks. Grassini sets up the background:

> The case was called *Dawn Renae Diaz v. Sugar Transport of the Northwest, Inc., et al.* The plaintiff was Dawn Diaz, who was severely injured in a cross-freeway accident. Dawn was heading southbound on the 101 Freeway when a Sugar Transport truck heading northbound was clipped on the front left side by a pickup passing it, causing the pickup to flip over the median divider and land on Dawn's car.
>
> Police report and witnesses put 100 percent fault on the pickup driver. We sued Sugar Transport (STN) for negligent hiring and their driver, Jose Carcamo, for negligent driving.
>
> The cross-examination is of a twenty-five-year employee of STN whose deposition we took as "the person most knowledgeable in hiring practices and procedures at STN and in hiring the driver, Jose Carcamo."
>
> It was important for us to show STN's hiring practices were terrible and that they didn't care about these drivers (from their office three hundred miles away) driving through Ventura.[3]

MR. GRASSINI: Do you believe, sir, as a—as the person in charge of hiring for STN, that before hiring someone or at the time you get the information back from the prior employers, you should take that into consideration in determining whether they are a

---

3. Personal communication from Larry Grassini.

safe or unsafe driver to protect the public on the motoring—motoring public?

STN CORPORATE REPRESENTATIVE: I believe it could be one consideration, yes.

Q: And that—and at STN, it can't be a consideration because you don't get the information. Isn't that right?

A: That is correct.

Q: How many years have you been in charge of hiring for STN?

A: It has to be in the fifteen neighborhood, fourteen, fifteen years.

Q: And for the past fourteen or fifteen years, as the hiring manager in charge of hiring at STN, you have never seen one of those previous employer's records like you got on Jose Carcamo. Isn't that correct?

A: That is correct.

Q: So, it isn't just a situation where you didn't see it for Jose Carcamo. The policy and procedures set up at STN are set up so that the person who hires the drivers never sees the information that's returned from the prior employers. Is that right?

[Grassini sets up the problem as not just leading to the issue for this driver, but systemic to the defendant company.]

A: That is correct.

• • •

Q: And, of course, that document, Plaintiff's 81, wasn't even considered when you decided to hire Jose Carcamo because you don't get it. Is that right?

A: I did not get that.

Q: And you saw on that, sir, that basically, that document, which you didn't have, gets told—said that the safety habits of Jose Carcamo were poor and that he had two accidents. Correct?

A: Yes, it is.

Q: And we asked you why you would hire someone if you had that kind of information, and you told us, "It's hard to find drivers where their DMV printout are not a deterrent, and we needed drivers; we needed bodies to work." Was that your testimony back then?

A: Yes, it was.

[This was a great admission, which, since it came in a party's deposition, through its corporate spokesman, could be read into the record as substantive evidence without trying to first set up a contradiction to impeach.]

* * *

Q: When you look at that employment application, do you see that he worked for three months immediately before he applied to you, for Southwest Processors?

A: Yes.

Q: And Southwest Processors is the one who said they wouldn't rehire him and he had poor safety habits. The next note shows that he had a gap in his driving from February of '05 for four years. Do you see that?

A: Yes.

Q: As a person provided—as the person most knowledgeable in the hiring of employees at STN and specifically Jose Carcamo, isn't that a red flag?

A: No.

Q: Is a gap in the employment history something that gets your attention?

A: We ask them about the, uhm—yes, it gets our attention.

Q: And you ask them what they were doing during the time there was the gap?

A: Yes.

Q: And do you know if that was done in this case?

A: I could not tell you.

Q: And then you didn't see the application; so, you, yourself, could not determine there was this four-year gap from the three months before he was hired, right?

A: That's correct.[4]

Grassini went on to prove through the same witness that the trucking company had a lackadaisical attitude about whether its drivers received the company safety manual or attended regular safety meetings. He showed that the documents from prior employers that no one at the defendant company had read revealed the driver to be a hothead with a poor driving history. And he closed the cross getting the witness to agree that it would violate company policy for a driver to speed up to prevent a passing vehicle from cutting in front of the truck, exactly what the plaintiff contended had happened here.

Takeaways

Some readers may protest, "I don't get those kinds of mistaken, ignorant witnesses in my cases." I respectfully dissent. Ignorant witnesses never reveal themselves readily. It's our job to sense when a witness does not know things he or she should know and push to plumb the bottom of their emptiness. Jim Leventhal, for one, had no idea that the expert he cross-examined wouldn't know the name of the hospital he was talking about, but careful listening gave a hint, and so he pounced. The lesson for all of us is this: you never know unless you ask.

---

4. *Dawn Renae Diaz v. Sugar Transport of the Northwest, Inc., et al.*, Case No. CIV 241085, Ventura County, California Superior Court, February 27, 2008.

11

Shooting It Out with the Hired-Gun Witness

The only two currencies that have any traction in our calcified political culture are fear and money.

—David Simon

In this chapter and the next, we study perhaps the most dangerous adverse witness we can face: the hired-gun professional expert witness who turns up, case after case, mostly or always on the same side, hired by the same lawyers. This witness has chewed up so many cross-examiners that we want to indict him for cannibalism. He is back in court, again, because he's so effective.

So the answer is obvious, right? You zero in on the expert's testimonial pattern, bring it out in two or three questions, add up how much money the expert has made from this one-sided work, then tussle with one or two inconsistencies in his testimony, then sit down, quickly, before you become the latest dish of cross-examiner sushi eaten raw.

Most of the time, that recipe doesn't work. Here's why:

- We fail to appreciate the danger: a slick professional witness who favors one side has heard this line of questions before and has some ready answers. If we're not prepared and persistent, the witness's plausible first line of defense defeats us.

- We assume it's enough to bring out the testimonial pattern and the money without more, saving our big attack on the witness for closing argument—when it can be too late to dispel a favorable impression the witness has created with the jury. (This "save it for closing," the tenth of the old commandments of cross, has probably caused as many lost opportunities for effective cross as the other wrong commandments combined.)

- We don't spell out for the jury *why* it's suspect for a witness to always or mostly take one side or work for the same lawyers. Why should they necessarily know? Lawyers always seem to take one side, so what's the big deal with witnesses?

- The witness may have some other response we're not ready for. Perhaps he or she claims to work for both sides evenhandedly, and we haven't done enough research to prove that's wrong or have enough questions ready to cast suspicion on the claim.

- The money cross that we often pair with the one-sided cross also doesn't get the attention it deserves, because we don't spell out what it means to be beholden to one side for this lucrative line of income. Worse, we can look like hypocrites when we establish no more than the other side writing big checks to its expert witnesses, because we do the same for ours. The risk here is jurors disgusted at both sides saying, "a pox on both your houses," which of course is exactly what the defense wants, since canceling both sides means the side with the burden of proof loses.

This is worth mulling over in depth, if for no other reason than one-sided and money cross could be the most common types of cross that we attempt on expert witnesses, thousands of times a year in courtrooms across America. Most lawyers think they know how to bring out bias and prejudice for a one-sided hired-gun witness, and that's part of the problem, because they may try the "one-sided" or "money" lines of questioning without thinking it through.

In this chapter, I will disassemble and put back together into a more effective weapon our money and one-sided cross-examinations. Plus, I will look at what the science tells us about hired guns and how to defeat them. Then, in the next chapter, I will take up another key weapon to show the bias of a professional hired gun: polarizing the witness and showing how truly extreme his or her opinions are.

Building Better Cross of the One-Sided Expert

Let's go back to the start. What are the hidden assumptions that attract us to the one-sided line of attack? How can we use these assumptions to build more powerful cross of the one-sided witness with a Rules of the Road approach?

The basic idea has sound logic and is almost a syllogism:

1. Expert witnesses are allowed to come into court and give opinions, not just facts, because they can help the jury understand some important aspect of the case. Opinions are squishy things, harder to cross-examine than concrete facts.

2. In return for the freer rein given to experts that other witnesses don't enjoy, expert witnesses are supposed to be objective and fair-minded, not advocates for one side or the other.

3. An expert who only, or predominantly, testifies for one side is likely to be biased in favor of that side—especially if this is a big source of the witness's income.

4. The jury is instructed that it can discount or ignore the testimony of any witness who jurors conclude has a bias or prejudice.

5. This witness is biased and should not be believed because he always (or nearly so) takes the same side (and makes a lot of money doing so).

Items 1 and 2 are rules or principles that are easy to establish in front of the jury, but we don't bring them out often enough in open court because principles that are obvious to us as trial lawyers become engrained, invisible, and therefore silent. Let's add them to our question outline that we're constructing.

Item 3 is more tricky. It contains both an asserted fact—this witness testifies mostly or entirely for one side—and a conclusion—one-sidedness means bias. Either the fact or the conclusion can become a pushback point for the witness, and so we have to be ready for both. If we can deal with it successfully, then items 4 and 5 will fall into place with jury instructions and closing argument.

Establishing the Fact of One-Sidedness

When we confront a witness with her testimonial pattern, there are only a few possible answers:

- *Deny:* "It's not true. I've testified plenty for your side."
- *Admit the pattern but deny the bias premise:* "I'm just here to tell the truth as best I can as a scientist."
- *Admit with a minimizing explanation:* "It's true I seem to only testify for one side, but . . . [fill in one of the following variations]"
  » I'm really unbiased; I have no idea why I only get calls from one side.
  » I used to testify a lot for your side, or I would if you would just call me.
  » I've done plenty of case reviews for your side, but the lawyer never follows up and calls me to court.
  » I hardly ever go to court, so it's just random chance that three times in ten years have been for one side.

Old-fashioned witness investigation should help you figure out the witness's true pattern, at least that which she has admitted to under oath in the past. If you read enough deposition or, better, trial transcripts from the witness, you will also see how she has handled the question in the past.[1]

The preview you get from transcript review will help you plan your own cross and also help decide the more important question of whether you want to venture down this road at all. This is one of those lines of questions (like many in this book) where I urge you to either go "all in" and go after the witness hard, or, if the witness has great answers about her testimonial history that you cannot impeach, figure out some other way to cross-examine the witness. Just dipping your toe into the water briefly is not going to work.

Establishing That One-Sidedness Means Bias

If you've done your homework and can establish that this is a truly one-sided witness, the most likely response from the witness will be to deny the equation between one-sidedness and bias. This happened to me not long ago, and I think I could have handled it better.[2] The expert, an obstetrician who specialized in high-risk pregnancies, had already testified on direct examination that in the last ten years he had consulted on legal cases only for defense lawyers. Maybe this was the defense lawyer's "disclose it first and take the sting out" strategy—a dubious approach because it highlighted the issue without ever providing an innocent explanation.

So I hit him hard with my first question on cross:

Mr. Malone: Did you ever wonder, Dr. Christmas, why your phone never rings from plaintiffs' lawyers?

---

1. See chapter 14, "Mining for Dirt," on investigating witnesses.

2. We visited this same piece, more briefly, in chapter 4, "Cross-Examination with Case-Building Rules," on the case-building rule of informed consent that the witness reluctantly agreed with.

Dr. Christmas: It never crossed my mind, no.

Q: It didn't possibly cross your mind that you were one of those guys who could always be counted on if there is any issue where it might be a little bit of ambiguity that you would slice it for the healthcare provider? That didn't ever occur to you?

A: With all due respect, I swore to tell the truth about three hours ago, and I take that very seriously.[3]

I elected to drop the line of questioning right there, figuring that the witness had "protested too much," but I could have done a lot more. Riffing off his last answer, I could have lobbed some of these:

Q: So you're volunteering that you plan to be truthful?

Q: And objective too?

Q: You agree your job on the witness stand is different from being an advocate?

Q: Your role is different from the attorney who hired you. He is supposed to be truthful in court but doesn't have to be objective. You, however, do have to be objective?

And I could have returned to the question he never really answered, which was whether his testimonial pattern indicated he really wasn't objective:

Q: So when I asked you about the fact that you always testify for one side, I take it from your answer that you agree that pattern raises at least the appearance of your not being objective?

And most direct:

Q: If you had a reputation for being objective, don't you think your phone would ring from lawyers on both sides, not just one side?

---

3. *Simpson v. Roberts*, Case No. CL04-213, City of Roanoke Circuit Court, Virginia, May 16, 2012.

I hesitated to ask all these, because I didn't know what he would say (and in truth, I had underprepared this piece of the cross). It was probably an unnecessary fear. Yet again, if these were questions he wasn't used to, maybe he didn't know what he would say either, and there you have a promising area for cross-examination: the unrehearsed answer, on a topic likely to bear fruit for your side.

Another way to improve the cross of one-sided experts is to bring out patterns in their testimony that go with that territory. For example, defense medical examiners usually show up in court to rebut the testimony of the plaintiffs' treating doctors. They do so with only the briefest exposure to the patients. That makes them vulnerable to this line of cross in these sample questions:

Q: You're here to say that Dr. Treater got it wrong?

Q: And you base that on your single visit with the patient, compared to Dr. Treater's [fill in number] times seeing him?

To this question, some professional witnesses like to say:

A: No, I base it on this six-inch stack of medical records that I've studied closely.

To which you can respond:

Q: Show me one important fact in those records that Dr. Treater didn't know about.

Q: And that's what you usually do, isn't it? You come to court and you testify for the defense that the treating doctor who testified for the plaintiff got it wrong?

Q: How many times have you testified in court that the treating doctor was wrong?

Your conclusion: "With this witness, everybody's out of step but Johnny."

Improving "Money" Cross

Now let's look at one-sided cross's first cousin, money cross. Both plaintiff and defense attorneys in civil cases are drawn to cross-examination of experts' lawsuit income like bees to nectar, or flies to . . . well, you know. Why? For starters, you don't have to be Einstein to figure that time equals money equals bias. We darned sure expect bias—uh, loyalty, let's say—from the experts on our side. Our own experts would cause us outrage and dreams of suing them if they entertained the notion of abandoning our side late in the game when a bad new dispositive fact should shimmer into view. But the experts on the other side? Oh, they've sold their souls, haven't they, for filthy lucre! And that pinpoints one big problem with cross about experts' income: our own hypocrisy. Mr. Green is okay for our side, but never for theirs.

So what do we do about it? Recognizing the Achilles' heel in our own position is a good start. That means being selective about when and whether we play the money card in cross so it doesn't blow back against us. For instance, just because the opposing counsel didn't make a big deal about our experts' consulting incomes when the experts were in the courtroom doesn't mean it's necessarily safe for us to blaze away at their experts on lawsuit income. The other side might have an expert disclosure from us or some other way to get this into evidence and make us look two-faced.

We also need to work hard to show that this witness is different from ours: not just well paid, but a sellout, a witness who couldn't possibly give objective testimony because it would bite the hand that has fed her so many times. That's the impression we're looking to create. So we need to fit money cross into a bigger equation:

$$\frac{\text{money}^4 + \text{one-sided testimonial history} + \text{evasiveness on the stand} + \text{contradictions}}{\text{a biased, untrustworthy witness}}$$

---

[4]. Preferably lots of it, over long stretches of time, from the same sources over and over.

That was the winning combination for Florida attorney Gary Fox, who faced off with an expert witness who had a long testimonial history. Fox started with one sidedness, then moved to money. (After he finished this one-two, he ended the cross with a contradictions point, which I excerpted at the end of chapter 9, "Fixing Contradictions Cross.")

Let's listen in.

MR. FOX: But, in any event, can we agree, Doctor, that in the 450 cases in which you've testified, either by deposition or at trial, that in 95 percent of the cases you've testified for the defendants and against the patient?

DR. RADETSKY: Well, again, sir, I don't testify for or against anyone. I try to give exactly as accurate a testimony as I can no matter who may have retained me. I think that's the job of an expert is to give accurate testimony. It is true that I would say 95 percent of the time, by the time it comes to a deposition or a trial, I'm brought there by a defense attorney, but my testimony is not for or against anyone.

Q: Yes, sir. You are brought there by and paid for by a defense lawyer to testify in a case against a baby or a baby's parents. Isn't that true, sir?

A: No. Mr. Fox, again, I'm not testifying for or against anyone. I think that that's really a mischaracterization of what my job is. My job is to try to give accurate and, I hope, scientifically based testimony to the jury for them to make the decision.

Q: Yes, sir. Well, how about you and I not quibble about words. In 95 percent of the cases you are paid by the defense. Can we agree to that?

A: Yes.

[This was a good turnaround question to get the witness to agree with what the cross-examiner wanted here. It was obvious that the witness would not agree with the fact that he "testifies *for*" someone, so specifically pinning down who pays him was a good way to step around that dodge. And after the witness had repeated, too many times for his own credibility, that he doesn't testify *for* or *against* anyone, this starkly highlighted the key point. The witness then finds a reason to reassert his objectivity. One could argue that the point had been made and the cross-examiner should have moved on, rather than hammer the point. But at some point here, the witness's protestations of objectivity come to seem overly slick.]

Q: And in 95 percent of the cases you come in and you tell a jury that the defendant did nothing wrong or anything the defendant did didn't cause an injury or death?

A: No, sir. That's not what my job is. My job is, first of all, to answer the questions put to me, but secondly, to try to give the jury as accurate and honest testimony as I can based on the science that I know. So, again, you're really mischaracterizing what I think the job of an expert witness—at least me as an expert witness—actually is.

Q: Doctor, can we at least agree that in 95 percent of these cases in which a lawsuit is brought by a parent or by a child against a doctor or healthcare provider, your testimony is paid for by the defendant?

A: I think you asked me the question already, sir.

OPPOSING COUNSEL: Objection, Your Honor. It's already been asked and answered. It's repetitious.

THE COURT: Well, just—I don't know that he had a straight answer. Was it a yes or a no? Can you just answer the question, whether it's accurate or not?

DR. RADETSKY: Yes, that's true, sir.

[It doesn't hurt when the judge steps in, which sometimes happens with overly slick witnesses. The questioning went on to highlight the corollary point—that a testimonial history of always being on one side meant that the witness was never on the other side—a point worth making.]

Q: In fact, Doctor, in all the twenty-five years that you've been doing this, you've only come in and testified for a patient or a patient's family how many times at trial?

A: Again, I don't testify for or against. But out of the trial testimony that I've given, I have been brought there by a plaintiff's attorney now I think four times.

Q: Four times in twenty-five years?

A: That's correct.

[Next, Fox tried to get a straight answer about the witness's total fees for the case on trial. Fox pursued his point with courtesy but persistence and, in the end, won something even better than a responsive answer: a clear impression of a witness who wants to hide what he's paid.]

Q: Now, Doctor Radetsky, how much are you being paid in this case? I know what your hourly rate is. I want to know how much—by the time you get back to New Mexico—what the total bill for the defendants is going to be for your work in this case?

A: Are you asking me what my bill will be for coming here to Tallahassee?

Q: No, sir. I'm sorry. I didn't ask the question right. What I thought I asked—well, I'll try to ask better—is what is your total bill going to be, what—for all of the work that you've done in this case?

A: I don't know, sir. I don't have that information.

Q: Well, I understand you may not know it to the nickel, but give our jury the best estimate as to what your charges are going to be.

A: You know, I just don't know. I've sent in invoices in the past and been paid for them, but I don't have that information with me today.

Q: Well, I understand that you don't—you don't have all the invoices. I'm just asking for an approximation. Give us your best approximation as to what your total charges are going to be.

A: I just don't know, sir. You know, the case was first sent to me four years ago. So, I'm sorry, I just don't have that information.

Q: So could it be 30, 40, $50,000?

A: I don't have the information, sir.[5]

Notice how, when the witness misconstrued the first money question, Fox took the blame on himself for the misunderstanding, then re-asked the same question (which of course was clear the first time he asked it). Then, when the witness showed he didn't want to answer, Fox gave him several other chances to respond. Many cross-examiners would have turned sarcastic or biting at the very first sign of evasion. That's a mistake born of the questioner knowing the witness a lot better than the jurors who have just met the witness for the first time and haven't read dozens of his depositions. What's better than quarreling is to try different but polite ways to get an answer. The old saw that you catch more bears with honey than vinegar applies to cross-examination most of the time. This works only with the right combination: right witness, right facts, *and* right you, the cross-examiner. On that last point, here is Gary's comment to me about what I believe was vital to his success with the witness: self-control.[6]

> It is way too easy to get angry and frustrated with the witness's evasion and deceit, and guys like Radetsky [a pediatric infectious disease doctor who has testified for defendants in malpractice cases hundreds of times] thrive on that. The importance of being emotionally and psychologically prepared for the evasion can't, in my opinion, be overemphasized. The cross-examiner scores a lot of points with the jury when dealing with a guy like this doctor in a calm and steady way. It is, of course, a lot easier to stay calm and together when we *expect* the witness to behave a certain way and we have decided in advance that, rather than get frustrated and angry by the deceit and evasion, we *welcome* it because it gives us

---

5. *Slayton v. Professional Park Pediatrics*, P.A., Case No. 03CA1622, 2nd Judicial Circuit, Florida, June 22, 2007.

6. See chapter 1, "Laying the Mental Foundation," for the full treatment.

additional opportunities to help the jury see the witness as he truly is.[7]

Look back again through the excerpt of Fox's cross-examination, and you will see numerous times when the witness seems to quietly try to bait Fox into blowing up, by offering gratuitous comments about his own objectivity that are not really responsive to the question:

- "I'm not testifying for or against anyone."
- "My job is . . . to try to give the jury as accurate and honest testimony as I can based on the science that I know."

Over and over, Fox declines to turn sour but politely persists in making his point. This is why preparing *yourself* for the cross-examination is just as important as preparing the subject matter and the questions themselves.

Another way that money cross often falls short of the mark is that it's too brief. Here are some points to expand our thinking about money and experts, followed by a good example. We need to remember this always: The issue is not money itself. The issue is whether money interferes with the expert's duty to be impartial and objective. Jurors reach their own conclusions about that, which we can influence with the way we shape our questions.

- Are both sides more or less evenly balanced in money spent on experts? Then you might not want to get into money, but the defense lawyer might do so in hopes of getting the jurors to condemn both sides for their hired-gun testimony (which means, the defending lawyer hopes, that you will fail to meet your burden of persuasion). It's a delicate tactic for the defense lawyer, who risks the charge of hypocrisy.

- Does the witness make what seems like a lot of money, either annually or for the day's appearance or both, especially measured by local community income standards?

---

7. Personal communication from Gary Fox.

- Does the witness show the marks of a well-oiled money machine? Professional corporations, relatives on the payroll, elaborate fee agreements (typically guaranteeing full pay even if the court appearance is canceled), consistently large income amounts year after year—all are potential signs.

- Is the money in this case part of a regular pattern of money received from a single source or related sources?

- How evasive is the witness in answering money questions?

On this last point, a really polished professional witness trains herself to answer money questions nondefensively and directly. She understands that the faster the cross-examiner gets in and out of this line of questions, the better for the witness. This is why a good cross-examiner, as in the example below, never lets the money line of questions die after one or two, but stretches the point out until it's obvious to half-attentive jurors.

STRETCHING THE MONEY POINT

Here, Roanoke, Virginia, attorney Tony Russell nicely stretches the point about the witness, an orthopedist named Dr. Andrews, making a lot of money from testifying and performing "independent" medical examinations. On direct examination, the defense counsel (Mr. Peake) had brought out Dr. Andrews's net income from testifying, but he omitted some details, such as money paid to family members who worked for the doctor's testimonial corporation.

Here's part of the cross:

MR. RUSSELL: Doctor Andrews, we know each other. Is that correct?

DR. ANDREWS: We have met before.

Q: I want to first start off with the financial information that Mr. Peake concentrated on in this case. The medical legal work that you were discussing with Mr. Peake, that does not involve people who you actually treat, correct?

A: No, these are not my patients. These are people whose records that I'm asked to read that I am not treating.

Q: And the medical legal work that you do as well as the record review that you discussed with Mr. Peake, you have set up a corporation to handle that, correct?

A: I have.

Q: And that corporation is William C. Andrews, Jr., MD, PC, correct?

A: That is correct.

Q: And that is the corporation that receives all of the proceeds from your medical legal expert work and your records review and all your nontreating doctor stuff, correct?

A: Correct.

Q: And you said, if I recall, Mr. Peake asked what you made in 2012, last year, from doing expert witness and record reviews and you said it was $340,000, correct?

A: That's correct.

Q: Now, that is just profit, correct?

A: That is correct.

Q: Because your corporation made much more than that in 2012 for your legal expert witness work as well as your record reviews. Is that correct?

A: That is correct.

Q: Tell us, if you would, how much money did your corporation make in 2012 for this stuff?

A: I didn't look that up last night. I think it made around $500,000.

Q: So a half million dollars?

A: Correct.

Q: Now, in 2011 when you told Mr. Peake that you made $288,000. That, again, was profit from these things, correct?

A: Correct.

Q: Again, that does not include all the money that your corporation made for what you did, correct?

A: Right.

Q: Now, Doctor Andrews, tell us how much did your corporation make in 2011 for the work that you do? Again, this is not treating work. This is not your clinical practice. Just the legal expert work and the medical reviews.

A: And, again, I did not look it up, but I think you can do the math and say probably somewhere around $425,000.

Q: And then in 2010, again, when Mr. Peake asked you what you made and you said a quarter of a million dollars, that again was just profit, correct?

A: That is correct.

Q: Tell us how much your corporation made in 2010 from the proceeds of the work that you do, like here today?

A: Again, an estimate would be around $400,000.

• • •

Q: So in the last five years, including this year, your corporation has made approximately $2 million dollars for this type of work that you do, correct?

A: That's correct.

Q: And you have made over a million dollars doing this type of work?

A: Correct.

• • •

Q: Did you have one or more of your children work for that company before?

A: I have.

Q: Do you still have one or more children working for that company?

A: They do.

Q: Do they get paid from the money that goes to your corporation?

A: They do.

Q: And you're a hundred percent shareholder in that corporation?

A: I am.[8]

The attorney went on to couple the money with the witness's one-sided testimonial pattern. This is the key linkage that shows why the money matters: it influences testimony.

The Pithy Point of Money Cross

Here's a famous quotation I showed on the screen to a witness, a lawyer testifying as an expert for GEICO insurance company in a bad-faith lawsuit. This came at the end of thirty minutes of my voir dire cross-examination—before the witness had given a single opinion about the case. I reviewed his bills in the case and established that his law firm had made over $10 million in billable time from its niche practice representing insurers in coverage disputes. So he could be counted on to take the insurer's side.

> "It is difficult to get a man to understand something, when his salary depends on his not understanding it."
>
> —Upton Sinclair

I asked the witness an open-ended question: "What do you think of this quote?" He didn't have an answer. Now, I may have lucked

---

8. *Patricia Rose v. MONCO Assocs., Ltd.*, Case No. CL12-549, Roanoke, VA City Circuit Court, November 14, 2013.

out, but is there any good rejoinder to this maxim that neatly summarizes the problem with high-paid witnesses?

The science about jurors' perceptions of experts is sparse but interesting. A group at Rutgers did an experiment where they played the same tapes of a plaintiff's expert and a defense expert testifying to mock jurors; the plaintiff's expert's testimony had four possible combinations of pay and credentials:

- high pay–high credentials
- high pay–low credentials
- low pay–high credentials
- low pay–low credentials.

The defense expert was held at the same pay-credentials level in all four renditions, to provide a "control." The jurors then voted on which side was more persuasive.

The *only* combination that caused significant discounting of the expert's credibility was the first: the expert with high credentials who also was paid very well. That was the expert that jurors thought was a hired gun whom they did not trust. Everything else being equal, the high pay–high credentials expert won the verdict for the plaintiff only 29 percent of the time, whereas the high pay–*low credentials* expert won over 62 percent of the jurors. The same high pay–high credentials expert scored higher than all three other categories in being annoying, and lower on being trustworthy, honest, persuasive, believable, and likeable. Remember, this is the same witness speaking for thirty minutes with a script of *identical* testimony, with only these two small facts of pay and credentials changed!

Jurors evidently made the common-sense conclusion that the high pay–high credentials expert had a bigger market for his services and could take on whoever would pay him well. Jurors assumed, without being told, that this expert likely testified a lot, whereas the high pay–low credentials expert, they reasoned, probably didn't testify that much but must have had some specific expertise suitable for the case.

Experiment number two in the same series kept the high pay–low pay variable. But instead of varying the expert's credentials, the researchers substituted number of times testifying in court. Half the jurors heard the plaintiff's expert was a frequent testifier—this was his fourteenth time in court, he said—and half that he was a novice, second time in court. Again, jurors heard the same thirty-minute audiotape, with only these two small variables: pay and frequency of testifying. The result: the jurors didn't like the highly paid, frequent testifier and didn't find him persuasive. Jurors found the highly paid *novice* expert twice as persuasive as the high-priced, frequent testifier.

The same Rutgers group found that technical jargon was a real turnoff for the jurors. Jurors have a hunger to understand what the witness is saying. When they can't, they judge the person.[9]

Takeaways: Handling the Hired Gun

Let's put together what we know about the hired-gun witness from experience, common sense, and the available science:

- This most dangerous of adverse witnesses requires careful study and a cool, meticulous approach. You're disassembling a bomb—fire and ire won't work.

- Your goal is to create a firm impression: here is a biased, untrustworthy witness. A one-angled shot generally won't work. Your best chance is with a combination approach that exploits all the witness's vulnerabilities: one-sidedness, money, long and cozy relationships with the other side, evasiveness, and, as we will see in the next chapter, a polarized, extreme view of the evidence that sees absolutely no merit in your side.

---

9. Joel Cooper and Isaac M. Neuhaus, "The 'Hired Gun' Effect: Assessing the Effect of Pay, Frequency of Testifying, and Credentials on the Perception of Expert Testimony," *Law and Human Behavior*, Vol. 24, No. 2 (April 2000), pp. 149–171.

- Strong credentials can backfire on a witness's credibility, especially if he testifies a lot. This is why you can sometimes build up the expert's credentials even more than the direct examination brought out. (If you're on the receiving end of this tactic, be ready for the "he's an ivory tower elitist" argument.)

- Jurors don't like professional witnesses even when they play both sides of litigation work, except when the witness can make a very good showing as a "man or woman of the people." In the right case, you can underline the hired-gun point by showing all the time the witness spends working on lawsuits rather than curing sick people, teaching students, and doing the other things that professionals in their fields typically focus on.

- Painting a portrait of a professional witness works all the better when the witness provides fodder, such as incorporating a special entity for his testimonial work, developing elaborate retainer agreements, and having intricate fee schedules with lots of opportunities for pocketing money for no work.

Exercise

Pull out your last cross-examination transcript of a hired gun. Ask yourself how much more you could have done to bring out the witness's bias. Do a new outline of questions that explores the key areas in more depth. At a minimum, see if you can achieve the following:

1. Spend enough time at the junction between money and one-sidedness that the point becomes clear that this expert could never testify for your side if he wanted to enjoy his usual source of income.

2. Show the witness has a pattern of taking extreme views where everyone is wrong but him.

Once you've done that, you'll face this same witness again with eagerness and confidence.

12

Polarizing the Extreme Witness

The opportunity of defeating the enemy is provided by the enemy himself.

—Sun Tzu, *The Art of War*

We just finished working on our main weapons that show the bias of hired-gun witnesses: their long testifying history, the narrow base of their income, their one-sidedness, and their evasion of simple questions. Another important tactic for cross-examining an implacable foe is to push the hired-gun witness to the extreme boundaries of his position.

Rick Friedman calls this *polarizing*. He wrote a book on polarizing as a way to confront so-called independent medical examiners who posture themselves as objective and fair-minded but in actuality are advocates through and through.[1] The technique involves

---

1. Rick Friedman, *Polarizing the Case: Exposing and Defeating the Malingering Myth* (Portland, OR: Trial Guides, 2007).

blending three of the basic tear-down weapons: bias, ignorance, and contradictions.

- First, typically, you show bias by bringing out the witness's tight relationships with the defense counsel and, if it's a corporate defendant, the company behind these lawyers.
- Then, you show ignorance by demonstrating how the expert has picked through the facts of the case—ignoring, distorting or conveniently forgetting about those facts that don't serve his preconceived opinions.
- Finally, you show how the expert stands in contradiction to a large number of disinterested witnesses: treating doctors, employers, family members. All of them, this witness contends when pushed, are wrong. This stark contrast never comes out unless we highlight it on cross.

Here is an excerpt from a successful cross-examination Friedman conducted that shows the polarizing method at work. This witness was the defense star in an insurance bad-faith trial. Friedman represented the plaintiff, a venture capitalist who claimed his career was ruined by chronic fatigue syndrome and who tried unsuccessfully to collect on a disability insurance policy. For four hours, as the final defense witness, the forensic psychiatrist raked through the plaintiff's life and wove a story that boldly accused the plaintiff of being a malingering faker.

Friedman's game plan was to accuse the doctor straight up of being a hired-gun advocate and then, when the doctor predictably denied it, show that he nonetheless could not bring himself to consider facts that might favor the legitimacy of the plaintiff's medical condition. Friedman forced the psychiatrist to the extreme view that *all* the witnesses who thought the plaintiff was a person of integrity who had a genuine debilitating medical condition were either wrong or were lying themselves. He also showed that the psychiatrist had not considered a host of relevant evidence from treating doctors and bystanders.

Note Friedman's frequent violations of the old commandments of cross-examination, as he invited the psychiatrist to use his own words to show how extreme his opinions really were.

Friedman first hit the psychiatrist with a quotation from a textbook to which he had contributed a chapter, to the effect that the forensic psychiatrist's job was to spin a one-sided view of the evidence.[2]

Then he went straight at the witness's cherry-picking of facts:[3]

MR. FRIEDMAN: Well, that's what you did in this case, isn't it, Dr. Rosenberg? You highlighted the facts that support your malingering theory and de-emphasized or ignored the facts that don't support that theory?

DR. ROSENBERG: Again I would grossly disagree with that. I wrote a thirty-plus-page report and reviewed hundreds of pages of documents. I think I did a very reasonable and balanced evaluation.

[The witness has just established the criteria by which he should be judged: "very reasonable and balanced." He also gives Friedman a nice bridge into a pointed question about that report.]

Q: Tell us the facts that appear in your report that support the theory that Mr. Mead is genuinely disabled.

[Friedman promptly challenges the psychiatrist to prove he's "reasonable and balanced," as he's just asserted. The question as posed is narrower than first glance might indicate. The key words are *"facts that appear in your report,"* which of course Friedman has read closely.]

A: Well, there are his—I give a detailed account in my interview section as well as in the review of records—his subjective claims that he's disabled and the nature of his symptoms, et cetera. It would be tough for me to give a reason in the opinion section in support since the facts are so overwhelming that it's a faked CFS [chronic fatigue syndrome] claim.

---

2. That segment is excerpted in chapter 6, "Using Treatises to Get to Yes," on using literature in cross.

3. The names of the plaintiff and associated bystanders are changed here to protect privacy.

Q: That's it? Those are the only facts you came up with in your entire evaluation that support Mr. Mead's claim of disability. Is that right?

A: Well, in addition I've mentioned in my depositions, and I'd have to look and see if I mentioned it in my report as well, I phrased things that there are no significant findings in support of his CFS claim. You can always find in this amount of information some little suggestion, some slight oddity, in the neuropsychological testing, and again in all of his subjective claims, but there's no significant information that would support a genuine claim.

• • •

[Friedman then challenges the psychiatrist's selective use of facts given from the plaintiff's ex-wife, Gena Mead.]

Q: Well, is it a subjective statement if she reports what she observed from living with him for twenty-eight years? Is that—do you consider that subjective?

A: Yes, I would consider it subjective. First of all, it's her personal interpretation colored by many factors, and it's also the fact again that she also has her own personal secondary gain at stake in a case such as this.

Q: And both of those things are true of you, aren't they, Doctor? What you've given us is your personal interpretation of the facts, just like Gena Mead did, and you yourself have an economic motive, don't you?

[A "sauce for the goose, saucer for the gander" question intended to highlight the expert's own financial bias.]

A: Well, again, I would disagree strongly with both. I've tried to lay out painstakingly the scientific basis for the extraordinary number of reasons in support, using what are generally accepted ways of making these analyses, and I get paid the same whatever the outcome, so I don't have the same kind of financial stake.

Q: Aren't you supposed to weigh the evidence in favor of your hypothesis as well as the evidence against your hypothesis?

A: Absolutely, you're supposed to weigh the evidence.

[The expert agrees he is supposed to weigh both sides, and Friedman immediately confronts his failure to weigh the other side here.]

Q: All right, and where on your report did you weigh the evidence of Gena Mead's reports of Cliff Mead's physical degeneration over a period of years?

A: Well, it would be tough because I didn't review that material until after my reports were done, but in recently reading her deposition, I highlighted the facts that were relevant when I was talking about the reasons in support of malingering.

Q: But not the facts that would be relevant in support of the theory that Mr. Mead is disabled. Is that right?

A: Not her subjective statements in support of that. That's correct.

Q: What you're doing is you're picking and choosing from Ms. Mead's deposition, taking the portions that support your theory and ignoring or de-emphasizing the rest. Isn't that right?

A: Again I would disagree. I started out with a particular opinion that the evidence scientifically supports malingering. I was giving reasons to support that opinion, and as I've just mentioned, there certainly is plenty of subjective information from her describing his CFS symptoms.

Q: Did you just say that you started out with the opinion he was malingering, and then you were supplied with reasons to support it?

[The witness has just slipped up and made an apparent admission that he started with the opinion first, then fit the facts to it. This is a good instance of the payoff from listening closely to the witness's responses and immediately challenging them.]

A: I think that—I apologize if I didn't state myself in what I said clearly.

Q: I'm sorry, is that what you psychiatrists call a Freudian slip?

A: I don't know if that's a joke or if you wanted me to give you an expert opinion, but in any case, if I could finish my answer, what I was saying then when I started to testify today with regard to the opinions—the opinion of malingering and then the reasons in support of it from a scientific basis, I was laying them out, and I integrated my recent review of her deposition.

• • •

Q: All right. Now, at the time you testified in *Abner*, in every case you could remember being hired by Barger and Wolen [the defense law firm] to defend Unum Provident, you had concluded that the plaintiff was a malingerer. Is that right?

A: I don't recall. I don't consider myself hired to defend Unum Provident, but I was hired as a consultant on several cases for Unum Provident through Barger and Wolen. I don't recall if I said that or not.

Q: By the way, these inconsistencies in your testimony today versus your testimony before, does that raise in your mind a credibility issue similar to what you've told us about Mr. Mead?

[Nice question! Of course the witness will say no, but the issue is flagged for the jury.]

A: No, I wouldn't say so.

Q: In each of the cases in which you were hired by Barger and Wolen, you disagreed with the treating doctors. Isn't that right?

A: I don't recall if that's the case or not.

• • •

Q: So is Gena Mead lying when she tells us about what she observed with regard to Cliff Mead's health over the years?

[This is an important polarizing-style question, to force the witness to admit how truly extreme his opinion is. The expert who accuses the plaintiff of being a fraud necessarily must view the plaintiff's long-time wife as either a fraud herself or as badly duped by her former husband.]

A: She may or may not be, or maybe to some degree, but it's sufficiently suspicious that it needs to be taken skeptically.

Q: All right, so you're basically saying, yes, you believe that information is not worth weighing in the balance as you decide—as you try to decide whether Mr. Mead's telling the truth or not.

A: Well, actually I weighed it in the way I just described to you.

Q: You weighed it and then threw it out?

A: Well, as I was saying, I weigh it just as I weighed Mr. Mead's subjective complaints over time. All of these things are weighed, but the information is still overwhelming for a faked claim for CFS.

Q: Who else can you tell us is lying, Dr. Rosenberg?

[Another polarizing question that seeks to clarify the exact numbers of witnesses whom the expert accuses of giving false observations. Note the power of the open-ended question.]

A: Besides Mr. Mead?

Q: And Mrs. Mead, Gena Mead, who else?

[The expert now tries to back away from accusing the former wife of lying. The point of the question is to force clarity and not let the expert get away with an ambiguous "skepticism" about the ex-wife.]

A: Well, again, I have to take exception to that because I think it's a misstatement of my testimony. I didn't say she was lying. I said there is sufficient evidence that you need to be very skeptical about her information and her vested financial interests in the outcome.

Q: You don't believe her, do you?

A: It's not that I don't believe her; it's that I'm sufficiently skeptical of it that I have to weigh that and all the other information that I considered because there's other evidence of, first, her financial interest and, second, her assisting Mr. Mead in the past with trying to twist the outcome.

* * *

Q: Dr. Rosenberg, just to be clear, your opinion is that all the treating doctors got it wrong. Is that correct?

A: Well, I don't think we make that broad of a statement, but any treating doctor who asserts that Mr. Mead does have chronic fatigue syndrome and it impairs his ability to function, with all due respect, I think that's incorrect.

Q: He fooled them all?

A: Well, in the manner I just described it to you, that would be correct.

MR. FRIEDMAN: Thank you, Dr. Rosenberg.[4]

HALO OR HORNS?

Let's look back at what Friedman was up against. This was the other side's chief expert witness, called, as they often are in a primacy and recency strategy,[5] as the final dagger-to-your-heart expert wrapping up the other side's case. The witness said things on direct exam that really hurt Friedman's case, and did so in a confident and persuasive manner. So he started out wearing a nice shiny halo.

A prime goal of cross-examining such a hired gun must be to knock off the halo and replace it with horns. Ordinarily this must be the *first* object of the cross (and if successful, it can be the only object). No fooling around with secondary subjects like minor errors in the witness's recitation of the facts. No trying to win concessions

---

4. [*Mead*] *v. Paul Revere Life Ins. Co.*, CV-S-00731-JCM-RJJ, U.S. District Court, District of Nevada, Dec. 10, 2004. (Note that the plaintiff's name in this citation is changed to protect privacy).

5. *Primacy* says that the first thing you say is more important than just about anything else, and *recency* says that the last thing you say is second in importance only to the first. In cross-examination, the maxim to "Start strong, and finish strong," captures a primacy and recency strategy.

first from this expert. This is a straight tear-down cross, not a case buildup. So Friedman's approach followed this basic format:

- First, announce a halo-disrupting theme directly to the witness. No subtlety, no pulling of punches. Friedman's theme was that the witness's job was to pick only those facts that supported his prefabricated opinion and ignore evidence that favored Friedman's side: in short, a biased cherry-picker, not a true objective expert.

- Second, pursue the creation of that impression until you are sure the jury has seen a whole new side of the witness. This is not a one-shot technique. Friedman's attack extended over many pages (I had room to excerpt only a small slice) and went at it from several angles: one-sidedness, money, relationships with the defense counsel, refusal to consider inconvenient facts, implicit accusations of false testimony by others, and much more. Friedman knows it's not easy to dispel an initial impression from the direct exam of a strong witness, so we have to go at it in a relentless, detailed way.

A Polarizing Plan for Your Case

What about your case? When can a polarizing strategy work? First, remember that this is a big-gun weapon for an oversized, difficult adversary. You are wresting off the witness's mask of objectivity. If the witness is truly fair-minded and objective, you'll hurt yourself trying to remove a mask that is genuine skin. So we limit the technique to the right witness: the one whom you know, by reputation and experience, is wearing a disguise.

Here's a checklist for the material we want to line up for a polarizing attack:

- All links between the witness and the adverse party and that party's counsel: number of prior cases, length of association, money. Don't count on voluntary disclosure. Discovery subpoenas, public court records, and intelligence from other attorneys on your side will help you find most of this. (We push to the top of the list for cross all those we know about that are not mentioned in the witness's direct examination.)

- Reports from other cases that show the witness always comes down on the same side. Again, to get these reports, you will need to construct a good list of the witness's testimonial history and get in touch with those lawyers who've faced the witness before. You need to do this as soon as the other side has identified the expert, because it takes months to gather this stuff.

- A list of good facts for your case that the witness ignores in his or her report. These need to be annotated with the source material—medical record, deposition, and the like—so you can confront the witness with each fact in rapid succession.

Then, you work on a list of questions. Here's a sampler of possibilities:

Q: When you say, "no objective evidence," do you mean it doesn't hurt?

Q: So is the patient lying, exaggerating, cheating? (Or crazy?)

Q: When the patient told Doctor Treater on [date] that pain was seven out of ten, was the patient lying?

Q: Did the patient fool the doctor?

Q: Did the doctor commit malpractice by writing a prescription for pain meds, instead of sending the patient away empty-handed?

Q: Did the patient's wife lie when she testified she saw him screaming in pain?

Q: Who else is lying here?

Q: All the doctors got it wrong when they concluded the patient has a genuine problem and needs treatment?

Q: All the lay observers got it wrong? The employer, when he said in his deposition, "___"? The minister? The coworker?

Q: What is the error rate for your opinion?

Q: The test that you say provides "no objective basis" for the patient's problems: Is that different from every other known test in medicine, all of which have known error rates? There are no 100 percent accurate medical tests? Every one has a false-negative rate, where the alarm fails to go off? Because no test is perfect?

Q: It could be that the lay observers are correct, and you are just drawing a much bigger conclusion from the test than any objective doctor would?

Takeaways

Most defense medical examiner (DME) doctors will back off any insinuation that the plaintiff's complaints are not real rather than put themselves in open opposition to the lay witnesses and treating doctors. Whichever way they go, you win by flushing the defense out into the open with a polarizing strategy that pushes the witnesses to take an extreme, noncredible position or abandon their opinions. The ones who want future business from the same counsel will stick to their position, even as it becomes more and more ludicrous. Others will start giving you big concessions. Either way, it's good.

13

FUNDAMENTAL ATTRIBUTION

Undermining the Expert Whose Credentials Don't Fit

> *Science is the organized skepticism in the reliability of expert opinion.*
>
> —Richard P. Feynman

Every "expert" who climbs up on the witness stand is in fact an expert—in some one thing, maybe in many things. But maybe not in what you think the case should be about. The expert may have a highly buffed curriculum vitae, but whether all his expensive expertise fits your case will never become clear to the jury unless you bring it out in cross-examination.

We first took up lack-of-fit cross in chapter 8, "Cross-Examination with Witness Tear-Down Rules," when we started developing witness-centered Rules for cross. We focused then mostly on what the witness *doesn't know* and *hasn't done* that makes her unfit for the case. And that's where most attorneys start and end. Because we're so tuned into legal relevance, we sometimes look at a witness's qualifications only through the lens of what's right for this case, and we blind ourselves to another side of lack of fit: what the witness *does know* and *has done* that makes her wrong for this case, despite having other credentials that do fit. In this chapter, we hone in on that. We introduce the psychological concept known as *fundamental attribution*, and we start to explore the diamond mine of independent facts that evoke fundamental attribution, a mine needing only the attorney's energy to reap treasure with many a witness.

This chapter is the last of our series in the middle of this book in which I give each of the four basic weapons of witness tear-down their own single-chapter spotlight. The one unique feature about lack-of-fit cross compared to bias, ignorance, and contradictions cross, is that the structure of trials lets us ask all our lack-of-fit questions, if we want, before the witness has given any opinions about the case. That's what the right to conduct voir dire on any expert gives us, and it's a powerful weapon with the right witness. You can always fold your lack-of-fit questions into the main part of your cross, but sometimes it's better to push hard at the witness's qualifications before the jury hears his opinions, even if you don't expect to win a motion asking the court to declare the witness unqualified. That's a tactical decision unique to each case, with no hard and fast answers, but one worth thinking about as we consider all we can do with lack-of-fit questioning.

Fundamental Attribution and the Cross-Examiner

The *fundamental attribution error*, as it's known in social psychology, is the tendency of all human observers to look for cause-and-effect explanations inside the actor—some fundamental attribute of the actor's—and not random chance or other external factors. When we watch a natural disaster unfold on television and think, "What kind of crazy people would live in a [flood, earthquake, or tornado] zone?" that's fundamental attribution at work. What flips the fundamental attribution switch on and off is often our own self-serving natures. Finding fault in others helps insulate us from the bad stuff: "Something's wrong with them; it couldn't happen to me."

Good trial lawyers, and especially the great cross-examiners, know and exploit this tendency of humans to make the fundamental attribution error, because it works in the courtroom. And, because it's an instinctive, natural tendency, you can evoke fundamental attribution without ever spelling out the logic (or in this case, the illogic) behind it.

Fundamental attribution works in several realms of cross-examination, but most especially in lack-of-fit cross. We bring out traits in the witness's character and background intended to make the witness look flaky and unreliable. It's not so much that the witness *lacks* expertise in the subject of the case, but that the expert has *too much* expertise in other stuff that has nothing to do with the case.

Attorney Jim Lees used this tool to defuse an adverse expert's opinions about the cause of a gas wellhead explosion. His cross-examination focused not on the case and the expert's opinions, but on who this witness was and how he was different. If you want the jury to find some fundamental attribute in the witness that lets them discount the entire testimony, you turn the spotlight away from the jury's thinking processes and conclusions and focus the klieg lights instead on who the witness is.

Lees teased out the witness's history as a jack-of-all-trades who owned—and on the stand, disowned—business after business over thirty years. There's nothing necessarily wrong with incorporating a new business every few years, as this witness had done, and nothing wrong with letting a corporate license expire, as this witness also had done. But the witness's lack of command over the history of his businesses and his ignorance even of the names of some of his enterprises cast a general pall over his testimony. The cross-examiner never showed any specific wrongdoing by the witness, and the back-and-forth never showed the witness displaying any ignorance of important facts that had anything to do with the case. Yet at the end, he seemed unreliable, weird, and flaky. That is fundamental attribution at play.

The case concerned an incident at a gas wellhead that killed a service operator who was pressure-testing the well with a rig from his pumper truck. The hose assembly that connected the truck to the wellhead came apart under high pressure, killing him instantly. Lees represented the man's family in a product liability suit against the manufacturer of the hose assembly.

On direct examination, expert Edward Ziegler testified that any number of other factors were to blame for the death: where the operator was standing, how his truck was positioned, his lack of training, and so on, but he steered clear of any opinion on the core issue of whether or not the hose assembly was defective.

THE POWER OF PUBLIC RECORDS

Attorney Jim Lees used public records for nine-tenths of what follows. The research did not require hiring an investigator or poring over hundreds of documents; no, the miracle of Internet-based public records databases produced most of what Lees needed in thirty minutes flat. His main source was the Secretary of State database for incorporations in the expert's home state of Texas. Lees also found a published appeals court decision criticizing the expert's tenuous grasp of the facts in another case, plus another juicy bit of database research on the expert's alma mater. Let's have a listen.

MR. LEES: Good afternoon. My name is Jim Lees, and I represent Colton Fluke. You and I have never met before today. Is that correct?

MR. ZIEGLER: I believe that's correct.

Q: When you took the witness stand, by the way, you were referred to as "Doctor," is that the way you prefer to be addressed, Dr. Ziegler?

A: Not—Well, no, sir, I'm not—I'm not a doctor.

[One hears the hiss as the expert's balloon of credentials begins to shrink.]

Q: Okay. You, in fact, have a bachelor's degree?

A: That's correct, yes, sir.

Q: And you have a law degree?

A: Correct.

Q: And you attended the University of Pittsburgh Law School for two years, correct?

A: Yes, sir.

Q: And then you left there, correct?

A: Yes.

Q: Because . . . ?

[This non-leading question had little risk of a bad answer, since it focused on a narrow piece of the expert's educational story.]

A: I went back to work for Marathon Oil Company, and I finished my Law Degree at South Texas College of Law, and I—I transferred my credits from Pitt.

Q: And just to follow through very briefly on your CV, your educational experience, Texas publishes, through the Texas Higher Education Coordinating Board, publications identifying those institutions whose degrees are illegal to use in Texas, correct?

A: Yes, sir.

[Note how the examiner jumps into the topic with a single well-honed question that attracts the jurors' attention with "illegal" and tells them to stay tuned for some fireworks. This is a dramatic and a bit edgy way to delve into the topic of credentials from a nonaccredited school. I don't know Texas law, but I have a strong suspicion there is no legal penalty for truthfully saying that one has a degree from a school not recognized by the state of Texas. Still, the witness agreed with the "illegal" characterization, so all is well.]

Q: One of the institutions that Texas says is illegal to use a degree from is Kennedy Western University, correct?

A: At this time, that's correct.

Q: Okay. And you list Kennedy Western University on your CV as a place where you got your MS safety engineering courses.

A: Like—courses, yes, sir, courses.

Q: Didn't you used to list a degree from there?

A: Yes, sir, because after I received a degree for several years it was not on the list you refer to.

Q: Says here you attended Kennedy Western University from 1994 to 2003?

A: Yes, sir.

Q: So you went to that college for nine years?

A: No, sir. I—I took my courses—huh—by correspondence all in one year, and then I finished my thesis, which was on the Brenham salt dome—huh—explosion, in 2003.

Q: And you were living in Texas at that time?

A: Yes, sir.

Q: And where is Kennedy Western University located?

A: Huh. It was a—At that time it was a program that was in—huh—Thousand Oaks, California, and all of the faculty members that I worked with for my correspondence courses were at the University of California, at Santa Barbara.

Q: Just so I'm clear, then, did you go to Santa Barbara, to the university, and attend there?

A: No, sir, it was a correspondence course.

Q: Correspondence course.

[Echoing a good answer is the cross-examiner's way to underline the point.]

A: I—I was sent there by the U.S. Department of Energy.

[The witness's explanation doesn't matter, because the message is clear: his master's degree in the topic for which he is testifying in court came from a correspondence school not recognized by Texas education authorities.]

Q: You—huh—you, in your past, have branched out in terms of the things you are willing to offer opinions on. Is that fair?

A: I—I don't know what you mean by "branched out." I've worked on a lot of safety areas—huh—OSHA, a lot of different things.

Q: Well, has a court ever said you weren't qualified to give an opinion in a court of law in Texas on something you were trying to give an opinion on?

A: No, I re—I recall one—huh—case that I gave a deposition in. I was working as an expert. I sat in that case. I did not have enough information. By the time the trial came along, I was not working on the case—huh—been several years. As I recall, the attorney tried to use my deposition that I'd said I didn't have enough information for, and the judge did not let that be read into evidence, so that's the only case I recall.

[The witness has just changed his answer from "no" to "yes, once." Rather than quibbling with that change or chasing the witness's explanation, Lees starts to unspool his source information. This might be hearsay, but because it is intended to impeach a witness's credibility, the recitation of what the other court said is not objectionable.]

Q: Well, I may be misinformed, then. I'm looking at an Appellate Opinion from the Fourteenth Court of Appeals, on a case called Memorial Hermann Hospital System—huh—from Harris County, Texas, in which there is reference to an expert witness that has your name. Were you involved in that case?

A: Yes, sir, that's the case I just referred to.

Q: Says here you were attempting to give an opinion—and I'm reading now from the Appellate Court of Texas—

A: Yeah.

[reading from court opinion]

> "As evidenced by his deposition testimony and accompanying exhibits, Ziegler concluded that Memorial Hermann Hospital System failed to properly select the patient food carts in accordance with the safety concerns for the employees who operate them."

Q: You gave a deposition on food carts?

A: Yes, sir, it was on—on training and the selection of the food cart—

Q: Attempting to help the lawyers who were suing that hospital, correct?

A: It was an OSHA issue, yes, sir.

Q: It was an OSHA issue?

A: Yeah.

Q: According to the appellate court, you had never even seen the food carts, correct?

A: Yeah, I seen—I'd seen pictures and the invoices and I went to the manufacturer and saw them.

Q: You didn't even know, according to the appellate court, how big the carts were, correct?

A: I—I doubt that because—Well, I don't know what they said, but I—I saw the exemplar carts.

Q: Well, I don't want you to—to think I'm trying to trick you here. I'll just read from the appellate opinion.

> "Yet he had not seen the carts in person. He did not know how big the carts were, how much the carts weighed, or how much they could or should carry. He also had no knowledge of the relevant factors in determining whether the weight of a loaded cart or amount of force to be applied to it would be excessive. Yet Ziegler concluded that the hospital failed to properly train its employees in how to operate a food cart."

Q: You gave a deposition on that subject?

A: Yes, sir. An OSHA issue.

Q: And the court said no way.

A: Well, for a reason, because the—huh—when I gave my deposition, I said I didn't have that information, but I did give an opinion they didn't have a training program because they didn't.

[Translating the court's holding into a crisp "the court said no way" works well to box in the witness. The witness retreats to his defense that the lawyer in the other case had failed to give him certain information. Lees could have insisted on a simple yes or no answer, but it wasn't necessary, since the answer was patently defensive.]

Q: You go around a lot and criticize hospitals and companies that they don't have training programs?

A: I criticize a lot of people for not having training programs, just like this case, yes, sir.

[Note how the witness has tried to lure Lees back into discussing the core of his opinions in this case, which Lees resists. Instead, Lees moves into the list of corporations obtained from his online research. Now Lees shifts from traditional lack of fit, which he nicely explored with the expert's correspondence school diploma and criticism from another court, and turns to misfit cross with fundamental attribution.]

Q: I'm sure you do. Let me ask you just a few questions about some of the businesses you've been in, and again, I may have this wrong, but I just got this off the Secretary of State's website—says you are or were the registered agent for Rini, R-I-N-I, Design, Incorporated. Is that a company you have been or are affiliated with?

A: Huh—I probably incorporated that for her or was—was a registered agent. That's—that's my wife and that's her—huh—comput—her—huh—graphic design company.

Q: Okay. So that's your wife's company.

A: Right.

Q: Let me go to the next one—Edward Ziegler Racing, Inc. Is that anything to do with you?

A: Yes, sir.

Q: What's that company?

A: Huh—I have a company that—huh—we—we both sponsor and have race cars—vintage—vintage race cars.

Q: I see. Is that company still in existence?

A: Yes.

Q: Because it says here in the Secretary of State "forfeited existence"—

A: Okay.

Q: —okay? Do you know why the existence was forfeited?

A: Probably because we didn't keep it as a—as a corporation and file the paperwork. We didn't—didn't need that anymore. We still have the company, but it's a sole proprietorship.

Q: Didn't file the paperwork, franchise taxes, things like that, right?

A: No, sir.

Q: No?

A: Filed—We—I mean, if—if you don't want to keep a corporation, you just simply don't file the paperwork.

Q: So you didn't want to keep that company?

A: As a corporation, that's correct.

Q: Do you still have a racing company?

A: Yes, as a sole proprietorship.

Q: And you race what, cars?

A: Vintage race cars, yes.

Q: Vintage race cars. Erebus, E-R-E-B-U-S, Energy, Inc., you're listed as a registered agent for that company.

A: Yes.

Q: What's that company about?

A: Huh—Doesn't exist anymore, but it was an oil and gas company.

Q: Did you start it?

A: We—huh—It was set up but I don't think we ever did any business with it.

Q: Who set it up, when you say, "we"?

A: My wife and I.

Q: Wife and I. And when did you start that oil company?

A: I don't recall, probably in the 1980s.

Q: That one says, "forfeited existence," correct?

A: I don't—.

Q: Did you decide not to pursue that company?

A: Yeah—yes, that's correct.

Q: Experts United, Incorporated, is that a company you're affiliated with?

A: Not—not sure anymore.

Q: You're not sure if you have a company called Experts United, Incorporated, or not?

A: Not—at this time I'm not sure. It was a company we set up.

Q: Well—

A: That—that was the company that did the business with—ultimately with—huh—Halliburton KBR Government Services, and we—we operated as Safety United, Incorporated.

Q: You got part of that government money for Halliburton to go do some safety consulting for safety in Iraq, didn't you?

A: Right, to supply equipment to our troops.

Q: And so Experts United, Incorporated, is owned by whom?

A: Probably by my wife and I.

Q: Your wife, and you. Is that still in existence or not?

A: I don't know.

Q: You don't know?

A: I don't know.

Q: I'll just tell you the Secretary of State says it, by the way, okay?

[The witness has now disowned an interest in four companies in a row that he had originally owned. His lack of knowledge about whether his company still exists paints a picture of someone spread so thin he doesn't know where he is.]

A: Okay.

Q: Okay. Dynamic Marine Engineering, Inc., is that a company you're affiliated with?

A: Used to be.

Q: Used to be?

A: Yeah.

Q: What was the purpose of that company?

A: That was my—huh—I—I owned a welding and maintenance company in Cameron, Louisiana, that did a lot of—huh—work in—in chemical plants in the offshore oil industry for several years back in the 1980s.

• • •

Q: So you're also an expert not only in food carts and oil and gas but welding?

[In a single sentence, the cross-examiner hopscotches the witness around his diverse fields of claimed expertise, highlighting their dubious nature.]

A: Well, the food—yeah, the food cart is OSHA, but, yes, I'm—I'm—I'm an expert in welding, yes.

Q: Okay. And I'm sorry, is that company still in existence or not, Dynamic Marine Engineering, Inc.?

A: Well, I haven't used it for twenty years, but it could still be in existence. I don't know.

∙ ∙ ∙

Q: Ziegler Investment Management, Inc., is that one of your companies?

A: I don't recognize that one.

Q: Says Edward R. Ziegler, list an address on Westheimer in Houston. Is that your business address?

A: That's correct.

Q: And you don't recognize Ziegler Investment Management, Inc.?

A: No, sir.

[No wonder the cross-examiner stays on this path. The witness keeps giving answers that don't help his credibility, as he fails to recognize even the names of some of his own companies.]

Q: Hmm. How about Ziegler slash Peru, Inc., does that one ring a bell?

A: Yes, sir, that's my current oil company. We drilled about a hundred wells in the last year.

∙ ∙ ∙

Q: So why did you start all of these other ones?

[Because the subject matter is completely safe for Lees, a "why" question works well to hand the witness a shovel and let him dig his own hole.]

A: Huh—dif—just different purposes at different times.

Q: You kept incorporating different business after different business after different business as I'm looking through the years of your professional life. Fair enough?

A: Yes, sir. In thirty years I've had about ten different businesses. That's correct.

∙ ∙ ∙

Q: What's Safety United? Is that another company?

A: Well, it's the one I mentioned earlier when you asked me about Halliburton KBR. That's our—that was our primary safety consulting business.

Q: I thought the Ziegler Operating Company was?

A: No.

[The purpose of the expert's various companies is now thoroughly confused, further undermining his credibility.]

Q: No. Okay. In addition to operating all of these companies at various times—and I know some of them are out of existence—you testify as expert witness a lot?

A: Not much anymore.

Q: Okay. Because you're kind of busy with this other stuff?

A: Yeah, I drilled a hundred wells— We have—we have four drilling rigs, and I've drilled a hundred wells in the last year.

Q: Well, you've testified against a hospital, right?

A: Yes.

Q: Who else have you given opinions against in a court of law, or attempted to, besides a hospital? Or, in this case, you're talking about Swan you're talking about Mr. Graves and EOG. What other kinds of businesses have you given opinions about?

A: Well, in—in the last—huh—thirty years, roughly a lot of businesses I've given opinions about, both positively and against—huh—dealing with almost every aspect of safety. When you go through the OSHA Training Institute for construction and general industry, that covers everything that's in OSHA, virtually every type of workplace, and as a certified safety professional, we deal with all industries.

Q: So you are the guy when it comes to safety in the—the workplace, right?

A: I am one of the guys, yes. I—I—

[Lees has now set up the witness to be someone of self-proclaimed vast and diverse expertise, who should know why the hose assembly failed. So he asks the $64,000 question at the heart of the case.]

Q: I want you to tell the ladies and gentlemen of the jury why the hose assembly came apart.

A: Well, I—I didn't look at that. That wasn't my area. I know why Mr.—I know why Mr. Fluke was killed, but I don't—I don't know why the hose came apart. That wasn't my area.

Q: Okay. Why was Mr. Fluke killed? I'll bite.

[Under the normal "rules" of cross-examination, Lees has just violated two commandments: asking a "why" question and asking the witness to repeat unfavorable testimony. It works here because it's a way of underscoring the cross-examiner's basic point: that this is a witness of vast and diverse self-proclaimed expertise—expertise already shown to have a dubious if not bizarre career trajectory—and yet the witness cannot bring himself to look at the core issue of the case: Why did the hose assembly fail?]

A: Mr. Fluke was killed because Mr. Graves, Mr. Wright left him and his truck in a bad position, let him pressure up. Mr. Fluke was not—huh—was not properly trained and did not have a proper safety program or the knowledge from his employer to—huh—be able to conduct the operation safely. Hoses come apart all the time, but if you're at the right place and do it correctly, and position your truck the right place, then you don't get killed or injured.

Q: And so you came all the way from Houston, Texas, to tell these people under oath that's why Tim Fluke was killed, correct?

A: Yes, sir.

Q: You can't even answer my question as to why that hose came apart?

A: I wasn't—I wasn't—huh—designated to be the person to decide why the hose came apart.

Q: Here's the fitting—

A: Yeah.

Q: —here's the hose. All your expertise, you want to take a look at it and tell me why it came apart?

[Lees keeps pushing for an answer because the witness has shown he wants to avoid the question. The answer cannot help the witness's side, and thus he evades. The more Lees gives the witness an open-ended opportunity to explain what happened to the hose assembly, the more evasive the witness appears. Lees is safe pushing the point because the witness's credibility has already been seriously undermined by what came before.]

[Bench conference not transcribed.]

Mr. Lees: Question stands. Based on your vast expertise, look at it, tell us, why did it come apart?

A: Don't—I don't know why it came apart. It could have come apart because it was abused. It could have come apart because it was pulled on. I—I mean, a number of different reasons—

Q: Wow.

A: —but the—but the—but the bottom line is, if Mr. Fluke had not by his supervisor and his employer be allowed and required to be where he was, he would not have been killed or injured.

Q: You know, if he had called in sick that day, with all due respect, he'd be alive today, right?

[A neat way to ridicule the witness's point.]

A: Well, maybe one of his coworkers would be dead but he might be alive, yes, sir.

Q: There's a million reasons in hindsight. You can look back and say, if, if, if, somebody would be alive today, but God doesn't give us do-overs, Mr. Ziegler, does he?

A: No, sir, that's why you have to do it right to start with. It's not—it's not if, if, if, it's if you have the proper training and if you're standing and required—allowed to be at the right place, that's why you don't need a do-over if you do it safely.

[The logic of the witness's position about safe practices should apply equally to the defendant, and makes for a good turnabout-is-fair-play question.

Lees knows this won't bring a positive answer, but will further show the witness's bias.]

Q: Right. And so if Makena and Bridgeport/Jacksboro had just done it safely, this young man would be alive today, wouldn't he?

A: I don't know what that means, because—

Q: I'm sure you don't.

A: —a hose can come apart for any reason. That's why you always stand the right place and do it safely as far as the procedures.

MR. LEES: Judge, I don't have any further questions for this guy.[1]

The fact that the witness claims to know why the victim was killed, but doesn't know how the hose came apart—and doesn't admit the fact that the hose coming apart killed the victim—makes him appear biased and untrustworthy.

Lees told me this:

> I started the cross with the intent to play around with this [incorporation] stuff for a very brief time. But it was going so well that I stayed with that theme. It was a much better cross than if I had tried to cross him on all the stuff he talked about in direct. The jury was laughing at him by the end of the cross. And the Judge said after the trial he was so amused by the cross he forgot to take notes.[2]

TAKEAWAYS

Witnesses' side stories, what they do completely unrelated to why they came to court, can tell us a lot about their character, and that in turn can seriously undermine whether they have any business testifying in the case. We cross-examiners have to recognize three things: first, these side facts can be very important; second, these

---

1. *Row v. Makena Sales Co., Inc.*, 266th Judicial District, Texas, March 7, 2012.
2. Personal communication with Jim Lees.

facts are just a few Internet keystrokes away; third, fundamental attribution can so undermine the witness's credibility that a strong cross-examiner, as we saw in this chapter, can safely invite the witness to explain his opinion and the witness still cannot recover his standing with the jury. Next, we'll dive into the research techniques that mine these facts.

14

MINING FOR DIRT
How to Prepare for Cross-Examining Any Important Witness

> "Upending Anonymity, These Days the Web Unmasks Everyone"
>
> —Headline in the *New York Times*, June 20, 2011

Most of us prepare for cross-examining a witness in a civil case by doing two things: we depose the witness, and we survey friends and colleagues for anything they know about the witness. Less often, we tread a third path: old-fashioned gumshoe work. Because that can yield the most spectacular rewards, discovering information that neither your adversary nor the witness knows you have, let's start with what you can learn with independent research. I will follow that with a good guide to a thorough deposition aimed at uncovering collateral attacks on the witness's expertise and credibility.

This chapter comes on the heels of chapter 13, "Fundamental Attribution," because a lot of the dirt awaiting our mining expedition goes to the witness's lack of fit with the case. But some of the research also supplies material for other tear-down weapons like contradictions (what the witness has said elsewhere) and bias (testimonial history, money, and the like). So it's a good concluding chapter for part 3, "Tearing Down the Witness," as we wrap up our survey of the four types of witness tear-down cross-examination.

I have little to say about what you can glean from friends and colleagues in your witness research, except this:

- Don't save these "reach out" inquiries for the last minute, unless you want to drive yourself and your staff insane, jack up your anxiety level, and distract yourself from more important tasks as you prepare for trial. Calendar this task for a minimum of thirty days before trial. That will give you time to pull the transcripts, sift through the chaff for the kernels of wheat, and do any necessary follow-up.

- Don't assume that the work of other lawyers in other cases can substitute for your own independent research about the witness. They had different goals and may have different work ethics. If it's an important witness, you should always do your own spadework, to which we now turn.

Independent Research about the Witness

When lawyers tell war stories about cross-examination triumphs, they almost never tell the one about how they crushed the witness at deposition and then did the same thing at trial, using the deposition as courtroom script. Why not? Maybe it's because when a lawyer squashes a witness in a deposition, one of two things happens at trial: the witness never shows up or the witness and the opposing counsel have cooked up a new set of answers that may not harmonize completely with the deposition but sound close enough to the ears of jurors not attuned to the subtleties and nuances that the cross-examiner knows. This song is called "Frustration in the Key of F."

Time is our enemy. The longer a witness gets to contemplate an answer, the more chance the other side has to frustrate our objective. When we give the witness months to ponder, along with a clear question-by-question guide to trouble spots, it's no wonder so many witnesses escape our noose when we have only a deposition transcript to work with.

Independent research lets us spring new stuff that neither the witness nor the opposing counsel have prepared for. It adds zest and spice to the trial, and for that reason alone is worth doing.

Guide to Everything You Always Wanted to Know about Witnesses

Here's a guide to sources of information about people that goes far beyond what you'll find with a few Google clicks. I am indebted to an ace crackerjack investigator, Scott Suddarth, for much of this information, which my assistant Ed Caughlan and I supplemented. Scott's contact information is in the footnote; he does nationwide searches for attorneys (hint, hint).[1]

According to Scott, the four most revealing documents from background investigations are these:

- **Traffic Tickets.** These provide vehicle description, license plate, driver's license number, date of birth, address, and full name. The Kansas database, for example, is found here: http://www.kansas.com/2013/02/28/2695405/searchable-database-traffic-tickets.html.

- **Bankruptcy.** These records provide a list of assets and liabilities, a list of creditors, marital status and dependents under eighteen, a list of income and employment for the last three years, and a list of addresses for the last three years. Records are available online through PACER (Public Access to Court Electronic Records), subscription information at

---

1. Custom Investigative Services, Inc., P.O. Box 935, Chesterfield, VA 23832, Office: (804) 751-9133, Fax: (804) 751-9134, www.custominvestigations.com.

http://www.pacer.gov/. An example of an individual state database is the New Jersey one: https://ecf.njb.uscourts.gov/cgi-bin/login.pl. Business filings can be found at http://www.bankruptcydata.com/BankruptcySearch.htm.

- **Marriage Licenses.** These provide full name, date of birth, date of marriage, address at time of marriage, place of birth, race, type of ceremony, current marital status, widow, divorced, number of marriages, full name of spouse, parents' names. GenWed (http://www.genwed.com/) provides links to records for states.

- **Divorce Records.** These provide full names, addresses, full names and dates of birth of children, work information, grounds for divorce, location of marriage, date of separation, and date of final decree. GenWed (http://www.genwed.com/) provides links to records for states.

A few more important ones:

- **Corporation Searches.** These are usually done through the office of the Secretary of State or State Corporation Commissions (SCC) for individual states and can provide a wealth of professional information. The complete list of such sites for all states can be found here: http://www.coordinatedlegal.com/SecretaryOfState.html. Virginia State Corporation Commission, for example (https://www.scc.virginia.gov/clk/bussrch.aspx), may be used to search for Virginia and foreign corporations, limited liability companies, limited partnerships, and business trusts. Business entity details available in SCC eFile are entity name, SCC ID, business entity type, date of formation or registration, status, principal office address (if required), and registered agent or registered office. You may also view an entity's eFile history, including images of documents that have been filed using SCC eFile.

- **Educational Institution Databases.** You can search through a comprehensive website operated by the Department of Education, found here: http://ope.ed.gov/accreditation.

This site provides a full listing of accreditations, scope of accreditation, and dates of accreditation for American institutions of higher learning, and also provides a search tool for internships and residencies. We saw in the last chapter how the cross-examiner discredited a witness who had once claimed a degree from the nonaccredited correspondence school, Kennedy Western University. A search on the DOE site no longer shows this school because, as shown by a Google search, the institution had (no surprise) changed its name in 2007 and ceased operations in 2009.

- **Professional Board Certifications.** This information shows whether people are board-certified. For medical certifications, use Certification Matters at http://www.certificationmatters.org/. Look up and verify nurses at NurSys at https://www.nursys.com/. For engineering licenses, which are often questioned in trials that involve mechanical safety liability, search Engineers Guide USA at http://www.engineersguideusa.com/engineer_license_lookup.htm. Some individual states, such as New York, have comprehensive databases for professional verifications in a wide range of fields: http://www.op.nysed.gov/opsearches.htm.

Scott Suddarth adds these points:

- When researching women, you must be aware that if they have been married or divorced and changed their last names, you have to research each name as a separate background check.

- We use a subscription to Skip Smasher to begin any background check. This is a database service only available to private investigators. We are able to obtain full Social Security Numbers, dates of birth, and middle names with this service. This is extremely important when researching common names through court records.

- There is a companion site, Crime Smasher, which is available to the public. You can run state-by-state or nationwide criminal records checks. You will need a full name and date of birth to conduct these searches.

- After that, we typically run a full database inquiry, using Accurint or IRB. This provides us with voter registration, professional licenses, relatives, criminal offenses, property ownership, and so on. This also gives us a twenty-year address history. Most crimes or traffic offenses are committed close to where a person lives, typically.

- Many states have court records online. For states that do not, allow for several weeks for background checks to be conducted.

- In open record states, like Florida and Texas, you can run a comprehensive, statewide criminal check online for a nominal fee. You still have to write to the individual courts to get copies of the court documents.

- Other states like North Carolina charge $25 for each individual county researched and the results can take several weeks.

- You can always hire a local private investigator to go to the local courthouses to conduct a thorough and speedier search for bankruptcies, divorces, and other legal cases that often contain ugly facts about the witness.

- Blackbookonline.info bills itself as the "free public records search site." This list is a treasure trove. Searches include arrest warrants, corporations, deaths, incident reports, motor vehicles, and on and on. You can look up topics nationally or state by state.

- Each state has an agency that regulates health professions and professional licenses. You should always verify a witness's licenses as well as any citations for misconduct.

- For looking up national sex offender information, we use the Dru Sjodin National Sex Offender Public Website, http://www.nsopw.gov/en. We search everyone through this site and statewide sex offender sites on every background check.

- For looking up social media and news sites, we use a site called PeekYou that scours sixty sites.

- We use a PACER subscription for all federal court records, such as criminal, civil, and bankruptcy.

- Another site we use frequently is called Records Room: http://www.daddezio.com/records/room/. This site covers searches for deeds, assumed names, wills, marriage licenses, judgments, liens, and real estate assessments.

- A site called opensecrets.org keeps track of political contributions at the state and federal level from 1990 to the present.

- Don't forget ordinary Google searches, using multiple creative search terms. For experts, you especially want to delve into Google Scholar.

- Other useful resources are LinkedIn.com, Classmates.com, and MyLife.com.

- Be sure to look up Facebook and MySpace accounts. However, do not try to "friend" an adverse party, and especially don't try to "friend" someone by hiding who you are. Those are ethical no-nos.

- Look up local newspaper archives in towns or cities where the witness has lived or done business.

- Look up Twitter feeds. Many professionals have them, and you can search their prior posts.

Always remember that databases are a good lead, but not a replacement for good legwork and courthouse searches.[2]

From that list you can see the verdict: you're criminally insane if you don't use these resources to scour the background of every important witness. Do you need to touch all these bases for each witness? Of course not. The scope of your research will depend on the witness's importance, your gut feeling on whether the witness's

---

2. Many thanks to Scott Suddarth for this extensive list.

background adds up, and your budget of time and money. But treasure awaits the diligent hunter, in the most unlikely places.

DEPOSING THE WITNESS ON EVERYTHING ELSE

Here is a checklist of areas you should cover in a deposition intended to prepare for cross-examining an expert at trial. I call it "everything else" because it doesn't cover case-specific facts (but gets close to them on some of the background questions). This checklist should set you up for good cross on bias and expert fit. (I used my own cheat sheets and borrowed from an excellent list put together by Paul Luvera of Seattle.)

Involvement and Connections

Q: Explain how you became involved in this case:
- Initial contact—letters, emails, phone calls?
- Written retainer agreement?
- Initial payment before sending case details?

Q: Explain any past connections to or cases with the counsel and firm who hired you. List all prior cases.

Q: Explain any connection with any lawyers in the hiring counsel's firm—social or professional. Give details.

Q: Explain any past work you have done for this firm: frequency, types of matters, other details.

Q: Explain any relationship or connection to the party for whom you are testifying. Social contacts? Business relationships? Blood or in-law relationships?

Q: Do you have any ties to the party's partners, associates, professional organizations, and so on?

Q: [If this is a professional negligence case] Do you have the same malpractice insurer as the defendant?

Experience as an Expert

Q: How did you get started as an expert witness?

Q: Do you advertise professional services as an expert witness—details, budget, and so on?

Q: Do any expert procurement firms send you cases? Explore financial relationships and history.

Q: What is your experience as retained expert? What are the numbers of each experience?

- Cases reviewed over the years, starting when?
- Reports written?
- Depositions?
- Court testimony?

Q: What is your ratio of plaintiff to defense work in cases, reports, depositions, and court testimony?

Q: [If the expert's history is heavily tilted toward one side or another] What is your explanation for the majority of your work being for [insurance companies, malpractice defense attorneys, and so on]?

Q: What are the trends over the years in types of attorneys or parties that retain you?

Q: Give details of the last time you testified for the cross-examiner's side of the case. For whom?

Q: In what states have you acted as an expert?

Q: Do you have a blog, website, Facebook, or Twitter account, about any professional or business issues? Give details.

Q: What is your current curriculum vitae? Are old versions of your CV available?

[I struck gold once when an expert had deleted from his CV an article he wrote helpful to my side of the case and not to his own. Lesson: do your own search for publications by the expert, and don't rely on his filter.]

Professional Attitudes and Biases

Q: Tell us about your peer review work.

- Manuscript review for journals?
- Quality of care review in hospitals, clinics, and so on?
- Medical society (or other peer group) review of expert witness testimony?
- Collaboration in consensus statements on clinical guidelines and so on?

Q: Have you done any lobbying of Congress or state legislature on any professional issues?

Q: Are you a member of any political action committee?

Q: Do you donate money or volunteer time to any political or social causes, candidates, office holders?

Q: Are you active in any professional societies?

Bias and Fairness Issues

Q: How do you perceive your role in this case? Describe the nature and scope of work as you understand it.

Q: Is an expert witness supposed to be fair and impartial? What does that mean to you? How do you keep yourself fair and impartial?

[Note: I usually save these broad Rules questions for trial.]

Q: Is an expert supposed to consider all the evidence in the case bearing on the opinion?

[Another one best saved for trial.]

Expert Fit for This Case

Q: Have you given a deposition or trial testimony on any subject relevant to this case? [Better is to list specific issues and ask about each, so it's not up to the witness to define what subjects are relevant to the case.] If so, identify the case by caption and court.

Q: Have you faced the same circumstances faced by the party for whom you are testifying? How did you handle it? What did you do different from what happened here?

Circumstances of Work in This Case

Q: What materials did you study for the purposes of this case? Please provide an exhaustive list of the following:

- Documents reviewed?
- "Real evidence" reviewed—images, photos, microscopic slides, scene of the event, and so on?
- Research done—Internet, books, and so on?
- People talked to?
- Consults with the opposing attorney—what was said, and so on?
- Notes taken?
- Reports written?
- Time and billings?

Q: Did you generate any notes about this case in the course of your review?

Q: Did anyone recommend you *not* take notes?

Q: Describe any documents you prepared in connection with this case, including reports, notes, chronologies, memoranda, bills, correspondence, and so forth.

Q: Also provide fee schedules, standard retainer agreements, and engagement letters, whether generated by you or the attorney.

Q: Identify any professional colleagues with whom you have discussed this case or the issues involved in this case.

Q: Did you ask the defense attorney for any information that was not or could not be provided?

Q: Is there anything you would ordinarily do to develop opinions in a case that you didn't do here, or you did differently here than your custom?

Q: Did you know when you started your review what the outcome of the event was, or did you deliberately shield yourself from knowing that?

Q: Identify any specific publications—including treatises, textbooks, articles, and the like—that contain any statements that you intend to refer to or which you rely on in connection with your opinion in this case.

Q: What further work do you intend to do in this case?

Q: What further work have you been asked to do by the counsel who hired you?

Q: Are there opinions you hold in this case based on facts actually stated in the medical records, or have you made any assumptions in arriving at your opinions?

Q: Have you made any credibility judgments as part of your analysis of this case? If yes, describe all such credibility judgments and your basis for making them.

Q: Were you asked by the attorney to consider opinions that you could not or did not give? Did you consider any subject matters in this case that you then decided not to testify about?

Q: Did you offer any opinions to the attorney that are omitted from the disclosure?

Q: What additional facts would you need to be 100 percent certain in your opinion?

Q: Is it possible to be 100 percent certain about your opinion?

Q: What is the strongest fact for the plaintiff?

[If the expert says, "I can't pick one," you can say, "Go ahead and pick two or three if you can't pick one."]

Other Sources of Knowledge

Q: List any professional literature that you read in connection with this case, giving specific citations.

Q: List all literature in your possession that you believe contains useful information about any of the issues on which you plan to testify in this case.

Q: If you wanted to check whether your colleagues whom you respect would agree with you in important respects about this case, what would you look up? How would you go about checking?

Q: List any professional peer-reviewed journals to which you currently subscribe.

Q: If you have published anything relevant to the case, identify them by exact citation or by publication number in your CV.

Q: Prior to this case, have you prepared any manuscripts, outlines, slides, or other oral or written presentations on subjects relevant to this case? If so, describe all such items and state where they are located.

INFORMATION TO SUBPOENA

The following is a checklist of items to subpoena so that you can review them.

Costs in This Case

Get details of all the witness's charges broken down by the following:

1. Initial retainer and written agreement
2. Hourly charge for review of records
3. Minimum fee for initial review
4. Deposition fees
5. Court testimony

6. Travel charges (Do they bill full rate even when traveling? Sleeping?)

7. First-class airfare, limousines, and so on

8. Total billings to date (Look at invoices.)

9. Future work planned

10. Nonrefundable fees or minimum fees (Nonrefundable fees are a hallmark of the professional witness, who likes to be paid whether or not he has to put in the time.)

Income from Expert Work

Subpoena financials: get the witness's Schedule C from his or her personal 1040, 1099s, corporate returns if the expert's business is incorporated, all sufficient to document the following:

- the percentage of annual income from work as an expert witness
- the total annual earnings as an expert for the last few years
- income broken down by source: insurance companies, law firms, and so on
- the highest fee ever earned on a case
- whether the fees are paid over to someone else or to an employer

MORE INFORMATION TO RESEARCH

For all medical experts, review the witness's specialty organization for expert witnessing ethical standards. These are compiled on my law firm's website.[3]

---

3. http://www.patrickmalonelaw.com/medical-society-statements-on-expert-witness-testimony.html

Fear Will Spur You Forward

Some of us work in jurisdictions that don't typically allow depositions of experts. Not to worry! In this Internet and social media era, we're almost better off without the crutch of depositions. Depositions tend to make us lazy; we obtain background material directly from the witness when we'd be better off getting it on our own. The side sponsoring the witness is lazy too, and distracted, and will rely on the witness to reveal any skeletons in the closet. For her part, the witness has every incentive to forget such unpleasantries. This means that the other side will likely be unprepared for any dirt you have independently unearthed on the witness, whereas they will be on high alert about anything turned over to you in the formal discovery process. So, with or without depositions, we should always do careful independent research on any important witness.

Takeaways

You don't have to follow each and every investigative trail in this chapter for each witness. But a sensible plan, tailored for the individual circumstances, will almost always pay off. At a minimum, you will gain a sense of the witness's character, interests, and strengths, and this will guide both the substance and the tone of your cross-examination. And, often enough to make the hunt worthwhile, you will dig up bombshells that you can detonate in the courtroom: unrevealed conflicts of interest, academic scandals, résumé exaggerations and fabrications, and sundry other low and high crimes and misdemeanors that will smudge if not destroy the witness's credibility.

PART IV

Problems and Solutions

We're in the home stretch! In the first three parts of the book, we've covered all the basics that, with practice, will convert you into a more-than-competent cross-examiner. But you're more ambitious than that, or you wouldn't have bought this book and wouldn't have read this far into it. So here we have a collection of four chapters on special issues that, once mastered, will take you to a whole new level of proficiency in the art of cross-examination.

- Chapter 15, "Evidence Rules Every Cross-Examiner Must Know," dives into some of the obscure evidence rules that tangle us up when our adversaries use them and present us with wonderful new weapons when we figure them out for ourselves. Bonus: one of these gives us a whole new window on expert cross, which I immodestly think is worth the price of the book by itself.

- Chapter 16, "Calling the Adverse Party," is about high-wire acts: calling the adverse party in our case, maximizing the thrills, and avoiding the spills.

- Chapter 17, "Technique Problems and Their Cures," sets out five technique problems and their cures: wandering, dangling, hastening, quibbling or quarreling, and dabbling.

- Chapter 18, "Controlling the Runaway Witness," collects all the control techniques that let us tame the runaway witness. Number one on our list, no surprise to anyone who has read chapter 1, is "controlling yourself."

15

Evidence Rules Every Cross-Examiner Must Know

Know the rules well, so you can break them effectively.
—Anonymous (wrongly attributed to the Dalai Lama XIV)

Everybody reading this book already has a basic grasp of the rules of evidence: relevance, hearsay, probative versus prejudicial, yadda yadda. Tucked inside these rules are some obscure but vital power tools that let you do amazing things that otherwise might not even cross your mind. In this chapter, I've gathered the ones I think cross-examiners know least and need to know a lot better:

- The rule of completeness, a shield against unfair, out-of-context quotes lobbed at a witness.
- The extrinsic evidence rule, which prevents a lot of prior-bad-acts impeachment that otherwise keeps us up at night.

- The rule that lets cross-examiners dive into all the stuff an expert says she has "relied on" to form her opinion.

- The bogus non-rule called "document speaks for itself."

- The discovery hammer we can swing when the witness refers to a refreshed-recollection document.

- Dealing with the "asked and answered" objection.

- Some nifty things we can do with inconsistent and consistent statements.

- How to prevent our adversaries from leading their own clients on the witness stand when we have called the adverse party as a witness in our own case.

There is one more critical rule, on authoritative literature. I've already covered that one in chapter 6, "Using Treatises to Get to Yes."

Rule of Completeness

Just when we think we've got the witness on the ropes, as we introduce the witness's prior statement with a flourish, the opposing counsel barks, "Objection, yohonnuh! Rule of completeness. He's left something out."

Here starts an interminable bench conference, one that gives the witness the breathing space to take the lawyer's hint and come up with a rejoinder about how our attempted impeachment has taken his words out of context. That's the best that can happen. The worst is that we're forced to add something else to the quoted prior statement in front of the jury, which takes the starch out of the entire line of questions and makes us look sneaky to boot.

So the rule of completeness is important to know about, not just in preparing and organizing for cross-examination, but as a powerful tool to prevent unfair cross of our own witnesses.

The rule is expressed in two parallel provisions of the Federal Rules of Evidence and Civil Procedure, both of which are in play at trial. (The same rule with some variations in language is found in most state court rules.)

Fed. R. Evid. 106:

> If a party introduces all or part of a writing or recorded statement, an adverse party may require the introduction, at that time, of any other part—or any other writing or recorded statement—that in fairness ought to be considered at the same time.

Fed. R. Civ. P. 32(a)(6):

> If a party offers in evidence only part of a deposition, an adverse party may require the offeror to introduce other parts that in fairness should be considered with the part introduced, and any party may itself introduce any other parts.

Pay special attention to these bits of the rule:

- Because *both* rules govern civil trials, this doesn't cover merely the witness's deposition—that's the Civil Procedure rule piece—but also *"any other writing or recorded statement."* (The Rule of Evidence piece.) And it's not limited to *this* witness's statements. It can be *any* writing that ought in fairness to be considered at the same time.

- This means if you want to quote a piece of professional literature to a witness, then the other side can force some other quotation in the same writing onto you—during your cross.

- Some judges won't take it that far and will tell the opposing counsel they can introduce the missing piece in their redirect. But the literal wording of Rule 106 arguably requires that the missing piece come in *with* your cross, not later. The rule says the adverse party "may require the introduction, *at that time*, of any other part . . ." of the writing or some other writing, "that in fairness ought to be considered at the same time." (emphasis added)

So what's the answer to the rule of completeness? Three points:

1. **Don't be sneaky!** If you try to slip in part of a deposition answer and not the whole thing, you're asking for trouble, unless the part you want to omit is truly unrelated. Same goes for anything within a page or two of your favorite quotation. Ditto for a literature quotation: If something on page three is golden for you, but the author does a 180 on page four, don't pretend the second statement doesn't exist. You will be caught, and eternal shame will shadow your soul.

2. **Use the whole quote.** This rule doesn't mean you shouldn't use a nice impeachment quotation just because it's nuanced somewhere else. It just means you have to use the whole thing. If the two pieces of a statement are enough at variance with each other, one way to play it might be that the witness contradicts herself continually, even page to page in a deposition. It depends on your goal, which we discussed in chapter 7, "Planning: The Essential Weapon for Speed," on outlining questions.

3. **Don't belabor points.** For deposition takers, the rule of completeness means not to belabor points. Get your point established, lock it down as best you can, and move on to something else. Then the other side won't have this potent weapon to needle you with.

Extrinsic Evidence to Prove a Witness's Prior Bad Acts

When venturing with a witness down the *bad-acts* road—the kind of stuff I taught you how to dig up in chapter 14, "Mining for Dirt," on investigating witnesses—you need to know Fed. R. Evid. 608(b) and its state counterparts. The rule says:

> (b) Specific Instances of Conduct. Except for a criminal conviction under Rule 609, extrinsic evidence is not admissible to prove specific instances of a witness's conduct in order to attack or support the witness's character for

truthfulness. But the court may, on cross-examination, allow them to be inquired into if they are probative of the character for truthfulness or untruthfulness of: (1) the witness; or (2) another witness whose character the witness being cross-examined has testified about.

The rule is written backward. It first says what you *cannot* do, then what you *can* do. When we flip it around, we see the rule sets these boundaries:

- You can ask about specific instances of the witness's conduct, "*if* they are probative of the character for truthfulness" of the witness or someone else's character the witness has vouched for on direct.

- *But* you must accept the witness's answer and you cannot impeach the answer with "extrinsic evidence" *unless* it's a criminal conviction that fits under Rule 609.

Lots of lawyers do not know this "no three-ring circus" rule barring extrinsic evidence to impeach a witness's character for truthfulness. But it's a powerful rule and often counterintuitive because the witness can escape from otherwise juicy impeachment.

For example, let's say a witness has been judged as untruthful in an administrative action by a specialty society of experts that the witness belonged to. What can you do with that nugget? You *cannot* ask what the specialty society did, because that calls for hearsay and also calls for extrinsic evidence. You are limited to asking, "In such and such case, did you act untruthfully?" When the witness replies, "Nope," Rule 608(b) bars you from offering the extrinsic evidence of what the specialty society concluded. (If it's your witness who was on the wrong side of one of these kangaroo court proceedings, a motion *in limine* may be prudent, and if you win, you will have the witness's eternal loyalty.)

The good news is that the bar on extrinsic evidence applies *only* to "character for truthfulness." It does *not* apply to the other means for undermining a witness's credibility, namely these:

- bias and self-interest
- inconsistent prior statements

- competence
- ability to perceive

All those forms of credibility attack are governed by Rules 402 and 403.

The Advisory Committee Notes for Rule 608(b) spell out all these details with helpful case citations. See especially the Note on the 2003 amendment to the Rule, which says, "[T]he absolute prohibition on extrinsic evidence applies only when the sole reason for proffering that evidence is to attack or support the witness' character for truthfulness."[1]

Using Another Witness's Testimony to Cross-Examine an Expert

Just about anything an opposing expert has looked at to form his opinion can become the basis for powerful cross-examination, if you do it right. The nearly universal rule, as set out in Fed. R. Evid. 705, is that out-of-court statements that an expert relies upon are fair game for cross-examining the expert.

Fed. R. Evid. 705:

> Unless the court orders otherwise, an expert may state an opinion —and give the reasons for it—without first testifying to the underlying facts or data. *But the expert may be required to disclose those facts or data on cross-examination.* (emphasis added)

The advisory committee note makes clear that the rule writers do not expect cross-examiners to engage in a suicide mission when they bring out such "underlying facts or data." The advisory note says,

> If the objection is made that leaving it to the cross-examiner to bring out the supporting data is essentially unfair, *the answer is that he is under no compulsion to*

---

1. Read it here: Fed. R. Evid. 608. https://www.law.cornell.edu/rules/fre/rule_608.

bring out any facts or data except those unfavorable to the opinion. The answer assumes that the cross-examiner has the advance knowledge which is essential for effective cross-examination. (emphasis added)

Many trial lawyers forget about this rule or misunderstand it only to apply to those out-of-court statements that support the witness's opinion. But the rule, correctly understood, isn't so limited. The rule takes in all the stuff the witnesses have *relied on* in forming their opinions, which usually is the entire universe of what they've looked at.

So this rule lets you pile up a cafeteria tray full of tasty morsels of testimony from other witnesses' depositions (plus other facts the expert looked at) and put them in front of the witness and jury, as soon as you establish that the source of the quotation was something the expert relied on in forming his opinions. Best of all, since these are other people's words you are quoting, the witness cannot protest that you've misunderstood the words that everyone can see in black and white on the page (a regular dodge when you're confronting a witness with his own prior statement).

How do you open this treasure chest? It's easy. If the witness didn't already mention in direct examination all the source material the witness read for the case, just ask the witness: "I take it you read the depositions of my clients, the defendant, and witnesses A, B, and C? And you *relied on* all that material in forming your opinions?" Most of the time, they will say yes, and bingo, you're in. If they start trying to hedge about relying on *this* but not on *that*, they've invited you down Cherry Picked Lane, where you get to point out that they have selected only certain tidbits for their opinion and have not relied on any inconvenient contrary fact.

Here's a neat example from Tennessee lawyer Randy Kinnard. In a malpractice case, he cross-examined an expert orthopedic surgeon who was defending another doctor's failure to detect that her patient was developing signs of a blood clot pressing on her spinal cord. An important issue was the defendant's failure to obtain key information from the patient that she, according to the records, had just told another doctor and a nurse.

MR. KINNARD: And the standard of care is to ask not only how are you, but what has led up to this. Correct?

EXPERT ORTHOPEDIC SURGEON: I think everybody would ask it in different ways, but, yes, you want to know how they are now and what is—what's been going on to lead to the pain or place that you are now. Yes.

Q: You'd want to know as a careful surgeon what has happened since I was last here to you, Bette Donathan. You'd want to know that, wouldn't you?

[Note how this question simply restates what the witness has just said, to reinforce and underline its importance for the jury.]

A: Yes.

Q: Well, what did Dr. White say she asked Bette Donathan?

A: I'm not sure that that was recorded, exactly what she asked. I mean, I remember well the note that Dr. White wrote, I believe, but what she asked, I'm not sure that I know where that would come from in the record.

Q: Did you read Dr. White's deposition to form your opinions in this case?

A: I did.

Q: You relied upon it?

A: I did.

[Randy Kinnard has just laid the technical foundation under Fed. R. Evid. 705 to show the witness a piece of someone else's testimony that otherwise might not be admissible at this point. Watch what he does next with it.]

Q: Well, to refresh your memory, page fifty-six, line twenty-four. The question to Dr. White was,

> Q: And did you determine that she even complained of that before you were trying to get an MRI done?

And her answer was,

A: I can't remember if she, if she had. I hadn't been told about it and she didn't tell me because when I sat down and I talked to her and I looked her in the eyes, and I said, describe your pain to me. Tell me exactly what you are feeling.

Do you see that, Doctor?

A: Yes, sir.

Q: I don't see anywhere in here that Dr. White said tell me everything that's happened to Bette since I was last here, what's been going on. Do you see that there?

A: That's not there, no.[2]

The deposition transcript wasn't as clean as it might have been, since the deposition questioner didn't ask, "Tell me everything you did to obtain the history that you wrote in your note." But most depositions are messy, and we are well advised not to let the perfect be the enemy of the good. In other words, don't forgo using a good impeachment quotation from a deposition just because the quotation isn't a model of clarity—especially if you can use the quotation with a different witness, so there is no risk of the witness saying, "That's not what I meant."

Here, the deponent's words—"I said, describe your pain to me. Tell me exactly what you are feeling"—seem to suggest the doctor asked only for the patient's present sensations, not what had come before. Of course, if there was another spot in the deposition where the doctor said she did ask the patient to recount everything that had happened since the doctor had last seen the patient, then that would make for excellent redirect examination, and would be a good reason not to use this particular piece of the defendant's deposition on cross of an expert. Since I know Randy Kinnard is cagey enough not to create openings like this for his opponents, it's safe to assume the quotation he did use was as close as the defendant came to describing in her deposition how she took the patient's history.

---

2. *Donathan v. The Orthopaedic & Sports Medicine Clinic*, United States District Court, Eastern District of Tennessee at Chattanooga, February 2, 2010.

Squashing the Document-Speaks-for-Itself Objection

Just when you're about to launch a good line of cross about a document that's already in evidence, your adversary totters to his feet and brays, "Objection, document speaks for itself." What do you do?

Let's start by recognizing that this objection has no anchor in the reality of any rule of evidence. Now, the objector will act like there is in fact some rule behind it, and judges sometimes go along, especially if they have a less than encyclopedic grasp of the actual rules.

When I hear "document speaks for itself," being a bit of a smart aleck now and then, I lean down to the table where the document rests, cup my hand to my ear, and listen intently. Maybe it's just me, but I've never heard a document talk to me. A silly response, you say, but it's a silly objection to start with. There is no such valid objection in the pantheon of sustainable objections.

The serious point is that documents don't talk until humans run their eyeballs over them. If those humans are deciding the case, they need to either see the document or hear somebody recite what's in it. Jurors are supposed to hear and absorb the evidence as it comes in, so the logical time to do this is when the document is admitted into evidence, or when a witness connected to the creation, transmission, or receipt of the document is testifying.

The objection sort of sounds good, though, maybe because it's so familiar. It's a bastard cousin of several rules of evidence, none of which turn it into a valid objection, but all of which we should think about.

- First, "document speaks for itself" could be a Rule 403-type, unnecessarily cumulative objection. How can this be valid, if the jury has never heard what's in the document?

- Second, if it's a contract, asking a witness to interpret its meaning could violate the parol-evidence rule. But of course, that doesn't bar publishing the actual contents of the document to the jury, without spin.

- Third, this could be a rule-of-completeness-type objection, that the cross-examiner is taking something out of context. The answer to that is that the other side is free to publish to the jury whatever they want from the document that relates to what you want to publish.

- Fourth, there is sort of a best-evidence objection here.[3] That rule says you cannot use a secondary document to prove the contents of another document unless the original isn't available. But you're not doing that. This *is* the original, or an identical facsimile.

- Finally, the rule in every court is that the judge has discretion to allow any document admitted into evidence to be published to the jury. But discretion doesn't mean whim. There has to be a good reason *not* to allow the jury to know the contents of a document admitted into evidence. Otherwise it's an abuse of discretion to sustain the objection.

You also have on your side the let's-save-the-jury-time point. Why force the jury to wade through the entire contents of the document when they only need to see one sentence? Bottom line: once you've shown there is no valid reason not to show the document, most judges will let you.

Mining the Refreshed-Recollection Documents

One of the best excuses for witnesses coming up with new or different testimonies is that their recollection has been refreshed. What would otherwise be a suspicious 180-degree turn can be sanitized

---

3. *See* Fed. R. Evid. 1002. That term, *best evidence*, is no longer used in the rules, because it's so easily misinterpreted. What it means, and what it only means, is the requirement of an original document. It doesn't mean, to take one example, that the availability of an official weather report would bar a witness who recalls what the weather was like on a certain day from testifying about it.

instantly with this explanation, which is why it's so dangerous. But we have strong weapons to test the witnesses' claims that their memory has been refreshed. Remember that you as cross-examiner have an absolute right to look at *any* document witnesses use to refresh their recollection while testifying, and if they testify that they were refreshed with some document *before* testifying, many judges will let you look at that document too. Attorney-client privilege won't stand in your way. Check out Fed. R. Evid. 612. Section (a)(2) gives the judge discretion over the before-testifying refreshing documents. But Section (b) is much stronger for the cross-examiner. It says,

> Unless 18 U.S.C. § 3500 provides otherwise in a criminal case, an adverse party is entitled to have the writing produced at the hearing, to inspect it, to cross-examine the witness about it, and to introduce in evidence any portion that relates to the witness's testimony. If the producing party claims that the writing includes unrelated matter, the court must examine the writing in camera, delete any unrelated portion, and order that the rest be delivered to the adverse party. Any portion deleted over objection must be preserved for the record.

Powerful stuff, yes? And even if you don't get to see the document on some sketchy grounds of privilege or "dog-ate-that-homework," this is a good fight to wage in front of the jury.

"Asked and Answered" and Its Work-Around

What about this ancient objection? The truth is it's not a real objection set out in any rule of evidence. It's a piece of alliterative folklore that, unfortunately, many judges buy into. There is no rule against repeating a question and an answer, particularly if it came out disjointed the first time.

The actual rule that "asked and answered" relates to is Fed. R. Evid. 403, which says, with italics on the relevant part,

> The court may exclude relevant evidence if its probative value is substantially outweighed by a danger of one or more of the following: unfair prejudice, confusing the issues, misleading the jury, undue delay, *wasting time, or needlessly presenting cumulative evidence.*

So, despite the folklorish nature of "asked and answered," we still must anticipate the objection and expect a knee-jerk "sustained" from some judges. The simple work-around is to stretch the point by one of the following means:

- Ask the negative of the question. For example, if the witness affirms what he *did* do, then ask what he did *not* do.

    Q: So you went to the store?

    A: Yes.

    Q: You didn't stay home?

    A: No.

    Q: You didn't go to the barbershop?

    A: No.

- Reverse the question in some other way, such as this:

    Q: You've testified for the defense ninety-five out of the last one hundred times?

    Q: So you've testified for my side only five of the last one hundred times?

- Break the question down into smaller time units. For example, if you want to establish that a witness has zero experience with the X procedure, instead of asking it once this way—

    Q: You've never done X?

    You would ask:

    Q: Last year, did you ever do the X procedure? And the year before? And the year before that?

And after a few of these, then you spring the wrap-up question:

Q: You've never done X, ever?

- Establish the general, then ask the specific. In Jason Itkin's cross of the safety investigator (excerpted in chapter 8, in the section called "Ignorance and Case-Building"), he first asked the witness which employees he had interviewed, got those identities, then went through a list of other employees whom the witness did not speak to. By breaking the question down employee by employee, the cross-examiner much more effectively made the point of a superficial investigation.

- Break the question down by some other logical unit, such as, in the example that follows, a witness's testimonial history in deposition and then the same history at trial.

- Feign loss of hearing or inattention:

Q: I'm sorry, what did you just say?

Inconsistent Statements Admissible for Truth

The old rules said that prior inconsistent statements of a nonparty witness did not come into evidence for their truth, but only to impeach the witness's credibility. Under the Federal Rules of Evidence, that qualifier no longer applies as long as the prior statement was given under penalty of perjury at a deposition, trial or hearing.

Federal Rule of Evidence 801(d):

> Statements That Are Not Hearsay. A statement that meets the following conditions is not hearsay: (1) A Declarant-Witness's Prior Statement. The declarant testifies and is subject to cross-examination about a prior statement, and the statement: (A) is inconsistent with the declarant's testimony and was given under penalty of perjury at a trial, hearing, or other proceeding or in a deposition[.]

In other words, a nonparty witness's prior inconsistent sworn statement, now defined by Rule 801 as "not hearsay," can be used for its truth, just like any statement of a party witness—sworn or unsworn—can be used for its truth.[4] This is not exactly earth-shattering news, because many lawyers, and probably the vast majority of juries, have long ignored this mind-bending distinction between truth-of-the-matter and credibility impeachment. But it's helpful to know, because it fits into our theme: you need to know exactly why the witness wants to use the prior inconsistent statement and tailor your questions to fit the goal. The evidence rule lets you argue straight up that it's the prior statement that should be credited as true. So remember: you can use *any statement* by a party, and any *sworn statement* of a nonparty witness, for their truth.

Using Prior Consistent Statements

Lots of lawyers think they can use a witness's prior statement only when it's inconsistent and they want to impeach something new and different said at trial. You can actually do a lot more with prior statements. Sometimes it's useful to use prior statements of a witness just to head off any inconsistent testimony before it happens. You can use prior *consistent* statements in at least three cross-examination situations.

Situation One

For any witness, you can bring out things the witness said before, as long as what she said is independently admissible as an exception to the hearsay rule. The most common instance is when the statement was written in a medical record or some other document made in the ordinary course of business. This falls under Fed. R. Evid. 803(6).

---

4. Fed. R. Evid. 801(d)(2).

Situation Two

Even if the prior statement isn't an exception to the hearsay rule, you can use it to refresh recollection. You know the drill: The witness hesitates and starts to pull out the "I can't remember" card, in which case you say, "Maybe it would help refresh your recollection if I showed you what you said way back when, much closer to the event?" To which any normal human will say, "Yes."

Situation Three

The witness is an opposing party or an opposing party's spokesperson. Then *any* relevant prior statement is fair game. You can use his or her prior statement, sworn or not, for its truth, whether or not it matches up with something he or she said in court.

Fed. R. Evid. 801(d)(2) states that if an opposing party wants to use a party's statement, it comes into evidence as nonhearsay—for its truth—if *any one of five* conditions in Fed. R. Evid. 801(d)(2) are met. That rule's text is Fed. R. Evid. 801(d):

> Statements That Are Not Hearsay. A statement that meets the following conditions is not hearsay: . . . (2) An Opposing Party's Statement. The statement is offered against an opposing party and: (A) was made by the party in an individual or representative capacity; (B) is one the party manifested that it adopted or believed to be true; (C) was made by a person whom the party authorized to make a statement on the subject; (D) was made by the party's agent or employee on a matter within the scope of that relationship and while it existed; or (E) was made by the party's coconspirator during and in furtherance of the conspiracy.

If it's a deposition, it's also admissible under the Rules of Civil Procedure, and it doesn't matter if it's different or the same from what's been said in court. Fed. R. Civ. P. 32(a)(3):

> Deposition of Party, Agent, or Designee. An adverse party may use for any purpose the deposition of a party

or anyone who, when deposed, was the party's officer, director, managing agent, or designee under Rule 30(b)(6) or 31(a)(4).

So when it's an opposing party or party's spokesperson on the stand, you can do a prior-statement-still-true cross. Your primary message to the witness is this: *you said these things before, and you still say them again (because you're a consistent truth-telling person).*[5]

WHO GETS TO LEAD THE WITNESS?

Well, that's obvious, you say. Any lawyer cross-examining any witness can use leading questions with that witness. Nope. There is one important exception every cross-examiner must know. If the plaintiff or the defendant in a case, or such party's corporate spokesperson, has been called as an adverse witness by the opposing side, the side calling the adverse witness gets to use leading questions, but *not* the witness's own lawyer. Not every judge will side with you on this distinction, and it's important to know the judge's leanings before you pull the trigger on calling the adverse party as a witness. But there is good language in the court rules and case law, which I set out in the footnote.[6] These rely on the core rationale for when

---

5. We saw a good example of this technique with Larry Grassini's cross of the trucking company's spokesperson in chapter 10, "Exposing the Ignorant Witness." See the exchange called "Example: Ignorance of a Corporate Defendant," with Grassini pulling out a great quote from the spokesperson's deposition and confirming it was still true.

6. *Erp v. Carroll* 438 So.2d 31, 37 (Fla. 5th DCA 1983): "When a party calls an adverse party as a witness, the adverse party's own counsel is not entitled to use leading questions as a matter of right during cross-examination. A Defendant is prohibited from employing the use of leading questions during cross-examination if Plaintiff's counsel calls the Defendant, or any other adverse witness, during the Plaintiff's case-in-chief.

"An obviously willing, forthright, and candid witness need not, and should not, be led without regard to the witness's formal status or interest of whether the witness is being directly examined by the person calling the witness or cross-examined by anyone else. Thus, as Wigmore concludes, the test for permitted or prohibiting leading questions is ultimately and essentially independent of

leading questions are allowed: to confront an adverse witness, not to let a lawyer lead his own witness just because of the formalism of who called the witness to the stand in the first place.

Takeaways

The path toward true mastery of cross-examination requires total familiarity with some of the least known rules of evidence. The magic is that what seems obscure and boring will become shiny and wonderful the very moment you have used one of these rules to beat back a wrongheaded objection or lever the right to plow a new furrow of cross. These are mighty weapons for those who know them.

---

the superficial circumstance as to which party originally put the witness on the stand. 3A Wigmore, Evidence Section 909 (Chadbourne Rev. 1970)."

See also Fed. R. Evid. 611(c): "Leading Questions. Leading questions should not be used on direct examination except as necessary to develop the witness's testimony. Ordinarily, the court should allow leading questions: (1) on cross-examination; and (2) when a party calls a hostile witness, an adverse party, or a witness identified with an adverse party."

Here is another example of a procedural rule helpful to the party who decides to call the adverse party in the party's own case. From the Superior Court of the District of Columbia, Rules of Civil Procedure, Rule 43(b): "Scope of Examination and Cross-Examination. *A party may interrogate any unwilling or hostile witness by leading questions.* A party may call an adverse party or an officer, director, or managing agent of a public or private corporation or of a partnership or association which is an adverse party, and interrogate the witness by leading questions and contradict and impeach the witness in all respects as if the witness had been called by the adverse party, and the witness thus called may be contradicted and impeached by or on behalf of the adverse party also, and *may be cross-examined by the adverse party only upon the subject matter of the examination in chief.*" (emphasis added)

16

CALLING THE ADVERSE PARTY

Promise and Peril

Never interfere with a man who is in the process of destroying himself.

—Attributed to Napoleon Bonaparte

Cross-examining an opposing party in a civil trial for professional or corporate wrongdoing is so hard that many top trial experts say you should put it off as long as you can, until whenever the opposing counsel calls the party to the stand. Put another way, the accepted learning is this: if you represent the plaintiff, never call the defendant as an adverse witness in the plaintiff's case-in-chief.

But there is much to say on the other side of the argument. The idea of getting the opposing party's damaging admissions into evidence first, before friendly questions from his own lawyer have brought out all the defenses, is appealing to the primacy and recency instincts of many plaintiff lawyers. And there's a "bring it on" machismo to yanking the opponent up to the stand at your time, on your terms, that adds to the attraction.

Let's first list the sobering reasons not to bring the opposing party to the stand:

- The witness has spent a lifetime learning and practicing his field. The cross-examiner is fighting on the witness's ground with the witness's chosen weapons.

- The witness has spent months to years thinking about the facts of the case. Surprises from the cross-examiner will be few.

- The witness is more sympathetic to the jury than the cross-examiner. In a medical case, for example, the witness is someone who saves lives and heals people for a living. The cross-examiner? He chews people apart for a living.

- The judge can allow a friendly cross-examination by the party's own attorney that repairs any holes created by the cross-examiner's assault. A weak judge may let the opposing counsel lead the witness, even in areas of examination that your adverse questioning had deliberately avoided. In short, the cross-examiner can quickly lose control of the scope of the witness's testimony.

- If the witness does well on the adverse examination, especially if she is called early in the plaintiff's case (remember the first-heard-last-heard rule for making strong impressions), it can be game over. And if you've called the opposing party in your case on the same primacy and recency theory, it's the overall impression of the witness that matters. The defenses tend to all come out at some point during the testimony, so whether they come first, last, or interwoven into both sides' Q&A probably matters little.

- Even though most courts have dropped the old rule that a party is bound by the testimony of any witness the party calls, sponsorship theory counsels that the jury might think that even if not so instructed. Why else would you call the opposing party unless you thought they had something important to say against their own interest?

On the other side, there are some very good reasons to call an opposing party as an adverse witness:

- A well-planned and well-executed adverse examination, like the one in this chapter from Denver attorney Jim Leventhal, can extinguish the defendant's chances of winning. The examiner gets to choose the structure and order of questions and can systematically deal with each of the defendant's major defenses or excuses as they come up (which they are sure to).

- Sometimes the opposing party has a key fact that you need for your case-in-chief, and you didn't obtain this fact in discovery. (This happens to the best of lawyers, when the harsh light of hindsight on the eve of trial shows all the holes in the deposition that the lawyer previously had thought was pretty solid.)

- In some cases, the counsel has good reason to believe the opposing party is not fully prepared and would otherwise use the unfolding trial to fully learn the case. This generally happens only with a less-than-skilled opposing counsel or an arrogant opposing party who thinks he is too good to study the case.

- If the opposing party created a poor impression at deposition, you may be convinced the witness is not trainable to do significantly better at trial. (This again requires a less-than-skilled adversary counsel. Usually a lawyer's best shot at an opposing party is at the deposition.)

- In some trials, the party's defenses may be weak on the merits, and the cross-examiner has the skill and focus, as Jim Leventhal did here, to thoroughly expose them.

- Calling the adverse party lets the advocate structure the order of proof. In a professional negligence case, for example, the advocate might try the sandwich approach: first call a friendly witness to explain the professional standards and rules, then the adverse party, then another friendly witness to explain why the adverse party's excuses don't add up.

PRACTICE TIP

If you call the adverse party, you can take some wise steps to ward off the prospect of a runaway witness spoon-fed leading questions by his own lawyer. You can file a motion *in limine* to ask the court to impose two conditions on the party's own attorney: 1) allow no leading questions, and 2) limit the scope of the cross-examination to clarifying matters raised by your adverse direct exam. See the last section of chapter 15 for case law on who gets to ask leading questions. On the scope-of-cross issue, it depends on the rule of procedure or evidence[1] and on the proclivities of the judge. Filing the motion will flush out the judge and will give the cross-examiner a chance to reassess the battle plan before pulling the trigger.

So there you have it. No one-size-fits-all answer applies. Everything depends on the vagaries of the individual case, the witness, the attorneys, and the judge. If that drives you crazy, because you like hard-and-fast rules, then welcome to the world of trial tactics, where part of the fun and excitement is approaching every case fresh, with no preconceptions, and with your best weapon an inquisitive, analytical brain.

Do not skip the rest of this chapter if you have made a firm decision never to call the opposing party under any circumstances. The case study that follows is still worth your time,

---

1. Fed. R. Evid. 611(b): "Scope of Cross-Examination. Cross-examination should not go beyond the subject matter of the direct examination and matters affecting the witness's credibility. The court may allow inquiry into additional matters as if on direct examination.

because many of the techniques used by Jim Leventhal apply equally when deposing the opposing side. And everyone gets the chance to do that.

The Defendant Confesses Fault

Leventhal's case was a medical malpractice lawsuit for a misdiagnosis of an aortic dissection—a split between the inner and outer walls of the aorta, the body's biggest blood vessel carrying high-pressure arterial blood out of the heart. Missing this condition happens not uncommonly in emergency medicine because the symptoms can mimic other, less catastrophic maladies. Correct diagnosis requires the doctor to pay close attention to the patient's story, as Leventhal brings out here.

The defendant under adverse examination here is a family medicine doctor who was covering an emergency room under contract to a hospital. He saw the patient on two occasions, four days apart, for severe chest pain radiating to the back. The doctor evaluated the patient for heart attack and correctly concluded the patient wasn't having one, but never looked into the other devastating source of this kind of chest pain, aortic dissection.

As you will see, this is a virtual Perry Mason examination; by the end, the witness has flatly conceded his care was substandard and he was at fault for the patient's death. Pay attention to these key aspects of the examination:

- Leventhal's style is persistent, relentless, but polite questioning.
- The examiner has anticipated all the avenues of escape and locks them down one by one.
- Key points are stretched out so they become more vivid than a single question-answer allows.
- The usual rule to never ask a "why" question is broken repeatedly, but only when the subject is narrow, escape routes have been blocked, and any answer may be helpful.

The transcript here is edited—heavily—for space. I will make the entire transcript available to interested readers.[2]

Mr. Leventhal: At this time, we will call the defendant, Dr. Perez, on cross-examination, pursuant to the Rules of Civil Procedure . . . Your Honor, I would request that the Court instruct the jury on the difference between calling somebody on cross versus direct.

[This is an optional prelude that heightens the drama and highlights for the jury the examiner's right to lead this witness on direct. A less experienced judge might have floundered. This one delivers a smooth and well-taken instruction that sets the table for any leading questioning that the examiner wants to do.]

The Court: The purpose of calling somebody on cross-examination is largely to be allowed to question them using leading questions. As you will see, you've seen leading questions on cross-examination of other witnesses; but basically, the plaintiff has the right to do that. That does not make Dr. Perez the plaintiff's witness. It simply means that the plaintiff is using this opportunity to question him in a certain way, that arguably the plaintiff feels is appropriate to present her case. The defendant, Dr. Perez, also has the right to be examined by his own attorney in the same fashion. You will see some of those same types of questions. Later on, Ms. Doig will be examining Dr. Perez on direct examination; which is the same way that the plaintiff has been presenting questions, which means questions that call for a story. You will see those different types of questioning here. You are to evaluate the testimony of Dr. Perez like any other witnesses, regardless of who calls him. Okay?

Mr. Leventhal: Thank you, Judge. Good afternoon, sir.

Dr. Perez: Good afternoon.

* * *

---

2. www.trialguides.com/resources/downloads/the-fearless-cross-examiner

[After some soft questions on the witness's general training as a family practice doctor (sounding much like a direct examination by the doctor's own lawyer), we now see the cross-examiner honing in on the defendant's specific training in the key subject of evaluating chest pain.]

Q: You heard some witnesses testify as medical students, third-year, second-year medical students, part of the training was evaluation of chest pain?

A: Yes.

Q: You had that same training, didn't you?

A: Yes.

Q: And, in fact, you had the same training that Dr. Magorien said that he teaches, and Dr. Duran, and Dr. von Elten say they teach, and they took when they were studying to become family practice doctors?

A: That's correct.

[Note how the cross-examiner frames what otherwise could be abstract discussion of "standard of care" into more concrete questions about "how you were trained in medical school." He also quickly links to the experts who have already testified for the plaintiff, who put the abstract standard into the concrete "what I teach." Now the cross-examiner marches directly into the heart of the case, the failure of the defendant to consider the aorta as part of the chest pain evaluation.]

Q: That training included, that when you evaluate somebody for chest pain, you look at worst first, right?

A: You look at life-threatening conditions, yes.

["Worst first" is a pithy way to put the diagnostic priority rule. Any time the cross-examiner can frame a Rule with two or three words is good.]

Q: That when you're evaluating somebody for chest pain, you have to consider the aorta?

A: Yes.

Q: That is part of your training, isn't it?

A: Yes.

• • •

Q: So, the types of patients that you've seen in the emergency room in Burlington include—it is not unusual for you actually to see chest pain patients, is it?

A: I see chest pain patients on a regular, basis.

• • •

Q: In fact, you believe that the standard of care for diagnosing a patient who presents in the emergency room for chest pain is the same, whether that doctor seeing him is a family practice doctor or an emergency room doctor?

A: In the initial evaluation of a patient through the emergency room, yes.

[The next question is a natural follow-through to the prior one, but one many lawyers don't follow because of the bad indoctrination so many of us get to "not ask one question too many" and to "save the point for closing." The next question is obviously important to validate the plaintiff's expert having a similar, but not the same, specialty as the defendant. Technically it doesn't *have to* be asked. The examiner has just established that the standard of care for family medicine doctors and emergency doctors in evaluating a chest pain patient in the ER is the same. So this next question is only necessary if the examiner wants the jury to understand the key points as they're being made, which every trial lawyer who wants to conduct an effective cross-examination should want.]

Q: So, it was fair to have an emergency room doctor come and evaluate your care and testify in this case. That was fair to you, wasn't it?

A: Yes.

Q: Just as it is fair to have a family practice doctor, or anybody who understands the principles of evaluating a patient with chest pain?

A: Yes.

[More questions that tie the witness's training to his job duties and to what happened to the patient in this case. You can see the relentless progression of logic.]

Q: Part of your job was to be able to recognize signs and symptoms of problems with the aorta, right?

A: That's correct.

Q: That was part of your duty to Mr. Epperly and any other patient that comes in with chest pain?

A: Yes.

[The cross-examiner begins a series of questions that close another escape route. In the Rules of the Road method, this is the "not important" escape for violating a rule. Here the lack of testing for what turned out to be wrong with the patient *was* important.]

Q: I want to begin with what is not contested in this case. You admit that Mr. Epperly died from an aortic dissection, don't you?

A: That's correct.

Q: You admit that when you saw Mr. Epperly on September 19, 2003, that he was, in fact, experiencing an aortic dissection?

A: In hindsight, with all of the information we have, with the autopsy report that we have in front of us, more than likely, yes.

Q: You admitted that [had] you done a CT on the nineteenth, had you ordered a CT examination at the Kit Carson Hospital, more likely than not, Mr. Epperly's aortic dissection actually would have been diagnosed?

A: Again, in hindsight, that is probably yes.

Q: In fact, you told us that was probable?

A: Probable, yes.

[Nothing wrong with having the witness repeat a favorable admission.]

Q: And had that been diagnosed on the nineteenth, that more likely than not, Mr. Epperly would have survived?

A: The probability would be in his favor, yes.

Q: You also admit that the signs and symptoms that Mr. Epperly presented with—the new onset or acute onset of chest pain that day, and the pain radiating from his chest to his back—that those signs and symptoms that he was telling you about were, in fact, from this aortic dissection that he was experiencing at that time?

A: With the information that we have now, in hindsight, yes.

[Note the cross-examiner's self-discipline in not taking the witness's bait about "hindsight." It would have been easy to take a detour into what was knowable only by hindsight versus what could have been known with a better examination or testing at the time. But hindsight is where the witness wants to go, not the examiner, not yet, and so the attorney continues to set out the basic admissions that frame the case.]

Q: You also admit that had you ordered a CT on the twenty-third, when you saw him, that more likely than not, the aortic dissection that he had, which started on the nineteenth, would have been diagnosed?

A: More than likely, yes.

Q: And that more likely than not, had you made the diagnosis on the twenty-third, in the morning when you saw him, that he would have received appropriate care and would have survived?

A: The probability of survival would be, again, in his favor, yes.

[The whole case has now been mostly admitted. The only surviving defense is whether the diagnosis could and should have been made at the time, or only through "hindsight." I've moved out of this chapter the next segment of Leventhal's cross, which is a particularly adroit use of literature, which you can now find in chapter 6. This segment established that a leading internal medicine text cautioned doctors not to rely on a chest X-ray alone to rule out an aortic dissection, and the defendant agreed with the treatise on that point. We resume the examination after that.]

Q: Now, Mr. Epperly came into your office on the nineteenth, and he came into your office at the clinic, which is directly across the street from the hospital, isn't it?

A: That's correct.

• • •

Q: And when he came in, he reported to your nurse that he had severe chest pain, right?

A: He reported that he had chest pain.

Q: Okay. That took him to the top of the list, even though you had other patients who had appointments. Other patients who had scheduled appointments, whether it was days or weeks in advance, Mr. Epperly became the priority. Didn't he?

A: Like many other patients before him and after him, that present to the clinic with a complaint of chest pain, yes, he took priority.

* * *

Q: Is that because when somebody complains of chest pain, it is possible that they may have an immediately life-threatening condition?

A: They would be—potentially, yes, in serious danger or trouble.

* * *

Q: And when you saw him, you then asked him what his history was, right?

A: Yes.

Q: You learned that he had this sudden onset of pain while he was walking that day?

A: He said a new onset of chest pain, not sudden. That is very important to verify. You have been talking about the standard of care throughout your whole presentation here. And I believe that I provided the standard of care. And to me, there is a big difference between sudden onset and a new onset.

Q: Okay.

A: Because on a regular basis, we do get patients with new onset chest pain. When we cover the emergency room, that is one of the top reasons why we see somebody at two o'clock in the morning; they have a new onset of chest pain.

[The thus far compliant witness now begins to defend himself, on the narrow difference between "new onset" and "sudden onset" of chest pain. A less skilled cross-examiner, hung up on receiving a discursive answer to a yes-or-no question, would have complained that the witness was saying too much, and would thereby lose control of the encounter and look weak. Instead, this cross-examiner calmly moves to take apart the new and sudden distinction.]

Q: So, do you have an answer then as to whether this was sudden? Start, you know, ten minutes ago, and I'm here—started an hour ago, and I'm here. Do you have an answer about whether that was sudden, or did you just know it was new?

A: I knew it was a new onset.

Q: You can't—you're not telling the jury, because you didn't ask the question about whether it was sudden, that you determined it was not sudden?

A: When the patient has a sudden onset, most of the time, like when he tells you other history, he will tell you it came on suddenly. In his case, he said that it was this—in the a.m., in the morning.

Q: Did you ask him?

A: I asked him when it started, and he said in the a.m.

Q: Did you ask him whether it was sudden?

A: I don't recall.

[Without a good deposition that closed this escape path, the cross-examiner would have been on difficult ground if the witness had a new memory of in fact having posed the critical question to the patient. Now with the critical admission that the witness couldn't recall having asked that question, the cross-examiner can underscore the point, which deflates the witness's only attempt so far in the examination to defend himself. The next few questions lock in the admission.]

Q: So, as you sit here, you don't know whether he had a sudden onset of chest pain?

A: I can't recall. I am not going to make up a story on that I knew it was a new onset, started in the morning.

Q: Okay. So, Mr. Epperly comes in and tells you that he had a new onset of chest pain that started the very morning he came in to see you, right?

A: Yes.

Q: It may have been sudden. You don't know?

A: Potentially.

Q: Okay. And he told you that it was a chest pain, and he told you that it was radiating to his back?

A: That's correct.

* * *

Q: But are you telling the jury, you didn't determine whether this was sudden, and that is somehow important to this case?

[It doesn't hurt to underline again the key point that the doctor had failed in his job to get an accurate history.]

A: The sudden onset of chest pain was not documented. I did not pick that up. It was a new onset. He did describe it as new onset. If he would have described it as sudden onset, that would have made a big difference, yes.

[The witness tries to push the blame for no "sudden onset" description onto the patient, and the cross-examiner shows he is instantly ready for the point.]

Q: But you're the doctor. You're the one that understands the significance. He comes in and says, "I got this pain this morning, and I'm here, and I'm concerned." That's basically what he said, right?

A: Yes.

Q: And you're the doctor. You're saying that if he had told you it was a sudden onset, that it would have made a big difference. What stopped you from asking him whether it was sudden?

[Is this open-ended question risky? Not very. The attorney has already established that (1) the "sudden" nature of the pain would be key to know, and (2) the witness didn't recall asking about it specifically, so another non-leading question that basically asks "why didn't you ask if it was sudden" is not one that leaves the witness any escape option, except to develop a new and noncredible memory that he did in fact ask the question.]

A: In getting the history, I asked, "When did it start?" I asked the severity of it. That's where the eight out of ten came from. I asked, "Does it go anywhere?" In that, the patient will usually elicit—if it is there, they will tell me it was a sudden onset.

Q: I understand you don't have that written down, and you don't know whether he said sudden or not; but what stopped you from asking him anything?

[Good cross-examiners listen carefully to each answer. The witness did not directly answer the question, so asking it again keeps the witness on the hook. Persistence then pays off in the next few questions when the examiner gets the witness to admit that if he had asked the key question, he would have taken an entirely different path with the patient.]

A: I just knew it started that morning.

Q: But there was no reason that you couldn't have asked him, "Was this sudden?"

A: I could have asked him, yes.

Q: You're saying if you had asked him that question and he said it was sudden—we have no reason to suggest that he wouldn't have said that because you heard what he said to Rana—"All of a sudden, I'm walking down the street, and it felt like I had one of our horses stomp on my chest." Are you telling the jury, if he had said it was sudden, it would have made, in your words, "a big difference"?

A: Yes.

Q: Are you telling the jury that if he had said it was sudden, you would have worked him up for an aortic dissection?

A: According to the standard of care and everything that you've been seeing, yes.

• • •

Q: You do admit, that virtually every textbook of medicine that deals with the evaluation of chest pain says you must include aortic dissection within the differential, especially when you're dealing with a middle-aged man. True?

A: Chest pain in general, you would have to consider aortic dissection.

* * *

Q: You did no tests which would have ruled out aortic dissection, true?

A: There was no test done to rule out an aortic dissection, true.

Q: There was a CT scan in the hospital, wasn't there? A CT scanner?

A: Yes.

Q: And if you wanted to order a CT for Mr. Epperly with contrast, that could have been done?

A: If an indication was present for a CT, a CT would have been done, and could have been done, yes.

* * *

Q: So a five-minute CT scan, and Mr. Epperly would be alive today, right?

A: With what we know today, in hindsight, he probably would be alive today, yes.

[The witness had already admitted, early in the examination, that a CT scan would have saved the patient's life. But here, adding the new detail about the amount of time a CT scan would have taken makes the repetition fresh and not boring: not just that a CT scan would have saved his life, but a five-minute CT.]

* * *

Q: Basically, what you're telling the jury is, if you had asked Mr. Epperly, "Was this sudden?" and knowing what you know today, he would have said, yes, he would be alive today?

A: In hindsight, if he would have conveyed the information, if I would have asked him, if he would have said "sudden," it would have [made] a dramatic difference.

Q: Dramatic is an understatement, isn't it? He would be alive?

A: Yes, potentially.

* * *

[Now the examiner asks the witness the ultimate question. Rather than using lawyer talk—"you breached the standard of care"—he uses the more forceful and direct, "your care was substandard."]

Q: Do you admit then, if in fact Mr. Epperly told you, in addition to the fact that it started that morning—do you admit to this jury, if he told you that, your care was substandard?

A: My care would have been modified to include a CT in the work-up, if I would have gotten the sudden component of the chest pain.

[Note how the witness has dodged the most damning admission, making only the lesser admission that his care would have changed. The examiner persists and then finally obtains the damning admission.]

* * *

Q: My question is, sir, if in fact you did get that information, if in fact Mr. Epperly said exactly what he told Rana, when she said that she heard, when she was in the emergency room, it came on while he was walking, felt like a—like his Belgian stepped on his chest. If he told you that and you didn't do a CT, do you admit to this jury, that your care was substandard?

A: If it was sudden, and I did not do a CT, a CT should have been included in the work-up.

Q: So you admit it?

A: From a sudden standpoint?

Q: Yes.

A: It should have been included in the work-up.

Q: And do you admit, sir, that because patients who come in, they might not even know what the aorta is. And even if they do, they may not know what is a sign of a problem with the aorta—that was your job, not Mr. Epperly's job, to ask him if it was sudden.

[Having received the critical admission, the examiner closes off the one tiny escape still remaining, that it could be the patient's fault for not saying "sudden."]

A: Yes, I'm not blaming anybody for that. In the history of pain, there was a new onset of chest pain.

Q: But it was your job to ask him, because it was so important to you. It was your job to ask him if it was sudden, not Mr. Epperly's job to tell you. It's your job to ask him.

A: Yes, I'm not blaming Mr. Epperly.

• • •

Q: So, when you, given your admission, and given your statement in the deposition, that the standard of care is to rule it out so that they don't die while you're thinking it is something else, and you didn't do that, you admit to the jury that your care, because there was a chance that this man was having an aortic dissection, given his presentation, that because you didn't rule it out, don't you admit that your care was substandard, truthfully?

A: In my heart, I still believe that the care provided for Mr. Epperly was appropriate.

• • •

[The witness still won't admit his care was substandard. But watch how the examiner persists, by taking another angle: the failure to disclose the option of a further test to the patient.]

Q: So, you took away any chance of finding out whether Mr. Epperly had this life-threatening problem, by making the decision for him, without telling him, without giving him the option that he shouldn't have a CT. Right?

A: Based upon his history and his physical examination, yes.

Q: His history did not rule out an aortic aneurysm, did it?

A: Again, with the presentation, the new onset, not knowing if it was sudden, that plays a role.

• • •

Q: You have no reason to believe that John Epperly had any medical knowledge of what was important or unimportant in evaluating either his heart or his aorta, true?

A: True.

Q: And so, isn't it true, Doctor, that if the turning point of this whole case, the turning point of whether to do a CT scan, is whether this is sudden, that it was your responsibility, your duty, to ask the question. Isn't that true?

A: Yes, again, I do not blame Mr. Epperly for that.

Q: Just like in this case, by not asking Mr. Epperly whether this was sudden, and you have no reason to believe that he wouldn't have told you that it was sudden, right? I think that probably, if this is the history, he's walking down the street, and he has a sudden onset of chest pain, if you would have asked him, he would have said it was sudden. True?

[More relentless questioning further undermines the defense of "not sudden."]

A: He might have, yes.

Q: Probably would have. There is no reason to hold that back. He's in there; he's letting you stick holes in his arm, take X-rays. He's letting you hook him up to EKG. If you asked him a simple question, and said, "Was this sudden?" he probably would have told you that it was sudden.

A: The chances are good, yes.

Q: So, isn't it true, Doctor, and don't you admit to this jury, by not asking the question, by not finding out that this was sudden—which is a life or death question in this case—that care was substandard? Don't you really admit that, sir?

A: By not asking the question, it did not warrant the CT scan, so, yes, it did affect the outcome.

[The witness makes one admission but not the core one of substandard care, so the questioner returns.]

Q: Don't you admit, because you didn't ask the question, and because your whole decision on whether to do this CT was based upon that question, don't you really admit that, in this case, that since that question was so important, and because the answer was likely going to be, it was sudden, that that reflects substandard care on your part? Isn't that true?

A: It reflects a substandard in the history taking.

Q: Is it the history that, in your mind—

A: Right.

Q: —is so important, about whether or not to do the CT? So, had you asked the question as you now admit that you were required to do, and you probably would have gotten the answer that it was sudden, it was substandard care, and cost this man his life? True?

A: Not having the sudden onset in the history affected the outcome with regard to ordering or not ordering a CT, and ultimately, yes, the death of Mr. Epperly.

Q: So, you agree with me, that your failure to ask the question cost Mr. Epperly his life, and that was substandard care?

A: The failure of not asking him the question did affect the result on whether or not to order a CT, which then affected his life, yes.

Q: And that was substandard care, true?

A: Yes.

MR. LEVENTHAL: No further questions.[3]

---

3. *Epperly v. Perez*, Case No. 08CV165, 13th Judicial District, Colorado, January 15, 2009.

There you have a brilliant close to a brilliant cross. Leventhal chose his words with great care and ended up describing the event so persuasively that he seems to have convinced even the defendant that his care was substandard. After this, the witness's lawyer made a game attempt on redirect at reviving the witness, but the corpse was cold.

Takeaways

Note the need for persistence when you are questioning the adverse party. In this case study, I count eight specific times when the cross-examiner directly asked the witness to admit he had violated the standard of care. In this last stretch, the witness admitted three times that not asking the right question in his examination of the patient had, as Leventhal put it, "cost Mr. Epperly his life," but avoided answering whether the care was substandard. Finally, he gave it up. How many questioners would have persisted this long? Most would have retreated long before the end, thinking that the early admissions were "close enough." As the old saying goes, "Close counts only in horseshoes."

17

Technique Problems and Their Cures

Courage is almost a contradiction in terms. It means a strong desire to live taking the form of a readiness to die.

—G. K. Chesterton

Jim Leventhal's cross in the last chapter was a great extended example of a master at work, the kind of cross-examination that avoids all the technique problems we take up now in this chapter. Up to now, I have mostly concentrated on what other cross-examination guides give scant attention to: the "what" of cross. I believe the lawyer's strategic choices of picking and developing the topics of cross far outweigh the "how" in importance. But some "how" issues need focus, because in looking at my own work critically and reading transcripts from other lawyers, I see technique issues that erode the quality of otherwise good cross-examinations.

Technique Issues

I've divided technique issues here into five categories: wandering, dangling, hastening, quibbling or quarreling, and dabbling. All are curable.

Wandering

There are good reasons and bad reasons to interrupt one line of questions to pursue another. Good is when you've just realized that you need to establish a related point before the current point will make sense, and the proper order just didn't occur to you before. That happens to the best of us. And it's okay, as long as we get back on track as soon as we can.

But there are a lot more bad reasons for wandering. Bad is when we're trying to mystify the witness so he doesn't see where we're going with a point. That usually ensures a mystified jury too. Bad is also when we're disorganized and lack a good structure because we haven't thought it through. Then the wandering isn't deliberate but is just as frustrating to someone trying to follow along. Another bad reason: we get faint at heart sometimes when we get close to making an ultimate point in front of the jury, and we decide instead to try to hammer the witness from another angle because we're afraid this particular nail won't go in all the way. My philosophy is that the nail either will or won't, but we'll never know unless we give it our all, and so we need to finish hammering the point we're on first, before moving elsewhere.[1]

Dangling

Dangling is a problem when our point floats in the air half-finished. We've never quite explained the relevance of the point, partly because of unfounded fear that it will blow up in our face if we make it too clear, partly because we're so close to the case that we don't appreciate what an outsider needs to "get" it, partly because we

---

1. F. Lee Bailey did a nice hammer-and-nail finish to a line of cross in his cross-examination of Mark Fuhrman, featured in chapter 18, "Controlling the Runaway Witness."

don't do enough posting of signs and laying out of Rules principles for agreement. And partly because we have not thought it through, and we're not sure where and how to finish the point. Dangling is a close cousin of wandering. Both leave points half-baked. Cakes half-baked are raw in the middle and feel bad in the mouth.[2]

Hastening

Another problem related to dangling is hastening: getting in and out of a point so quickly that no one notices. Unlike dangling, when we hasten we do actually make finished points; the problem is the rapidity with which they rush by. The stone sinks into the water with barely a ripple. Clever professional witnesses encourage hastening when they make bland and quick concessions to our good points, so there is no tussle back and forth in front of the jury to underscore the point.

Quibbling and Quarreling

We've seen examples in this book when the cross-examiner received an answer that was a degree or two off from what she was asking, or that was a hair different from the same answer in a deposition, or that volunteered more than she was calling for, but the wise cross-examiner resisted obsessing over the variance. It's much better, most often, to follow Jim Leventhal's model: take the witness's answer and run with it. When we stare too closely at a deposition transcript, even the slightest deviation from the words on the page can loom huge in our minds. A sense of perspective and practicality helps here. Does the discrepancy really matter? I mean, really, really matter? If we cannot say yes, then let it go. Jurors hate quibbling. They hate quarreling too. Quibbling wastes their time and makes the cross-examiner look weak. Jurors ask themselves, doesn't she have any strong points to cover? Quarreling has similar problems

---

2. If you want to watch a non-dangler at work, a lawyer who makes his points with crystalline clarity and finishes each point he starts, you can do no better than read Jim Leventhal's adverse examination of a defendant in chapter 16, "Calling the Adverse Party." Another outstanding example will be featured later in this chapter from Randy Kinnard.

and can be even worse, because the cross-examiner's image as a fair-minded, stand-up human gets smeared.

Dabbling

Dabbling is a whole shelf of half-baked cakes, a messy combination of all of the technique problems in this chapter. The cross-examiner wanders, hastens, dangles, quibbles—he tries to make a lot of points in a very superficial way, and ends up making none. The other day I winced my way through the transcript of a dabbler's cross: every time I thought he was about to make a point, the attorney flitted off to the next topic on his list. He brought out that the witness, a semi-retired orthopedic surgeon who made his living examining plaintiffs for automobile liability insurance companies, had not operated in many years, saw patients only in the office, and made hundreds of thousands of dollars each year from just one insurance carrier. But he allocated only a single question to each point, and thus each of them vanished without a trace of an impression on the jury.

CURING THE AILMENTS

Each of these ailments has its own distinct cure.

- The main cure for wandering, as we'll discuss next, is in the way we organize our material for cross.
- Dangling's cure: Finish the point! Leave nothing unsaid.
- For hastening, we slow down and stretch the point, as we will soon see with a neat example.
- Quibbling (along with its more heated cousin, quarreling) is cured with listening and using judgment (and a dose of strategic decision-making science), as we'll discuss at the end of this chapter.
- Dabbling is fixed by curing the other technique problems and also with a healthy dose of judgment and prioritizing your best topics and leaving the middling ones unasked.

The Wandering Cure: Rules, Principles, and Goals

In the heat of the moment, it's easy to lose sight of exactly what our point was. If only we were fishermen fighting to bring a big catch into the boat. As the rod strains and the line zooms out, our mind and body merge into one, focused on reeling it in. Of course, what we're doing with a wiggling, squirming, fighting witness is a lot like what anglers do. It's just less clear how to bring the sucker into the boat.

In chapter 7, "Planning: The Essential Weapon for Speed," I laid out a simple organizing tool: Write down the precise point of each line of cross ahead of time on a piece of paper, with nothing else on that paper but the facts that lead toward that point. Then do the same on a new sheet for every other key point you need to make. I didn't invent this; Pozner and Dodd get the credit.[3] But it works, because it keeps your mind focused when the witness, the opposing counsel, and even the judge are trying to throw you off.

What are these key points that each get a headline and a sheet of paper? They start with our case-focused Rules and principles: the important plain-English rules of conduct that the other side accepts as true and that we can show were violated.[4] That's the master set that applies throughout the case. Then, we line up the concessions and agreements we know we can force from the other side and figure out which concession or agreement matches with which witness. We set up a line of cross that can go either way: the witness accepts what she conceded before, or if she wants to fight, we can prove that the previous statement is more reliable and the jury should accept it as the truth. That sets up the closing argument:

---

3. Larry S. Pozner and Roger J. Dodd, *Cross-Examination: Science and Technique*, 2nd ed. with cumulative supplement (LexisNexis, 2012).

4. For more about Rules, see chapter 4, "Cross-Examination with Case-Building Rules."

- We win because the other side agrees with our key points.

Or

- We win because the other side's witnesses agreed with our key points until they realized they would lose, and now they want us to forget what they said and accept a new story made up solely to win a lawsuit.

Nice, eh?

THE DANGLING CURE: LEAVE NOTHING UNSAID

When it comes to dangling, we cross-examiners are our own worst enemies. We know the point we're trying to make, but we stop short because we haven't fully plotted how to reach the end, or we hear the little whisper of fear, warning us, "save the ultimate point for closing" and "don't ask one question too many." The example here shows how wrong the old advice is and how we can score spectacular points by following the simple exhortation: Finish the point! Leave nothing unsaid!

Sometimes we need careful advance plotting to really finish the point, but other times, as here, a good lawyer who is presented with a new opportunity plows a path to the end with the adrenaline of the moment. Randy Kinnard was trying a medical malpractice case when the defendant surgeon called, as an expert witness, an orthopedic surgeon. During the direct examination, the defense counsel referred repeatedly to a key date in the case, April 16, as "Easter Sunday." "Dr. [name], on this Easter Sunday, did the orthopedic surgeon come to the hospital at about 6:30 a.m.?" And, "Dr. [name], on this Easter Sunday morning at about 7:30 a.m., was the orthopedic surgeon by the bedside of the patient, carefully looking after her?" And, "Dr. [name], in your opinion, on this Easter Sunday, did the orthopedic surgeon deviate from the standard of care in any respect?"

The questioning seemed to imply, without stating directly, that the patient was lucky to have the attention of any health care provider on this religious holiday.

Kinnard could have waited for closing argument to point out how flimsy the "Easter" excuse was. As I note at the end of this segment, his adversary had used a cognitive trick that would have been dangerous to leave alone.

So Kinnard wisely did this instead:

Mr. Kinnard: Good morning, Doctor. My name is Randy Kinnard, and I represent Bette and Ben Donathan.

Expert Orthopedic Surgeon: Yes.

Q: We haven't met before, have we?

A: No, sir.

Q: I notice defense counsel referred to April 16 as Easter Sunday. You were born in 1962?

A: Yes, sir.

Q: When you were six, I was in Vietnam. Okay?

[Witness moves head up and down.]

Q: We had New Year's Day, Easter, July 4th, Thanksgiving, Christmas Day. We were in the jungle fighting the enemy. Do you think we let our guard down on Easter?

A: No.

[A quick slice of personal biography can work well to connect cross-examiner to jury. It might be technically objectionable, because the counsel is arguably "testifying" about his own personal experiences, but it works here because it happens fast and is immediately linked to a relevant bit of the witness's testimony.]

Q: You're right. In your profession, not only in your profession, but there are a lot of professions where people have to work on holidays. True?

A: Yes.

Q: Firemen, policemen, pilots, air traffic controllers, all kinds of people have to work on the holidays, don't they?

A: Yes.

[A good cross-examiner like Kinnard instinctively looks for ways to broaden the point from the profession in the trial spotlight, medicine, to more familiar callings that relate to the jury and, not coincidentally, help gently pull medical professionals off their pedestals.]

Q: And they still have to be careful and be safe. True?

A: Yes.

[The motto here might be, Regular words for regular people! Think how much less effective this would have been had Kinnard not used "careful" and "safe" and instead talked about "following professional standards of care."]

Q: So, in your profession, you have to be careful on a holiday just as any other day. Is that fair?

A: Yes, sir.

Q: So, the standard of care in this case on April 16 was the same as it would have been on Monday or Wednesday. Do you agree?

A: Yes, sir.[5]

See how a non-dangler works? A more cautious, and less effective, cross-examiner would have stopped at least one or two questions before Kinnard did. After all, he made the point, sort of, at least enough to get by on a "save it for closing" theory. But the last two questions drive home the point and fully pulverize the "Easter" defense.

Although set up on the fly, this piece of cross was structured as a logical syllogism that marched from general to specific:

1. Lots of professions or occupations require working on holidays.

2. Everyone who works on a holiday has to be as careful and safe as on any other day.

3. Medicine is one of those professions.

---

5. *Donathan v. The Orthopaedic & Sports Medicine Clinic*, United States District Court, Eastern District of Tennessee at Chattanooga, February 2, 2010.

4. Therefore, the medical standard of care is the same on a holiday as on any other day.

A broader point comes out of this cross. Many of us have faced adversaries who repeat the same wrong idea over and over in a trial. It's usually something so obviously dumb that we scratch our heads that anyone would try it. Research on decision-making shows it's dangerous to delay your rebuttal of these kinds of points, because they can become engrained in the minds of listeners until it's too late. In his book *Thinking, Fast and Slow,* Daniel Kahneman says,

> A reliable way to make people believe in falsehoods is frequent repetition, because familiarity is not easily distinguished from truth. Authoritarian institutions and marketers have always known this fact.[6]

And add to that: certain trial lawyers.

THE HASTENING CURE: STRETCHING

One of the key principles taught in this book is to make sure the jury understands your point, and that often means asking the same question multiple times or, better, in multiple ways. This is the opposite of three of the old, wrong commandments of cross: the ones that urged cross-examiners to "be brief" and "save the point for closing" and "not ask one question too many." Effective cross-examiners know the lightbulbs don't go off over the jurors' heads until you make the point really, really obvious—in a way that is not boring or tedious.[7]

---

6. Daniel Kahneman, *Thinking, Fast and Slow* (New York: Farrar, Straus and Giroux, 2011).

7. For more on this technique, see chapter 15, "Evidence Rules Every Cross-Examiner Must Know," in the section called "'Asked and Answered' and Its Work-Around."

Example: Stretching a Professional Witness's Testimony History

Tony Russell, an excellent plaintiffs' lawyer in Roanoke, Virginia, faced off with a professional witness and drew out (as we saw in chapter 11, "Shooting It Out with the Hired-Gun Witness") that the witness's professional corporation, established solely to run his testimony business, had been paid more than $2 million in the past few years. Then Tony asked these next questions. Note how this could have been a single question, but by breaking it down between deposition and trial testimony, and between testimony on one side versus on the other, Tony stretched the single point into four questions and answers.

Mr. Russell: Now, you had mentioned that Mr. Peake was asking you about, in medical malpractice cases, the breakdown of your work, and I just want to be clear here. Have you ever testified in a deposition anywhere in the country that a doctor deviated from the standard of care?

Dr. Andrews: No.

Q: You have testified several times that doctors complied with the standard of care?

A: I have.

Q: Have you ever testified at trial that any doctor anywhere in the United States deviated from the standard of care?

A: No, I have not.

Q: You have testified at trial several times that doctors, like here today, did not do anything wrong, correct?

A: That's correct.[8]

---

8. *Patricia Rose v. MONCO Assocs., Ltd.*, Case No. CL12-549, Roanoke, VA City Circuit Court, November 14, 2013.

The Quibbling and Quarreling Cure: Game Theory

I like to bring science to the understanding of good and bad cross-examination because that helps us make intelligent choices when we get conflicting advice about how to go about cross-examining witnesses. The science isn't strictly necessary, just helpful if you have a skeptical mind like mine and you want reasons for doing something more than "because that's the way we've always done it."

The advice not to quibble and not to quarrel with the witness rubs against some of our combative instincts as trial warriors. In the cross-examination battle of wills, we want to give no quarter! We fear that backing off of an encounter will be the first step down the path of defeat.

But it's not. And there's solid scientific evidence that we win more in the long run when we pick our fights judiciously, when we let go of points not worth the trouble, and when we even go so far as to forgive the witness's minor transgressions.

Evidence from Game Theory

The evidence comes from game theory, the study of strategic decision-making. This interdisciplinary branch of behavioral science is widely used in economics (eleven Nobel Prizes to economist game theorists so far), political science, and psychology. And now, trial lawyering.

The prisoner's dilemma, the most-played exercise in game theory, asks what happens when two prisoners arrested for a crime are confronted with these choices:

- Cooperate with each other (and remain silent to police questioning).

Or

- Betray the other guy.

If they cooperate, each serves a short time in prison. If one betrays the other, the traitor goes free and the other guy who stayed silent serves a longer sentence. If both betray and blab, they both go down for a long time. The choice for each prisoner, not knowing what the other fellow is going to do, is devilishly tough.

Things get really interesting when the two prisoners play successive rounds of the game, each with the fundamental choice: cooperate (stay silent) or betray (and blab)? And that brings us to cross-examination, where something very similar happens when we volley questions and answers back and forth.

- Ask a polite, simple question; get the answer you want. That's cooperation mode.

- Ask another question; get an answer that blabs on and on and seems different from what you expected. That's betrayal mode.

What do you do next? Do you stay in cooperation mode with another polite, simple question? Or do you move to match the witness's betrayal mode with a sharper, more quarrelsome question?

Game theory says that if you want to win the long game, and not just this volley, you should overlook the betrayal and stay in nice cooperation mode. Not that you surrender the point, but that you stay polite and avoid matching transgression for transgression. Here's why.

When scientists first started running repeated rounds of the prisoner's dilemma on computers, it looked like a *tit-for-tat* strategy would be the long-term winner. *Tit for tat* means you start in cooperative mode, and then match whatever move the other player made in the prior round. So as long as both sides cooperate, all is smooth, but as soon as the other player betrays, the first player matches that betrayal in the next round. And the game can quickly spiral out of control as betrayal follows betrayal.

Political scientists saw that strict tit for tat was the same theory behind nuclear arms deterrence: each side warns the other, "play nice and things will be fine, but launch a missile and we will destroy you." The problem with strict tit for tat is that one side's mistaken perceptions of what the other side is doing—or "noise," in electronics parlance—are catastrophic for both sides. And noise can never be totally eliminated. A bit of fuzz on the radar screen, misperceived as a missile, and nuclear annihilation rains down on all.

So in both real life and in computer simulations, the researchers quickly saw that the better strategy than *strict* tit for tat was *forgiving* tit for tat, or as it's now enshrined in the social science literature, *generous* tit for tat. When the other guy seems to betray you in a round, you don't go ballistic; you offer measured retaliation. Then in subsequent rounds, you generously assume your adversary's departure from cooperation was a mistake, and offer him a chance to prove you're right by reverting to cooperative mode yourself.

The fundamental insight of generous tit for tat led to a landmark book by Robert Axelrod, *The Evolution of Cooperation*. This also led to the insight that self-interest can be much broader than what we usually think, and that *reciprocal altruism* can be a working strategy for defeating an implacable adversary. Generous tit for tat was President Kennedy's winning strategy in the Cuban missile crisis. Later, computer modeling proved generous tit for tat was the most successful strategy for winning repeated rounds of the prisoner's dilemma game. Here is the basic approach:

1. *Start nice.* Round one starts in cooperative mode, not betrayal mode. Let the other guy be first to betray.

2. *Stay nice* while the other side stays nice. Return cooperation for cooperation.

3. *Be ready to retaliate* when the other side betrays.

4. *But return to cooperative mode* as soon as you can. Don't overreact to a betrayal move by the other guy.

It's important to remember: This is not a strategy to win the Mr. Nice Guy beauty pageant but lose the long war. No, this is a strategy for winning a protracted, difficult, multi-round game against a wily adversary, just the kind of game we all play when we stand up to cross-examine.

Lessons for Not Quibbling from Game Theory

How is cross-examination without quibbling like repeated rounds of the prisoner's dilemma? When cross begins, wariness typically rules. We try to size up how cooperative the witness is going to be.

At the same time, from the witness's viewpoint, everything about the courtroom and their pretrial preparation sessions shrieks the need to watch out for attack. Hypervigilance becomes the watchword, but we can quickly disarm this with genuine politeness and nonhostile questioning.

In cooperation mode, we ask the witness to agree with something, and the witness does agree. We need to avoid open confrontation and stay in the realm where the witness can agree without being humiliated or losing personal integrity.

In betrayal mode, either we or the witness does something disagreeable. On our side, betrayal mode comes about whenever we veer into attacking the witness's integrity in a way that is obvious to the witness and bystanders.

On the witness's side, betrayal means evasion or some other form of a "gotcha" nonanswer. The witness disagrees with the question or avoids clean agreement by festooning the answer with all sorts of qualifications and argument. This, of course, prompts us to sharpen the next question and go into more aggressive questioning. Tit for tat has switched to betrayal mode.

Game theory can inform our choices of both what topics we cross-examine and how we go about the cross.

Lesson One: Search for Common Ground

First, find common ground. The most important common areas where the witness agrees with elements of your case will be most fruitful for cross-examination.

Lesson Two: Look for the Witness's Self-Interest

Second, look for ways you can align the witness's self-interest with your case. Questions that align the witness's self-interest with yours are more likely to succeed in getting the answers you want. What is the witness's self-interest?

- Every witness wants to be perceived as a truth-teller.
- Every witness wants to be respected.
- Every witness wants to avoid humiliation.

Those universals always apply. Add to that: Most witnesses also want to help the side calling them to the stand. (One exception is if they're the adverse party and you have called them to the stand.) But for a nonparty witness, wanting to help the other side is a weaker motive than the motive to help himself. Effective cross-examiners recognize that when they can create a conflict between the witness's self-interest and his desire to help someone else, self-interest always wins out. See chapter 5 for more on understanding witness self-interest.

Playing the Game: Start in Cooperation Mode

The tactical lessons from game theory for cross-examination align nicely with our discussion of self-control and stress reduction in chapter 1, "Laying the Mental Foundation."

Game theory tells us that we can more easily undermine a witness's testimony with adroit, cooperation-seeking questions without reaching for the harsher betrayal-mode questions. The exception is when the witness clearly asks for betrayal by giving a betrayal response to a cooperative question. The strategy for us then is to look for "nice guy" ways to bring the witness in line. Start with an open posture and a nonaggressive, calm tone of voice. Assume the witness is a good person. Don't look to humiliate. Unless you are really sure otherwise, assume an innocent explanation for his betrayals in your tit-for-tat game.

By the same token, avoid ruinous mutual destruction. Don't overreact to trivial disagreements or minor departures from the language the witness used in a deposition. It's easy to be hypervigilant on our feet during a cross-examination, but that is when we let the pieces of lint on the radar screen fool us into thinking massive retaliation is in order, when a generous tit-for-tat approach tells us we should move on and just make our next point, unless we have proof positive that the other side has launched a real missile.

Of course, many lawyers over the years have intuitively recognized and adopted the principles behind a game theory approach to cross-examination and have become successful attorneys in their own right without any fancy theorizing. Here's a description of a nineteenth-century cross-examiner. Readers will recognize the name:

> If any obstinate witness appeared and was determined to conceal facts which Lincoln desired brought out, Lincoln would neither show resentment nor attempt to coerce the witness but would go after him in a nice, friendly way, questioning about things which were foreign to the point desired, thus placing him at ease, making him forget his antagonistic ideas, and, before he was aware of the harm he was doing his side, the whole story would be laid bare, and then Lincoln would compliment the witness on his fairness and the witness would consider himself a hero.[9]

So that's a long segue about the science behind avoiding quibbling and quarreling, but it's worthwhile because it adds another dimension to what we first started discussing in chapter 1, about cross-examination excellence beginning with you, the cross-examiner.

Example of Not Quibbling: Seat Belt Case

Now here's an example: an excellent lawyer cross-examining an auto industry seat belt expert, in a case where a little girl suffered a catastrophic neck fracture when her head tangled with a shoulder belt too big for her. Kentucky attorney Peter Perlman was making the point that crash tests that qualify a car to be sold in the United States don't account for how children sit in cars. A quibbler would have spent far longer making the point, since the witness doesn't directly give the attorney the precise concession he is seeking. But Perlman has the wisdom to judge what's close enough, and move on.

> MR. PERLMAN: You've made some comments to the jury about movements and expected movements. Isn't it a fact, sir, that hardly anybody, especially children, ever sit upright, straight dead center in their seat? Isn't that a fact, sir?

---

9. Joseph Benjamin Oakleaf, *Abraham Lincoln as a Criminal Lawyer: An Address*, (Rock Island, IL: Augustana Book Concern, 1923).

EXPERT WITNESS ON SEAT BELTS: I don't think anyone sits in the designated posture for a crash-test dummy, which basically is like a marine sitting at attention, but we do that because we want to have comparability from test to test. But you can look around this room. There are no two people sitting in exactly the same way, and yet we're all more or less upright.

Q: And I could find it, if it was necessary, but you have testified that hardly anybody sits upright. Have you not, sir?

A: True. I mean, you don't see many people—

Q: And that's especially true of children, isn't it, sir? They squirm, they move, they do a lot of things, but you don't expect them to sit upright?

A: I don't expect any more of children than I do of their parents.[10]

Example of Not Quibbling: Patient's Pain Complaints

Here's one more example, from Nashville attorney Randy Kinnard. He is deposing a defense expert about the patient's complaints of pain recorded in the hospital record, and the issue is whether they qualify as "serious."

MR. KINNARD: It's in my bones. Right?

DEFENSE EXPERT: That's what it says, yes, sir.

Q: That's deep, isn't it?

A: Yes.

Q: This is a serious problem, isn't it?

A: Well, I don't think we know that yet. I mean, those are certainly serious complaints. We don't know what the problem is yet.

---

10. *Starks v. Nissan*, Franklin Circuit Court, Kentucky, August 25, 1999.

[When the cross-examiner encounters minor quibbling with his question, he adjusts the next question accordingly by echoing what the witness has just said.]

Q: We don't know what the problem is, but the patient is telling these people things that are serious. Right?

A: Well, again, we don't know if they're serious or not. The patient's complaints sometimes lead to not serious findings. Those are complaints that she was hurting significantly. I agree with that.

Q: It does say moaning. This patient is moaning, crying, and diaphoretic. It means she's sweating she's in so much pain. This is not good. Fair?

A: Again, those are very significant complaints, yes.[11]

There you have a focused, practical-minded cross-examiner repeatedly adjusting his questions to deal with the witness's answer. Notice how his last question translates medical jargon into English and then immediately asks for a common-sense opinion: "Not good. Fair?" He refuses the witness's bait to tangle up in a definitional battle over whether or not the complaints qualified as "serious." That's how a non-quibbling, non-quarreling cross-examiner gets the ball across the goal line.

The Dabbling Cure

Dabbling is a bad brew of all of the above technique issues, so we defeat it by solving the other technique problems. But the dabbler has an extra burden. Not only does he end all lines of cross-examination before finishing them, he tries too many topics and doesn't prioritize between the good, the middling, and the weak points. Here's a solution:

◆ Write out a list of goal-oriented topics.

---

11. *Donathan v. The Orthopaedic & Sports Medicine Clinic*, Eastern District of Tennessee at Chattanooga, United States District Court, February 2, 2010.

- Now do a separate page for each goal. Put the topic at the top of the page, then list all the facts you can establish below it, and all the questions that will pull out those facts.

- Don't scrimp on your questions: brainstorm as many questions as you can on each page. If you cannot fill the page with a good list of ten or more questions, that's a sign you may not have enough juice to win your goal on that topic.

- Now analyze what you're left with. What are your strongest topics? Can you create a coherent impression of the witness with this set of strong topics? Keep those, and throw out the rest.

TAKEAWAYS

We now have some simple antidotes to technique issues that keep us from reaching our very best.

- We can fix wandering away from a topic, before it's done, with better organization.

- We can fix dangling, or cutting ourselves off from finishing a point out of fear that it will blow apart, with courage and by observing some models of excellent cross that leave no point unmade.

- We can fix hastening, or getting in and out of a good topic too fast to make an impact, by slowing down and stretching the point with new questions that make the point in different but nonrepetitious ways.

- We can fix dabbling, or doing a mix of all of the above, with brainstorming and analyzing our questions and with ruthless pruning to a strong core.

- Finally, we can squash quibbling and quarreling with good judgment and a dose of strategy science that tells us why it is that we ultimately win more points when we keep the witness in cooperation mode. But some witnesses will never go along, and to them we turn next.

18

CONTROLLING THE RUNAWAY WITNESS

In cross-examination, as in fishing, nothing is more ungainly than a fisherman pulled into the water by his catch.

—Louis Nizer

Ah, the runaway witness. Every word that drips from the witness's mouth is like acid spritzed into our ear canals. Why is he so determined to torpedo our case? Why, over and over, does she keep repeating what we don't want to hear? More important, what can we do to make this witness stop and answer our questions? The answer: plenty.

We don't need to surrender to a runaway witness. When we ask simple questions that should yield narrow answers, sooner or later, the witness must respond. In the process of fighting, he or she often does us a big favor. Any hard-won agreement from a witness looks all the more important compared to one given up quickly and blandly.

The ways that top lawyers exercise subtle control over witnesses in cross-examination appear throughout this book. But here are the basic techniques, which you need to adapt to your own personality.

Control Yourself

Make sure you don't read this chapter until you've absorbed the lessons from chapter 1, "Laying the Mental Foundation" (which is first for a reason!), on stress and self-control. These witness control techniques can never work if you haven't first mastered your own emotions. Remember, whoever yells first loses the exchange.

It's not just a matter of staying calm and cool on the inside. On the outside, you need to calibrate your own reactions to the witness. Not all runaways are enemies. Some just have logorrhea and soothe their nerves by spreading a fog of words before them. Nothing personal, counsel, they just like to talk. Others have a script in their heads that they cling to in the unfamiliar terrain of the courtroom. Again, nothing personal. With still others, of course, it *is* personal, intensely so. Witnesses have a range of personalities between these poles. The good cross-examiner assesses the witnesses' and the jurors' reactions and adjusts the intensity and severity of the control measures to match. The good cross-examiner also evolves in the course of the cross. The opening sally usually should be mild in tone, as we were reminded again in our "quibbling and quarreling" section in the last chapter. Severe measures ordinarily should await some clear signal from the jurors that they too find the witness exasperating.

Control the Question

Here are some techniques in your question design to keep witnesses under control.

- Make the question smaller—not bigger. Long questions with too many *ands* and *ors* have way too many escape hatches for the witness to wiggle out through. Pare it down. One fact at a time, then a question mark. Then the next fact.

- When someone says, "I cannot answer that because . . ."—sometimes there really *is* a problem with our question. And even if we think the question is a model of clarity, a little humble pie never hurts. Listen to the witness, especially a nonpartisan witness, and respond to simple requests for clarification.

Here's how New Jersey attorney Dennis Donnelly responded to an opposing expert's question:

EXPERT WITNESS: I guess I need to know how you're defining the word *immediately*?

MR. DONNELLY: As if it was a fireman, as quickly as he could get his pants on. If it's a nurse, it's as quickly as she can go unless she's giving lifesaving care to another patient.

A: Okay.

Q: That's what I mean by *immediately*.[1]

Here's the *wrong* thing to say when the witness asks you a question:

Q: Ma'am, this is my turn to ask questions. When you become a lawyer, you can ask questions too.

Or:

Q: Sir, I'm not allowed to answer questions.

Both responses are rude and not even correct. A polite questioner can always rephrase a question or do something else on a civil plane to figure out what the problem is.

On the other hand, when the witness wants to fight with you over the meaning of ordinary words, it might be your turn to ask the witness what he means by a regular word like *urgent* or *nearby*—or *sex*. So just say to the witness:

Q: Let's use your definition. Go ahead and tell us how you define *nearby*.

Then repeat your question.

---

1. *Nimaroff v. Overlook Hospital*, Morris County, New Jersey Superior Court, June 11, 2009.

Control by Repeating the Question

These techniques apply when the question is important and the witness is obviously dodging it. It's also often really difficult to discipline yourself enough to ask the same question again and again. One high-tech, if pricey, helper with this is real-time stenography. You see your question and the nonanswer pop up on the monitor, and you can read the question back exactly as before.

Here are variations on the ask-and-repeat technique:

Q: Let me try that again. [Repeat the question exactly, a little slower than before. This only works with nice, short questions.]

Q: I must not have asked that clearly. [Repeat the question.]

Q: Sir, do you remember what my question was? [Often, they do not. Repeat the question.]

Q: That's not my question. My question is . . . [Repeat the question.]

Q: We'll get to that. What I want to know now is . . . [Repeat the question.]

Q: I hear what you're saying. Now can you answer *my* question? It is . . . [Repeat the question.]

Q: That didn't answer my question, did it? . . . [Pause and repeat the question.]

Write the question on an artist's pad. After a nonanswer, point to the board and ask this:

Q: Will you please read this question and answer it? [This is a late tactic, not an early one, unless you know it's going to be a key fighting question and you can have it all set in advance.]

Try a humorous quotation, like this:

Q: Have you heard the saying, 'A journey of a thousand miles begins with a single step?' So maybe we could try that here, and you could focus on my question. Which is . . . [Repeat the question.]

After an especially long digression by the witness following a simple question, turn to the court reporter and quietly ask for your question to be repeated. Everyone in the courtroom will be focused as the reporter reads it back. (On the other hand, if your question was convoluted, this will be a painful reminder.) This technique does not often work with impatient judges, and certainly do not try it near the end of a long trial day.

Q: John Paul Jones [or whatever the witness's full name is], this is my question . . ." [Repeat the question.]

This comes at the end of the list because it's a little stronger, but nearly always effective. The only person who addresses most of us by our full names is our mother, and it usually spells trouble with a capital T. You have to have an obvious reason to lever the witness with a strong crowbar like this one.

In extreme cases, keep shortening the question as you repeat it:

Q: So was the car black?

A: The car barreled through the stop sign and . . . blah blah. [nonresponsive]

Q: Car black?

A: Blah blah. [nonresponsive]

Q: Black?

A: Yes, it was black.

Control by Reversing the Question

This is a neat variation of the control-by-repeating method. First you give the witness a couple of chances to answer your question. Then you flip the question around:

Q: So you wrote this operative report?

A: This is just a summary and . . . blah blah blah.

Q: You wrote this operative report?

A: As I said, there is no way anyone could put all the details in here. This was dictated and . . . blah blah blah.

Q: So you did *not* write this operative report?

A: Yes, I wrote it.

Control with Agreement

You can bring around even a runaway witness with a simple list of obvious facts that everyone must agree with or look foolish. This is the heart of the Rules of the Road method. Since you're a case-builder before you're a witness-demolisher, you have a list pertinent to this witness set up in advance. So here we go:

Q: Let's see if we can make a list of things we agree on. Do you agree that . . . ?

Then start into a list of noncontroversial facts, leading with the blandest and most clear-cut first, which can edge closer and closer toward controversy as the list progresses. That's one of the reasons we advocate separating out the descriptive principles in a case from the prescriptive Rules. Principles are less confrontational than Rules, so they usually belong earlier in the list of agreement points than the Rules that squarely aim at the defendant's wrong behavior.

You can bring out a list of Rules and principles supporting your case theme as Randy Kinnard did. Cross-examining an expert witness about a patient who suffered brain damage after being taken off a breathing machine, Kinnard wanted to establish the Rule that *a doctor must believe his patient.* He did this by first asking questions about the need for patients to trust their doctors, and for doctors to trust their patients. He started softly: "I want to talk to you a minute about the doctor-patient relationship. It's a special relationship, isn't it?" You can see the full excerpt in chapter 4, "Cross-Examination with Case-Building Rules."

> **PRACTICE TIP**
>
> Put your key Rules or principles on a poster board, no more than six or eight, so they're legible from a distance. When a witness agrees with an item, put the witness's name or initials next to it. By closing argument, you should have an impressive collection of names.

Another simple agreement technique works following a long answer to a simple question:

Q: So can I take that as a "yes"?

CONTROL WITH DOCUMENTS

You can use any document that is admitted in evidence with any witness, as long as the document has even a shred of relevance to this witness. As soon as you put the document in front of everybody—ideally on a poster board, on a display screen, or in a tabbed jury notebook that everyone flips open—the courtroom spotlight automatically swivels from the witness to the document.

At that time, ask a series of simple questions focusing on the who-what-when of the document's creation and the who-what-when of how it got to its audience. (You don't strictly need to "lay a foundation" for a document already admitted, but it usually doesn't hurt to remind and orient everyone to the document's provenance.) Then you can saunter at your leisure, one at a time, through the various facts set out in the document. The only question to the witness is, "Did I read that correctly?"

If the document makes a point that contradicts what the witness said on direct, you can then move into a variation of the inconsistent-statement cross. The focus, as stressed in chapter 9, "Fixing Contradictions Cross," is on showing that this document is more reliable than the witness's contrary testimony.

Here is a good way to do this, if the facts are right:

Q: This document was written by your colleague shortly after the day of the event?

Q: Long before anyone was notified about a claim or a lawsuit?

Q: You wrote nothing back then that supports what you're now saying, different from this document?"

Two things can cut this exercise short:

- First, the witness pulls a Sergeant Schultz on you.[2] "I know nothing! Nothing!" The witness, of course, must have a plausible excuse for why the document would have never crossed his desk in the ordinary course. The answer for you is to move on to another document closer to the witness's nest.

- Second, your adversary says, "Objection. Document speaks for itself." This is a dumb, nonsensical objection. But it comes up a lot. I hashed out all the reasons why it makes no sense in chapter 15, "Evidence Rules Every Cross-Examiner Must Know." Here, it's enough to say that you're not trying to change what's in the document. That's all given, and so yes, this document does "speak for itself," sort of. But you're entitled to use it with the witness if it's relevant to the witness, as long as it's been admitted into evidence.

CONTROL WITH PACING

Dead time during a cross is usually boring to the jury and therefore bad. But slowing the pace can be good, especially if you're building anticipation for what comes next by a good setup. One natural candidate is a deposition impeachment.

---

2. Sergeant Schultz, played by John Banner, was a character from the TV show *Hogan's Heroes* (1965–1971), who frequently looked the other way when the prisoners he was overseeing misbehaved.

Here's Denver attorney Jim Leventhal with a defendant:

MR. LEVENTHAL: . . . Do you remember giving a deposition in this case?

DEFENDANT DOCTOR: Yes.

MR. LEVENTHAL: May I approach the witness, Your Honor.

THE COURT: You may. You may do so.

MR. LEVENTHAL: [to the witness] Doctor, I'm going to hand you the original of your deposition.

THE COURT: The record will reflect the seal has been broken on the original.

Q: This deposition was taken November 14, 2006; do you remember giving that deposition, sir?

A: Yes.

Q: Do you remember that when you gave the deposition, that you were under oath?

A: Yes.

Q: Do you remember that I told you that not only—and you were aware that not only—were you giving a deposition that was being taken down by a court reporter, but you were also videotaped?

A: That's correct.

Q: And I told you that if you changed your testimony during the deposition or at trial, that change could be pointed out to the jury, for them to consider whether you were telling the truth?

A: Yes.

Q: I want you to turn—and you also had an opportunity to make corrections to that deposition, didn't you?

A: Yes.

Q: But you made no corrections, did you?

A: No.

Q: I want you to turn to page 115 of your deposition. I want you to read to yourself from line two through line seventeen. Just read that to yourself quietly. Megan, I would like for you to play for the jury, please, line two through line seventeen.[3]

You can almost feel the crackle of suspense in the courtroom as this is unspooling. That's another mark of a skilled cross-examiner: not rushing through the foundation for impeachment with a deposition. Stretching the foundational point here heightens suspense because everyone knows that a critical juncture has been reached. It also maximizes the cross-examiner's control. Whenever you are following a familiar and time-honored path of cross-examination, you will get leeway to stay on that path until you reach the end.

Control by Listening to the Witness and Closing Escape Doors

The best way to handle an evasive witness is to listen to every excuse and dismantle it. Here is F. Lee Bailey's cross-examination of police detective Mark Fuhrman in the O. J. Simpson murder trial in 1995 that closed off all escapes and bought Fuhrman a perjury conviction.

Note especially the rejoinder to the classic witness evasion, "Not that I recall." If Bailey had stopped after that answer, as a commandments-obeying lawyer would have, he still might have had decent impeachment when he later played the audiotape of Fuhrman using the n-word, but he wouldn't have elicited provable perjury.

Mr. Bailey: Did you tell the lawyers in that room that you never used the word *nigger*?

---

3. *Epperly v. Perez*, Case No. 08CV165, 13th Judicial District, Colorado, January 15, 2009.

Ms. Clark: Same objection, Your Honor.

The Court: Overruled.

Mr. Fuhrman: It was never asked.

Mr. Bailey: I'm asking. Do you?

Ms. Clark: Objection, Your Honor.

The Court: That is vague. Rephrase the question.

Mr. Bailey: Do you use the word *nigger* in describing people?

Ms. Clark: Same objection.

The Court: Presently?

Mr. Bailey: Yes.

The Court: Overruled.

Mr. Fuhrman: No, sir.

Mr. Bailey: Have you used that word in the past ten years?

A: Not that I recall, no.

Q: You mean if you called someone a *nigger*, you would have forgotten it? [emphasis added]

A: I'm not sure I can answer the question the way you phrased it, sir.

Q: You have difficulty understanding the question?

A: Yes.

Q: I will rephrase it. I want you to assume that perhaps at some time, since 1985 or 6, you addressed a member of the African American race as a *nigger*. Is it possible that you have forgotten that act on your part?

A: No, it is not possible.

Q: Are you therefore saying that you have not used that word in the past ten years, Detective Fuhrman?

A: Yes, that is what I'm saying.

Q: And you say under oath that you have not addressed any black person as a *nigger* or spoken about black people as *niggers* in the past ten years, Detective Fuhrman?

A: That's what I'm saying, sir.

Q: So that anyone who comes to this court and quotes you as using that word in dealing with African Americans would be a liar, would they not, Detective Fuhrman?

A: Yes, they would.[4]

CONTROL BY SIDESTEPPING THE BAIT

Sometimes an especially clever witness will answer your narrow question in a bland way and then will innocently add, "May I explain?" If you take the bait, you will stand by helplessly as the witness launches a long explanation harpooning your position. I know; I've been there. Sometimes in the heat of the moment, we let the witness take over because we don't want to look unreasonable and cut them off from explaining. But then we regret it. So here's a neat way to cut through the dilemma:

Sidestep the bait by responding to the witness like this: "We'll get to that, but first . . ." and then launch another question. Keep asking new, narrow questions, and eventually no one will remember that the witness wanted to explain something and that you put off the explanation.

CONTROL WITH YOUR BODY

Adjust these whole-body techniques to your personality. Bear in mind that a small gesture can be as effective as a big one, and maybe more so, because you're not calling undue attention to yourself with theatricality.

---

4. Text taken from http://www.languageandlaw.org/texts/trial/fuhrcros.htm.

- *Keep eye contact* with the witness as much as you can. It makes it harder for the witness to embellish or evade. This also helps minimize professional witnesses' annoying habit of turning to the jury with every answer as they were taught to do back in witness prevarication school.

- *Raise your hand*, palm out to the witness. This universal *stop* signal will stop most witnesses in their tracks. Then repeat the question.

- *Shake your head no* as the witness blathers on. Again, this has to be proportional.

- *Shake a finger* (not the middle one) at the witness. Again, be proportional.

- *Nuclear option:* Sit down at the counsel table and stare at the table. Eventually the witness will run out of steam. This should not be employed as a first, second, or third resort, because you risk looking rude if the jury is not already inclined toward your view of the witness.

COMMON CONTROL TIPS I DON'T RECOMMEND

Following is a series of tips I *don't* recommend:

Q: I move to strike the answer as nonresponsive.

Q: Your Honor, could you instruct the witness to . . . ?

There's nothing wrong with getting the judge's help with a difficult witness. But the judge has to volunteer first. Seeking the judge's help shows that you are weak and have lost the control battle with the witness. The best that can happen is the judge helps you, which shows you cannot stand up to the witness on your own. The worst is that the judge overrules your objection and leaves you foundering, looking even weaker. Another bad thing that can happen is the judge *does* intervene but then acts like she needs to start refereeing all questions after this. Not a good thing if you are trying to stay in control.

Q: May I have your agreement that if I ask you a yes-or-no question, you will answer "yes" or "no"?

Q: Can you just answer this next question "yes" or "no"?

The trouble with this and similar let's-make-a-deal questions is twofold: first, they make you look unfair, someone who has announced up front that he wants to cut off the witness's explanations before even asking the question; and second, they make you look weak. Why would you need to issue this kind of admonition to a witness you didn't fear? Remember: this is a battle of perceptions.

On the other hand, a request to "just answer yes or no" *can* work, but usually only after the witness has played dodgeball several times with the same simple question. At the end of that line, when everyone in the courtroom is feeling exasperated, that's the time to try something quiet like, "If you can answer that 'yes' or 'no,' please do so."

Q: Are you finished?

Usually it's very obvious the witness has finished the answer, and this response sounds petty and sarcastic. Humor is good, sarcasm bad.

Q: [Interrupting the answer.]

This works only when the question was very simple and the witness has launched into an obviously long-winded digression. Usually an interruption sounds rude. You can make it work if you do it quickly, at the first sign of veering off the path, and politely, something like, "Excuse me, but can you focus on my question first?" But just talking over the witness never works. You annoy the court reporter and lose the jury.

Takeaways

We see again that true mastery of cross-examination starts with mastery of yourself. Once you achieve self-control, you can control the witness so much more easily. There are good and bad ways to do that, and the good ways far outnumber the bad ones. The bad ways make you look weak, whiny, and, well, cross. The good ways make you look like the real you: strong, confident, fair—the kind of attorney jurors want to vote for.

PART V

Bringing It Home

19

PULLING TOGETHER WHAT WE'VE LEARNED

Behold, I am sending you like sheep in the midst of wolves; so be shrewd as serpents and simple as doves.

—Matthew 10:16

Let's pull together the lessons we've learned in the last eighteen chapters. I will start with a checklist for lawyers in mid-trial who are parachuting into this book for some emergency guidance. Next, I will put the checklist to work for a commonly encountered witness: the defense medical examiner. Finally, I will end with some bigger issues that will take us back to where we started: preparing ourselves to be the shrewd yet simple cross-examiners imagined in the Biblical verse at the top of this page.

The checklist has two parts: topics and techniques.

Hunt for the Best Topics

1. List the case-building Rules and principles important to your side's case theme. Write them down on a single sheet of paper in plain English. Do not limit yourself to liability; add damages too, on a separate sheet.

    » Chapter 4, "Cross-Examination with Case-Building Rules"

2. Evaluate the witness's character and personality traits. Figure out if the path to agreement with this witness will be crooked and steep, or smooth and straight.

    » Chapter 5, "Witness Self-Interest and Case-Building Cross"

3. Look for the witness's self-interest and how you can recruit her to defect, and on which points.

    » Chapter 5, "Witness Self-Interest and Case-Building Cross"

4. Line up whatever credibility dirt you have on this witness that the other side might not know. Remember, independent research is your friend.

    » Chapter 13, "Fundamental Attribution"

    » Chapter 14, "Mining for Dirt"

5. When you've finished the above steps, you will know if this will mainly be a case-building agreement cross or a witness tear-down cross or some combination.

    » Chapter 3, "Choosing the Weapons Right for You"

6. Now, if you need to do any tear-down, study the four main witness-centered types of cross and figure out which works best with this witness.

    » Chapter 8, "Cross-Examination with Witness Tear-Down Rules"

    For each category, write at the top of a single sheet of paper, "The jury should conclude this witness is [unfit, biased, mistaken, or contradictory] because . . ." Then write all your points in that category on the sheet, with references to deposition page numbers and exhibits.

   a. *Lack of Fit:* the witness's background and suitability for this case. Remember that a witness can be *unfit*, with not enough credentials for the facts of this case, or a *misfit*, with lots of wildly irrelevant credentials (like the life-care planner in the paralysis case—in chapter 8, "Cross-Examination with Witness Tear-Down Rules"—who gives cosmetic treatments to her clinic patients).

   » Chapter 13, "Fundamental Attribution"

   b. *Ignorance and Mistakes:* what the witness doesn't know that she should, or thinks she knows but is wrong.

   » Chapter 10, "Exposing the Ignorant Witness"

   c. *Bias:* the witness's partiality and lack of objectivity.

   » Chapter 11, "Shooting It Out with the Hired-Gun Witness"

   » Chapter 12, "Polarizing the Extreme Witness"

   d. *Contradictions:* the pattern of conflicts between the witness and his own prior statements or conduct (depositions, writings, and so on), between the witness and others on his side, between the witness and the majority of other witnesses in the case, or between the witness and what we all know is true.

   » Chapter 9, "Fixing Contradictions Cross"

7. Prioritize and winnow the topics down into some combination that creates a coherent *impression, in a single sentence or phrase,* for this witness.

   » Chapter 3, "Choosing the Weapons Right for You"

   » Chapter 8, "Cross-Examination with Witness Tear-Down Rules"

   » Chapter 17, "Technique Problems and Their Cures"

If you're already in mid-trial, save this nugget for your next case: Set a realistic time line for planning out the cross-examination of important witnesses. In civil litigation with liberal discovery, you can do "inside research"—this is information the other side knows about and is hence less valuable than "outside research," which you can do in any case once you know the witness's name. In either case, do all such research well before the start of trial because it's too late in mid-trial to start inundating your brain with sorting through piles of irrelevant facts to find something pertinent to your case. Plan at least one practice play-acting session for the key adverse witnesses before trial, and another shorter one the night before they testify. Think of the preparation process as an upside-down pyramid. Lots of facts and issues at first, sifted down as you get closer to the witness's testimony to the very few key points that represent your best lines of inquiry that will shape one coherent impression of the witness.

Techniques to Pull It Off

1. Prepare yourself first: calm, confident, collected, polite. *Not* a hypercontrolling suit-and-tie bullying the witness.

    » Chapter 1, "Laying the Mental Foundation"

    » Chapter 2, "Freeing Yourself from the Ten Commandments of Cross"

2. Organize your material. I like manila folders. But you can use anything that works to get the material for each line of cross into its own home so you don't have to go back and forth.

    » Chapter 7, "Planning: The Essential Weapon for Speed"

3. Plan your questions. Put everything related to proving a specific point on a single page.

    » Chapter 7: "Planning: The Essential Weapon for Speed."

4. Plan several moves ahead: Sketch the possible answers to a question. Focus on developing those lines of questioning where

you can deal with any answer. Prepare yourself with sample responses to witness excuses for inconsistent statements.

» Chapter 9, "Fixing Contradictions Cross."

5. Set up graphics. Hot documents, specific rules, prior admissions—gather anything that you can display during a line of cross.

» Chapter 7, "Planning: The Essential Weapon for Speed"

6. Try to keep questions simple—one basic fact each.

» Chapter 18, "Controlling the Runaway Witness"

7. Ask leading questions when you need to, but remember to draw out strong points in the witness's own words whenever you can.

» Chapter 2, "Freeing Yourself from the Ten Commandments of Cross"

8. Don't be afraid to ask a question when you don't know the answer, as long as you know you can handle any answer given.

» Chapter 2, "Freeing Yourself from the Ten Commandments of Cross"

9. Prioritize: limit the cross to topics that can make a difference in the outcome of the case or that can neutralize this witness. Along the same lines: be proportional to the harm perceived. A witness who hasn't hurt your side needs little time; the one who tries to torpedo your entire case requires sustained attack.

» Chapter 7, "Planning: The Essential Weapon for Speed"

10. Keep going to the surrender point on any topic worth exploring.

» Chapter 17, "Technique Problems and Their Cures"

11. Stretch good points when you can; don't let them go with a single in-and-out volley.

» Chapter 17, "Technique Problems and Their Cures"

12. Announce: Make sure the jury understands the point of each line of questions. Do not save it for closing.

    » Chapter 11, "Shooting It Out with the Hired-Gun Witness"

    » Chapter 16, "Calling the Adverse Party"

13. Put yourself in the witness's skin. Play-act with colleagues so you can learn new ways the witness might answer. Think more about the self-interest pressure points for the witness that you've already considered in the topics list.

    » Chapter 5, "Witness Self-Interest and Case-Building Cross"

    » Chapter 19 (this one).

14. Subpoena the witness to bring her complete case file to court and show it to you before testimony begins. Focus on notes about the case and billing documents. (The other side hates this because it's so effective. Just remember, turnaround is fair play, so you might want to hold off until your witnesses have already testified.)

    » Chapter 14, "Mining for Dirt"

There we have two good lists. We've replaced the old ten commandments of cross-examination with something more practical, robust, and winning. Now let's show how it works for one commonly encountered expert, the so-called independent medical examiner.

THE CHECKLIST IN ACTION: CONSTRUCTING A CROSS OF A DEFENSE MEDICAL EXAMINER

I had a chance recently to help a colleague retool a cross-examination for an "independent" medical examiner who works for the defense in the Washington, DC, area. This type of witness will be familiar to many readers: he regularly roams courthouses throughout the mid-Atlantic region, an aging man in a plaid sports jacket and a comb-over, carrying only a thin manila folder with his report on the latest injured plaintiff whom he has skewered for the defense. He retired from operating on patients two decades ago and replaced the lost surgical income with testimonial work. He claims to maintain an office-based practice with an orthopedic surgery group, but sends all patients who need an operation to one of his colleagues.

For research material, I had his report in the current case, a curriculum vitae, transcripts of three cross-examinations from other cases (usually in a video deposition a week or two before trial), and some Internet research I did on his credentials.

Here is how I developed the cross from my checklist of strategies and topics.

Study the Witness's Self-Interest

Surgeons make their living by doing surgery. Seeing patients in an office generates a paltry income by comparison. This orthopedist hasn't operated in twenty years and, not coincidentally, started building his testimonial practice shortly after hanging up his arthroscope. I see in one of the depositions that he reveals in passing that his testimonial income is paid to him directly, not to the group orthopedic practice where he supposedly still sees patients. A sweet deal. (Imagine a law partner who has all his lucrative fees paid directly to him, and who shares with his partners only his itty-bitty hourly fees.) This is a witness interested in making money. And he does that by being Doctor Reliable to the defense lawyers who call on him. This will give us some fodder for a tear-down cross that we'll consider in more detail below. But first, is there anything in the medical substance of the case that he will help us with?

Look for Agreement Cross with Case-Building Rules

Case-building is Strategy 1 in this book, which I also call "defection" cross, because we're working to win over the witness to our side on important points. For an honest medical witness, you could develop a bunch of common-sense propositions about the human response to trauma. Principles like "Everyone recovers from injury at his or her own rate" or "There is no medical test for pain" or

"Pain is real" or "The injured person is in the best position to describe his or her own pain."

But there are two problems with case-building cross with a wily, one-sided adversary. First, your questions treat the witness with too much respect and play into the wrong impression of this witness: by starting the cross asking for agreement on medical issues, you're treating the witness as though he's still a real doctor, and not a bought-and-paid-for so-and-so. Second, the witness uses every question as an excuse to restate his opinions on direct or to fence with you. You will hear the following from any defense medical examiner to whom you pose general medical questions:

A: It depends.

A: I wouldn't expect that, no.

A: Not necessarily.

A: Yes, but there's no objective evidence of that here.

And each of these answers becomes the launching pad for as many damaging volleys against your case as the witness can get away with.

Now, you can venture some of these questions, but only once you have first softened up the witness with bias questions that have tamed the witness to show a reasonable demeanor. But most of these DME witnesses sprinkle ground glass on their breakfast cereal just to toughen up their bite before coming to court, so don't count on sweetness and light from their mouths.

Create Witness Tear-Down Cross

So I lay aside any thought of getting this witness to agree with any of the medicine in our case. Instead, I look for tear-down strategies, starting with the most basic: Is he qualified?

Lack of Fit

In reading his old transcripts, I see that other lawyers have tried to cross this witness on the fact he doesn't operate anymore. The impact fizzles most of the time because it doesn't really tie into the rest of the cross. What we need to develop is a pattern of this witness being out-of-date.

I find some promising lack-of-fit material with a modest bit of independent research, with websites of a hospital and a medical specialty certifying board. The bonus part is, it's easy to create exhibits with basic screenshots of the key website nuggets. Total time expenditure: ten minutes.

This witness likes to say he is on the faculty of the orthopedics department of a prestigious university medical center. But he's not, according to the current directory of "voluntary faculty" at the department's website. Then I check his orthopedics board certification. Yes, he's on the official certified list of the American Board of Orthopaedic Surgery, but with an important "grandfather" caveat. Every board-certified surgeon starting in 1986 has to take a recertification exam every ten years to prove current knowledge. His certificate dates from 1971. That means that thousands of orthopedic surgeons, everyone certified since 1986, have objective evidence of current knowledge in their field, but this witness does not.

So now I can construct a good lack-of-fit rule for this witness:

- A medical witness should be current in his field of specialty.

Or, a sharper version:

- A medical witness should not exaggerate the currency of his credentials.

And I have three ways the witness has violated the rule:

- He claims to be on the current faculty of a major medical center, but the institution says he's not.
- He has a "grandfathered" board certification and no objective evidence of current knowledge, other than his own say-so.

- He hasn't seen the inside of an operating room in twenty or more years.

There is one more lack-of-fit possibility here. This witness is a general orthopedic surgeon. The plaintiff's treating doctor witness is a hand surgery specialist. Here are some *generalist versus specialist* questions we could try:

Q: So when was the last time another doctor referred you a patient for [this type of injury]?

Q: When did a specialist in [this injury] last consult with you about recommended treatment?

Q: How many operations for [this injury] have you done in the last ten years?

Q: How many doctors in our city specialize in [hands, feet, shoulders, spines, or knees]?

Q: Did you consider recommending to the defense counsel to drop you and hire one of these specialists?

Q: Do you know more about [body part] than the surgeons who specialize in [that body part]?

Ignorance or Mistakes

I look through the witness's DME report carefully for errors and omissions of facts that favor the genuineness of the injury and its causal relationship to the defendant's conduct. I find a couple of small things, but I elect not to use them for a few important reasons:

1. They're not flagrant misstatements, just omissions.

2. I cannot develop a good cherry-picking bias pattern out of these omissions.

3. Delving into the medical facts and injury chronology of the case moves the cross back onto comfortable ground for the witness and lets him assert that the omitted facts are trivial compared to what he relied on.

I can see a Pandora's box looming here: the potential for questions along this line to let the witness restate his entire opinion, so I close the lid on the box and let this line of questions pass.

Before we leave the subject, here's a short checklist of important facts and observations we should gather to test whether the DME doctor is ignorant about what is important to the case:

- Exact particulars of the event causing the injury (speed of vehicles, crush, direction of impact, and so on).
- Observations of non-MD treaters (physical therapists, occupational therapists, nurses).
- Medication use as shown by pharmacy records (often far more complete than prescriber records).
- Friends and family observations.
- Actual imaging versus reports (many lazy DMEs look only at reports).

Bias

We have a good general rule here, one the witness cannot dodge because his own professional society, the American Academy of Orthopaedic Surgeons, has endorsed it. The rule:

- An expert witness must be objective, impartial, unbiased.

But I see in the old transcripts that the witness has wrapped himself in the objectivity blanket, and no one has really stripped it off. The witness testifies he performs an "independent medical evaluation." That's the headline on the top of his report, and it means, he says, that he gives the same opinion about the patient no matter who has sent the patient to him. He also claims that he doesn't know who has sent the patient to his office until after he does his "independent" exam. Can we blow the cover on this tidy pose?

Prior cross-examiners have done a good job obtaining the 1099s that show the amounts and sources of the witness's testimonial income. In the three old transcripts I read, each cross-examiner has done a money cross, the upshot of which is that the witness has a nice six-figure annual income from expert witnessing. But I think there's a stronger point to be made: exams funded by defense firms and insurance carriers are a major source of income for this witness. If he lost the business, it would have a big impact on his finances. So to continue getting the business, he has become Doctor Reliable for the defense bar. It doesn't matter if he knows specifically where each patient comes from; he has a pretty good idea of the sources of his income.

The defense lawyers who hire this doctor get only one shot at an independent exam under Rule 35. There are no makeovers allowed if the first DME comes out helpful to the plaintiff. So the lawyers favor witnesses they know can deliver the goods. This is one of those facts that every lawyer knows but few jurors do, so it's ripe for bringing out at trial.

But how do I prove this on cross, when the witness hasn't been asked these blunt questions before? I find two helpful facts in the old transcripts:

- First, the witness has received $175,000 income in the last reported year from the same law firm representing the defendant in this case. By most people's lights, that's a lot of money. His total testimonial income is around half a million dollars a year, so a sizable portion comes from this one source.

- Second, the witness admits to testifying 90 percent on the side of the defense when he comes to court. In truth, it probably edges closer to 100 percent, but we can live with 90 percent.

Now we do some educated speculation. Can we imagine the defense calling this witness to court, and paying his testimonial fee, when he concludes the patient is as bad off or worse than the plaintiff contends? The witness will likely feign ignorance on this, but he does know one thing we can ask: when he gets called to court, it's always by the lawyer that paid for the so-called independent exam. He never gets subpoenaed to court by the patient's own lawyer when he's done an exam for the defense.

Are we absolutely sure of this? Since the question has never been put to the witness, no. But it stands to reason with his admitted

90 percent defense pattern and his concentration of work for a few favored defense firms. So it's worth a question to him.

Now I find one more fact to stymie any of the witness's efforts to feign ignorance on who pays him. It turns out that all of what he calls his "nonclinical" work is billed from his home computer, not from the office he shares with a group of orthopedic surgeons. So he has to know where he is sending bills and who is sending him checks and 1099 forms at the end of the year.

One more way you can nail down the defense-minded pattern of the DME doctor: send a subpoena calling for all his reports in the last two to three years in which he found the plaintiff had suffered a permanent injury related to the event at issue. If he says it's too burdensome to sort these out, then fine, you'll take all his reports and do your own sorting. New Jersey plaintiff lawyer Ed Capozzi reports he uses this tactic with great success.

Contradictions

Our final checklist item focuses on contradictions:

- between the witness and himself
- between the witness and other witnesses
- between the witness and common sense[1]

Here we find one more promising line of cross for this witness. What is the reason that brings this witness to court thirty or more times a year? Who is it this witness always contradicts? Yes, it's the patient's treating doctor. That doctor is called to court by the plaintiff to describe the injuries and her treatment of them, and often will testify about the link between the event that's the focus of the lawsuit, and the patient's long-term outlook.

---

1. Close readers will notice that a fourth contradictions item isn't on this list: Contradictions between the witness and published authorities. That's because we've decided to forgo crossing this witness on any general medicine topics where such treatises might be useful. With a non-hired-gun witness, treatises can be helpful, but not in this situation.

Of course, the defense never says, "The treating doctor is wrong, and I'm bringing to court the man who says the treater is always wrong." It's our job as cross-examiners to bring out that contrast. And more: the treating doctor came to see the patient not with any lawyer fingerprints on the referral (we hope, anyway), but because the emergency room had assigned this doctor to trauma call that night (or some other medical-based steer). The treater's motivation is to heal the patient. What is the defense examiner's motive? Well, it certainly has nothing to do with healing. And of course, he sees the patient only because the same lawyer who sends him so much business has sent yet another patient.

Another contradictions or bias line of cross comes when the testifier has done a records review without ever seeing the injured person. It fits into the contradiction box because it's flagrantly contradictory to the way medicine is actually practiced. Every clinical doctor (radiologists and pathologists excepted) *always* takes a careful history from the patient and examines the person before issuing any opinions or giving recommendations.

The line of cross might include these questions:

Q: How many of your patients have you reached final diagnoses on without ever seeing them?

Q: How many of your patients have you reached final diagnoses on without ever touching them?

Q: You decided that *nothing* my client could say would make *any* difference to you, true?

Q: [Sometimes] You even made credibility judgments about someone you've never met, correct?

Q: Whether "necessary" or not, it's simple *respect* to meet patients before you draw final conclusions on them, correct?

Q: Are the conclusions that you might draw about patients ones that could have important consequences if they were believed?

In this case, the DME doctor has done an actual examination of the plaintiff, so the records review line of questions doesn't apply.

And he is careful not to cast any doubt on the legitimacy of the actual pain and disability; he just says the patient's condition has nothing to do with the original event. He's playing the old "spontaneous injury–unknown cause" card. Still, that leaves us with a good line of contradictions or bias cross, based on "You always say Dr. Treater is wrong."[2]

Cross Outline for the DME Expert

The impression we can now weave from our best points? This is an out-of-date expert who exaggerates his credentials and cannot be trusted to be objective and fair. So let's put together a good outline of cross that aims to create that impression. Here is mine.

Point One—Lack of Fit—Exaggerated Currency of Credentials

The order for what follows:

1. Establish the principle and Rules
2. Lock in what the witness claims
3. Show a violation of the Rule

Here is the heading on the top of this section of the outline:

It's wrong for an expert to exaggerate his or her credentials in court (but you've done that).

Establish the principle:

Q: Being up-to-date is important for experts—especially in medicine.

Q: One thing that is important for the jury to evaluate—when comparing experts—is who is more current and up-to-date.

---

2. I set out a sample line of "Dr. Treater is always wrong" questions in chapter 11, "Shooting It Out with a Hired-Gun Witness."

Derive the Rule:

Q: It's wrong for any expert witness to try to make his or her credentials sound more current than they really are.

[Show the Rule on the screen.]

Lock in the claim:

Q: You claimed on direct that you are currently assistant professor at [name] University Medical Center?

Q: You also claim this on your website—it's the *first* thing you say after your training in orthopedics?

[Show slide—website screenshot.]

Violated Rule re [name] University Hospital faculty:

Q: But you're not on the [name] University Hospital faculty?

[Show [name] University directory slide.]

Lay down a foundation for the directory if needed:

Q: Big medical institutions like [name] University Hospital commonly put their faculty on their website. So any patient can look up credentials?

Q: We clicked on the list and here is the download.

[Show the downloaded faculty list.]

Q: You haven't been on [name] University Hospital faculty for many years?

Q: [Name] University Hospital holds out a lot of orthopedic surgeons as being on their faculty?

Q: Do you have anything on you that proves the directory is wrong—like an ID badge that lets you in the door. *Or anything else* that says, "Dr. D. is currently on our faculty, notwithstanding his absence from our directory"?

Q: *When* was the last time you taught residents at [name] University Hospital? Ten years ago?

Q: So no surprise that they would kick you out of the directory of current voluntary faculty?

Q: When you said to the jury on direct exam, "*I am*" an assistant professor, you left out the fact that you have not been in the hospital seeing patients as assistant professor in *many years*?

You're also not current in other important ways—you stopped surgery years ago.

Q: Dr. D., have you exaggerated the currency of your credentials in any other way today?

Q: On direct exam, you told us you'd been an operating orthopedic surgeon for many years?

Q: *But you left out* that you stopped operating at least twenty years ago?

Q: It would have been more accurate if you had said, "I used to" or "I did"?

Q: Ulnar nerve decompression—the kind of surgery my client had—you cannot even pin down when you last did one? Maybe fifteen years ago, maybe twenty—maybe more?

Q: So when you told the jury about all the kinds of surgery you'd done, you did not mean to imply that you were currently a surgeon? You just omitted that?

Q: Nowadays those nerve decompressions are typically done by a specialist? Not a general orthopedist like you?

Show that the board certification is grandfathered.

Q: In the upper left corner of your report, the first thing it says is "American Board of Orthopaedic Surgery"?

[Show a screenshot of the report.]

Q: This is the board that certifies ortho surgeons as being qualified and current in the field?

Q: You mentioned you've been board-certified since 1971?

Q: But you have done *nothing* to be retested in your board certification since 1971?

Q: The American Board of Orthopaedic Surgery says everyone since 1986 has to pass recertification every ten years—to prove currency?

[Show a screenshot of ABOS website.]

[Note: the website proves that an oral exam is required, not just sending in a form every ten years: https://www.abos.org.]

Q: American Board doesn't exempt you from retesting just because you're better—they just have an old-timer's rule?

Q: You don't legally have to take an exam—but have you ever *voluntarily* taken the recertification exam, to *prove* you're still current?

Q: So you agree the fact that you were board-certified in 1971 does not prove that you are current in orthopedic surgery knowledge as of 2015?

Q: If we asked *any* other board-certified orthopedic surgeons who were first certified after 1986, they'd be able to prove their knowledge was current in the last ten years—with this objective certificate?

Summarize the exaggerated currency of credentials.

Q: So, just to put together the currency of your orthopedic credentials:

Q: The most recent outside objective authority for your current qualifications as a board-certified orthopedic surgeon is your certificate dated 1971?

Q: The last time you could claim current practice in an orthopedic operating room dates back at least twenty years?

Q: You have no proof you are currently on the faculty at [name] University Medical Center, contrary to what you said in direct exam?

Point Two—Bias—One-Sided Testimonial Pattern

This witness shows a pattern of testifying for certain firms over and over, and for the defense in general. This shows bias or the appearance of bias.

[Show the rule of objectivity on the screen.]

Q: This is the court's rule about expert witnesses: "Expert witnesses are supposed to be fair and impartial."

[Show the quote from the American Academy of Orthopaedic Surgeons.]

Q: This is a quote from the American Academy of Orthopaedic Surgeons: "I will conduct a thorough, fair, and impartial review of the facts and the medical care provided, not excluding any relevant information." This is from the academy's website: http://www3.aaos.org/member/expwit/statement.cfm.

Rule violation:

Q: Dr. D., you claim to be an independent examiner, but you're actually *dependent* on the law firm representing the defendant here for a very large sum of money every year?

Q: You made $175,000 in one year alone according to the 1099?

Q: You and the defense lawyer have worked together many times over the years?

Q: This lawyer could know, without ever speaking to you, that he could count on you for a favorable opinion for the defense. *Even before* you first laid eyes on the patient?

Q: So it's no surprise that he could *name* you as his sole expert witness in an official court document, filed *six weeks* before you ever saw my client?

Q: Because that's your pattern over and over?

Q: First, they name you as their sole medical witness?

Q: Second, you examine the client?

Q: Third, you report that the injuries are either exaggerated or have nothing to do with the defendant's conduct?

Q: You agree that working *over* and *over* for the same lawyers all the time raises at least the *appearance* of bias by you?

Q: You don't work both sides of the street evenly?

Q: At least *nine times out of ten*, you are in court testifying for the defense?

Q: That's what defense attorneys want—someone who will *reliably* give favorable opinion to them?

Q: The defense attorney gets one shot—no makeovers if the first defense medical exam came out favorable to the plaintiff?

Q: And doesn't that nine-out-of-ten pattern raise the *appearance* of bias by you?

Q: Can you tell me *any plaintiff lawyers* who call on you with the same regularity as defense lawyers to do medical exams on their clients?

Have available his personal billing of all DME work: hold this for an opening if he raises the subject by feigning ignorance of billing.

Point Three—An Objective Doctor Would Not Do This

An objective doctor would not continually contradict treating doctors like this witness does.

Show further violation of the objectivity rule.

Q: This case falls into your usual pattern?

Q: The treating doctor testifies for the plaintiff that this is a genuine injury, caused by the event at issue?

Q: You testify the doctor got it wrong?

Q: That's what you always do?

Q: Whenever you're in court, your unstated theme is, "The treating doctors are wrong"?

Q: The defense never calls you to court when you conclude the plaintiffs' doctors are right?

Q: You never testified that the patient is worse off than his or her own doctors found?

Q: If this happened, then after a defense medical exam, the plaintiffs' counsel would subpoena you to court?

Q: You've certainly never testified in a courtroom where the defense lawyer here was on the other side, and was cross-examining you?

Distinguish his motive versus the treating doctor's motive.

Q: Dr. Treater was hired to treat the patient?

Q: The patient got to Dr. Treater totally independent of any lawyer fingerprints? [We hope.]

Q: Dr. Treater was on trauma call for the emergency room the night my client was hurt?

Q: You have not taken trauma call in many years?

Q: Dr. Treater's goal is to help the patient get better?

Q: Your goal is to be a persuasive witness for the side that hired you?

Q: Because you want to be hired again by the same defense attorneys who hire you over and over?

Q: If you were 50-50, and you had diverse sources of business, you wouldn't care?

Q: Then you could call yourself independent?

Q: But you have a reputation to uphold. You're a 90 percent defense witness?

Q: *Show me* some independent evidence that you are an unbiased, objective witness. *Some fact*—outside your say-so.

So there you have my approach to a one-sided witness like a defense medical examiner.

My number one goal (and number two, and number three) with a witness like this is to replace the halo he is wearing for the direct examination with a sharp set of horns. This has to start with the first question on cross.

The sequence of topics outlined above is not important if you do the entire cross in one piece, because they all go to bias and credibility. I put the lack-of-fit topic first because that goes with a segmented voir dire cross that you can do before the witness has given any opinions at all about your client. I like to put a taint on the witness as quickly as I can, if I have the material. Then I can save the bias points for the substantive part of the cross.

Did you count the number of questions I asked about the medicine of the case, or medicine in general? That's right: zero, none, zip. With a heard-it-all DME expert, such questions, even on "safe" subjects, invite the witness to quibble and leave him in his comfort zone. Worse, they convey the impression to the jury that you think enough of this witness's medical acumen to ask him medical questions. I've said throughout this book that we need to always think of the *coherent* impression we want to create of the witness. If we're looking to show this is an out-of-date doctor with exaggerated credentials, why would we ever feed him medical questions to let him show off his medical knowledge?

If we didn't have a strong lack-of-fit cross, we could possibly venture some medical questions along the lines of "everyone's experience of pain is unique to that individual," but only *after* we've first established the witness's thorough defense-minded bias. Then, if he fences and refuses to make concessions, it's more evidence of his bias, and if he does make concessions, we can say later, "See what even a biased witness is forced to admit."

My questions are probably stronger and sharper than most of us are used to. Bear in mind that this kind of skeptical questioning can become even more effective with a mild, bland delivery. When you get heated in tone, you invite cries of "argumentative" from the other side.

A word to the wise for cut-and-pasters: Do not just copy these questions into your witness notebook for your next trial. You must custom-craft every line of questions. For another DME defense witness, like the one Jim Gilbert faced way back in chapter 3, "Choosing the Weapons Right for You," an ignorance or mistakes approach can prove devastating. Or in another case, where the witness insinuates that the plaintiff is exaggerating or faking, a polarizing-style cross may do well. It all depends on the witness.

Does it take courage to execute a pointed cross like this one? Especially when we don't know all the answers the witness is going to give, and we ask some open-ended questions that carry some risk? Most definitely. And so, as we wind down, a few more words about fear and courage are in order.

THE PARADOX OF COMPETENCE: REALISTIC FEAR

As you near the end of this book, I hope you're excited about trying my approach in your next cross-examination. But I imagine you're also wary and fearful. My approach is all about taking calculated risks, asking questions to which you don't know the answer, holding nothing back, and pressing forward to finish each point. If that scares you, even a bit, that's a good thing! It means you're competent. You don't labor under what social psychologists call the *Dunning-Kruger effect*.[3] That's a term for people too dumb to appreciate their own incompetence, and so they walk around with a sunny, fearless disposition, one that gets them into a lot of trouble because they're also lazy and grandiose. There is a paradox at work here. Bertrand Russell put his finger on the problem when he said,

---

3. Here's one of the original articles on the phenomenon, by Drs. Dunning and Kruger (no coincidence): "Unskilled and unaware of it: how difficulties in recognizing one's own incompetence lead to inflated self-assessments," *Journal of Personality and Social Psychology* 77, no. 6 (Dec. 1999): 1121–34, http://www.ncbi.nlm.nih.gov/pubmed/10626367.

"The fundamental cause of the trouble is that in the modern world, the stupid are cocksure while the intelligent are full of doubt."

THE NECESSITY OF COURAGE

For cross-examiners, the problem is striking the right balance between a necessary self-confidence to take on a formidable witness and the healthy fear that comes from a thorough preparation. Which brings us to the necessity for courage.

What is courage exactly? I like this definition from British writer G. K. Chesterton:

> Courage is almost a contradiction in terms. It means a strong desire to live taking the form of a readiness to die.

To similar effect, Nelson Mandela said this of his years in prison:

> . . . I learned that courage was not the absence of fear, but the triumph over it . . . The brave man is not he who does not feel afraid, but he who conquers that fear.

And finally, Teddy Roosevelt's speech at the Sorbonne in 1910 had these lines that I always thought were spoken for the cross-examiner:

> It is not the critic who counts; not the man who points out how the strong man stumbled or where the doer of deeds could have done them better. The credit belongs to the man who is actually in the arena, whose face is marred by dust and sweat and blood; who strives valiantly; who errs, who comes short again and again . . . who knows great enthusiasms, the great devotions; who spends himself in a worthy cause; who at the best knows in the end the triumph of high achievement, and who at the worst, if he fails, at least fails while daring greatly, so that his place shall never be with those timid souls who neither know victory nor defeat.[4]

---

4. From "Citizenship in a Republic." Read the whole speech here: http://www.theodore-roosevelt.com/trsorbonnespeech.html.

So you've read what the greats have said. The only thing left is to go out and do it! Our clients, who need our very best, will be grateful. And if anyone tells you to forget it, that only the genius cross-examiners can break the commandments the way I have advocated in this book, tell them you don't buy their brand of defeatism. Then prove it, first by practicing with some of our chapter-end exercises here and throughout the book, and then by executing what you've practiced in court.

Exercises

Some final exercises before you lay this book down:

- Think through the lessons and plan how to apply them to your own cross-examinations. That means working up your own detailed cross-examination outlines, with your own case-specific Rules of the Road adapted for each witness. No shortcuts! No last-minute unprepared, "I can wing this one!"

- Practice cross-examination in role-playing sessions with friends and colleagues. Make everyone stick to a chosen role for an extended Q&A, at least ten minutes at a time. Switch sides now and then so you know what it feels like to be on the receiving end. Putting yourself in the witness's shoes will help you realize how the witness may try to deflect your best questions.

- Practice cross-examination in depositions as if you're in a courtroom. That means crisp, tight questions in plain English, as if you're being watched by a jury. That means making your points, locking them down, and moving on. This will give you better transcripts for impeachment should the case go to trial, a better shot at a good settlement in the meantime, and valuable practice about how to ask questions and get answers. One major caveat: Never try to crush a witness in deposition whom the other side can opt not to call at trial. So for experts, for example, you want to lock down in deposition the factual basis of their opinions but not take the next step of showing that they are ignorant or mistaken. Save that for trial.

Appendices

Appendix A

Truisms and Rules

Truisms are folk knowledge that pretty much everyone accepts as true. Those who don't can get into trouble on cross-examination. In chapter 8, "Cross-Examination with Witness Tear-Down Rules," we saw how to use a truism to set up a contradictions cross: *Actions speak louder than words.* In the right case, any applicable truism can make a good Rule to start or end a segment of cross. If the witness agrees, fine; you've established a signpost for this phase of the cross and a point of departure for your questions. If the witness disagrees, the cross can become even more interesting as the witness tries to refute that which seems self-evidently true.

Here are some useful truisms for trial lawyers, with a few suggestions by me about how they could be used. Some can go right into the cross-examination; others can be saved for closing argument comment on the witness. Creative lawyers will find many more opportunities than I have listed.

Note that when the truism uses a good literary device like alliteration, rhyming, or parallel phrases, it becomes more memorable and thus looks more "truthy." Thus, "a fault confessed is half redressed" sounds a lot more profound than "a fault admitted is half made up for" and "woes unite foes" beats "shared adversity brings enemies together." Using memorable truisms is part of the cognitive ease strategy for effective persuasion.

There may be others that apply to your case. Witty and wise sources of truisms, only a few of which I've been able to borrow for this list, include G. K. Chesterton, Albert Einstein, Richard

Feynman, and, of course, Abraham Lincoln and Mark Twain. (But be careful about all the fake Twain and Lincoln quotes swirling around the Internet.) I also recommend checking a website like *1001 Truisms*, http://www.freewebs.com/1001truisms/truisms.htm, or http://www.aphorism4all.com for other possibilities.

Compendium of Handy Truisms for Trial Lawyers

A bird in the hand is worth two in the bush.

A fault confessed is half redressed. (for coaxing an admission of wrong from a reluctant witness)

A fool and his money are soon parted.

A house divided against itself cannot stand. (for conflicting witnesses who should agree)

A job worth doing is worth doing well. (for adverse parties whose conduct is at issue)

A journey of a thousand miles begins with a single step. (to control a witness who doesn't want to give simple answers to simple questions)

A lie, told often enough, becomes the truth.

A picture's worth a thousand words. (for impeaching with visuals)

A wise head makes a closed mouth. (for the witness who wants to run on)

Actions speak louder than words. (for the hypocrite witness)

All that glitters is not gold. (for puncturing an adversary's fancy exhibit)

An apple doesn't fall far from the tree. (for noting family history predicts children's occupations)

An ounce of prevention is worth a pound of cure.

Beggars can't be choosers.

Better safe than sorry.

Better the devil you know than the devil you don't know.

Better to be healthy than wealthy.

Birds of a feather flock together.

Broad is the path, but narrow is the way.

Chance favors the prepared mind.

Common sense is not so common.

Confession is good for the soul. (for a witness on the edge of telling the truth)

Count your blessings.

Cross that bridge when you come to it. (to bring back a witness who wants to get ahead of the cross-examiner's story)

Dead men tell no tales.

Desperate times call for desperate measures. (to suggest to a witness that a contradiction or change of story or inconsistency is a mark of desperation)

Divide and conquer.

Don't beat a dead horse. (for the witness who wants to keep repeating his party line)

Don't believe everything you hear. (to counter hearsay that has spilled into evidence)

Don't bet the rent (ranch) on it.

Don't bite off more than you can chew.

Don't bite the hand that feeds you. (to explain why a high-paid witness makes no concessions)

Don't borrow trouble.

Don't cast caution to the winds.

Don't change horses in midstream.

Don't confuse me with the facts. (for when a witness won't acknowledge the truth of an established fact)

Don't count your chickens before they're hatched.

Don't cry over spilled milk.

Don't cut off your nose to spite your face.

Don't do the crime if you can't do the time.

Don't get caught with your pants down.

Don't give up the ship.

Don't go against the grain.

Don't go off half-cocked.

Don't go off the deep end.

Don't grab the tiger by the tail.

Don't kick someone when they're down.

Don't kill the goose that lays the golden egg.

Don't kill the messenger. (to soften the blow from a pointed question)

Don't knock it 'til you've tried it.

Don't look a gift horse in the mouth.

Don't make a federal case out of it.

Don't make a mountain out of a molehill.

Don't make promises you can't keep.

Don't nitpick.

Don't pour salt on the wound.

Don't put all your eggs in one basket.

Don't put the cart before the horse.

Don't quit your day job.

Don't ride the fence. (for the wishy-washy witness who won't commit)

Don't rob Peter to pay Paul.

Don't rub people the wrong way.

Don't send a boy to do a man's job.

Don't split hairs. (or "hares," as Bugs Bunny pleaded to Elmer Fudd)

Don't start something you can't finish.

Don't sweat the small stuff.

Don't throw out the baby with the bathwater.

Don't throw stones in the well you drink from. (for a witness reluctant to commit to a fact that hurts his side)

Don't toot your own horn.

Every little bit helps.

Everyone has their price. (for the high-priced expert)

Everyone must know their limits. (for the know-it-all witness)

Everything should be made as simple as possible, but not simpler. (Albert Einstein) (for witnesses who want to leave out inconvenient facts that complicate the story)

Expect the unexpected.

Figures don't lie, but liars can figure. (to puncture the fancy statistical argument)

Follow the money.

Fortune favors the brave.

Garbage in—garbage out. (for the witness relying on shaky assumptions)

Go where the money is.

Good fences make good neighbors.

Haste makes waste.

Hindsight is always twenty-twenty.

Honesty is the best policy. (for any witness caught in a lie)

If fifty million people say a foolish thing, it is still a foolish thing. (Anatole France) (for when you need to attack conventional wisdom)

If it ain't broke, don't fix it.

If it sounds too good to be true, it probably is. (for when the witness tells an improbable story)

If it walks like a duck, and quacks like a duck, it's a duck.

If the glove doesn't fit, you must acquit. (Johnnie Cochran)

If the shoe fits, wear it.

If you fail to plan, you plan to fail.

If you find yourself in a hole, the first thing to do is stop digging.

Ignorance of the law is no excuse.

In this world nothing can be said to be certain, except death and taxes. (Ben Franklin's rule) (for the overly certain witness)

Injustice anywhere is a threat to justice everywhere. (M. L. King Jr.)

It don't take a genius to spot a goat in a flock of sheep.

It is better to light one candle than to curse the darkness.

It's better to ask dumb questions, than to make dumb mistakes.

Jack-of-all-trades, master of none.

Judge not, lest ye be judged. (Matthew 7:1)

Just because you can, doesn't mean you should.

Justice is blind.

Keep-it-simple-stupid (or K.I.S.S.).

Less is more.

Let the buyer beware.

Let the chips fall where they may.

Let the facts speak for themselves.

Let your conscience be your guide.

Life can only be understood backwards; but it must be lived forwards. (Kierkegaard) (to combat hindsight certainty)

Little strokes will tumble great oaks.

Look before you leap.

Measure twice, cut once. (a good carpenter's rule that applies to surgeons)

Money is a good servant, but a bad master. (for a pricey witness)

Monkey see, monkey do. (for when witnesses on one side are more in lockstep than they should be)

Necessity is the mother of invention.

Never ask a barber if you need a haircut.

Never let the facts get in the way of a carefully thought out bad decision.

Never let the facts get in the way of a good story. (for pointing out all the facts inconsistent with the witness's story)

Never put off until tomorrow what you can do today.

No man is an island.

No one can serve two masters. (for the witness with a conflict of interest)

Nothing ventured, nothing gained.

Numbers don't lie.

Oh what a tangled web we weave, when first we practice to deceive. (Sir Walter Scott, for the lying witness)

Old and smart beats young and fast every time.

Once bitten, twice shy.

Opportunity always knocks at the least opportune moment.

Opportunity knocks but once.

Out of sight, out of mind.

Out of the frying pan, into the fire.

Out of the mouths of babes . . .

People only want the truth when the truth is convenient.

Physician, heal thyself.

Pick your battles carefully.

Power tends to corrupt, and absolute power corrupts absolutely. (John Dalberg-Acton)

Practice makes perfect.

Practice what you preach. (for the hypocrite witness)

Pride goeth before a fall. (for an arrogant witness)

Proverbs are short sayings drawn from long experience.

Question assumptions. (for the witness with lots of "ifs")

Revenge is a dish best served cold. (for the cross-examiner's self-reflection)

Safety first.

Speed kills.

Stop, look, and listen.

Test, don't guess.

That's the pot calling the kettle black.

The best defense is a good offense.

The best things in life aren't things.

The buck stops here.

The customer is always right.

The devil's in the details. (for when the witness doesn't know stuff and has a simplistic story)

The early bird gets the worm.

The ends don't justify the means.

The grass is always greener on the other side of the fence.

The hand is quicker than the eye.

The law, in its majestic equality, forbids rich and poor alike from sleeping under bridges, begging in the streets, and stealing bread. (Anatole France)

The leopard can't change his spots.

The only stupid question is the one that is not asked.

The operation was a success, but the patient died.

The perfect is the enemy of the good.

The right tool for the right job.

The road to hell is paved with good intentions.

The squeaky wheel gets the grease.

The truth hurts. (for the reluctant witness)

There are lies, damn lies, and then there's statistics.

There are old pilots and bold pilots, but no old, bold pilots.

There is nothing so small it can't be blown out of proportion.

There is nothing to fear, but fear itself.

There's none so blind as those who will not see.

Those who ignore the lessons of history are doomed to repeat them.

To a hammer, everything looks like a nail.

To thine own self be true.

To whom much is given, much is required.

Too many chiefs and not enough Indians.

Too many cooks spoil the broth.

Two wrongs don't make a right.

United we stand, divided we fall.

Virtue is its own reward.

We must all hang together or surely we will all hang separately. (Benjamin Franklin)

What doesn't kill me only makes me stronger. (Nietzsche and Kanye West)

Whatever can go wrong, will go wrong (aka Murphy's Law).

What's sauce for the goose is sauce for the gander. (for confronting double-standard behavior)

When in doubt, check it out. (to show why testing is usually a good idea rather than relying on one's educated guess)

When life gives you lemons, make lemonade.

When the going gets tough, the tough get going.

When the train of history hits a curve, the intellectuals fall off. (Karl Marx) (for how facts tend to upset expert predictions)

When you have eliminated all which is impossible, whatever remains, no matter how improbable, must be the truth. (Sherlock Holmes, as quoted by his creator, Arthur Conan Doyle)

When you play with fire, you get burned.

Where there's a will, there's a way.

While the cat's away, the mice will play.

Whom the Gods would destroy, they first make mad.

Woes unite foes.

Worst first. (differential diagnosis priority)

You are known by the company you keep.

You can catch more flies or bears with honey than with vinegar.

You can fool *some* of the people all of the time, and *all* of the people some of the time, but you can't fool *all* of the people *all* of the time!

You can lead a horse to water, but you can't make him drink.

You learn something new every day.

You snooze, you lose.

You've got to play the hand you're dealt.

Appendix B

WRITING BETTER RULES FOR CROSS-EXAMINATION

In writing Rules to put to witnesses on cross-examination, the main rule is to be absolutely clear, and to be true to what you are trying to say. You want to avoid giving the witness any excuse to dodge your smooth stone by claiming not to understand what you mean. You want to strive with each sentence and each word to maximize clarity and minimize ambiguity. Here, I offer some simple writing tips that work for any kind of lawyer work product, and especially for writing Rules for cross-examination.

1. Keep each sentence (or question) to a single thought. As soon as your sentence drones on past the simple subject-verb-object, you create escape hatches for the witness. The witness or opposing counsel says, "Which part of the question do you want answered?" You back and fill, and you lose control. How do you keep sentences to a single thought?

    a. Watch for each "and" and every "or." Those usually signal multiple thoughts.

    b. Check the need for a comma or semicolon. They often signal the same problem.

    c. Read the sentence aloud. If you have to take a breath in the middle of the sentence, you're in trouble. Even in writing meant to be read silently and not spoken aloud, the human eye has a limit of around twenty words before it wants to see a period. (And that sentence nudged over the twenty mark by a bit.)

Example from a premises liability case:

Before:

Q: Do you agree it's a bad idea to set up a building garage exit with a double blind spot where neither the driver nor the pedestrian can see each other until a split second before their paths cross?

After:

Q: Did you set up this building garage exit so neither the driver nor the pedestrian can see each other until a split second before their paths cross?

Q: Would that be called a double blind spot?

Q: Do you agree it's a bad idea to set up a building garage exit with a double blind spot?

2. Keep the target actor in the spotlight, usually as the subject of the sentence. In cross-examination, the spotlight should ordinarily shine on either the witness or the adverse party. A simple way to do that is to put the target into the subject of the sentence. For a should or must type Rule of the Road, that means, for example: *"An expert witness should be fair and impartial."* Not: *"It is important to be fair and impartial."* See how the "it is" construct hides the actor and creates ambiguity? Who is "it"?

3. Avoid starting with a vague word like "there" or "it." *"There is a need to be fair and impartial"* is like the "it is" problem above. When you start a sentence with "there is" or "it is," you start down the shadowed road of hidden meaning. Now, granted, you can bring the sentence back to the land of clarity with a few more sentences, but why start off vaguely when you don't have to?

Example: Our rewritten question from number 1 above can be improved even more with this edit:

Do you agree it's ~~a bad idea to~~ *an architect should not* design a building garage exit with a double blind spot?

4. Prefer the active voice to the passive. Active voice adds clarity and energy to your sentences. And it avoids hiding the actor. Politicians and others who want to duck responsibility love the passive voice; "bombs were dropped," "money was spent," and "mistakes were made." By whom? Zombies, I guess. An easy way to hunt down passive sentences is to search for any "to be" verbs—is, was, are, were. These usually signal passive sentences. Root them out, substitute active verbs, and you will see a big difference.

Example: Here's a triple passive effort at a Rule of the Road:

- For an employee who is accused of misconduct to be fired without being given a chance to be heard is wrong.

Rewrite:

- Before firing any employee for alleged misconduct, the employer must hear the employee's side.

5. Substitute specifics for generalities. I see a lot of liability rules written by plaintiff lawyers that give me no clue what the case is really about, because the lawyer wrote them at a high level of generality. A recent example: *Doctors must perform tests to diagnose problems to protect patients from preventable harm.* It turned out the case concerned a delayed diagnosis of a surgical injury to the small intestine from "blind" insertion of a trochar into the patient's abdomen. My rewrite:

- A surgeon must do the right tests to figure out if he's caused an injury.

6. Avoid "plaintiff" and "defendant." Use their real names. It's a lot easier for the judge and jury to keep track of whom you're talking about that way.

7. Avoid pronouns, especially when you use more than one in a sentence. Pronouns are really trouble whenever you are talking about more than one person, because pronouns create a question about whom exactly you mean. It's especially bad when you use something like "he" or "him" more than once in a sentence, because often you are referring to more than one person. Why not use the actual name or the title or position of the actor? (See tip number 2 about keeping your actor in the spotlight.)

8. Use plain words. Avoid jargon, acronyms, and any other words that need translation into lay English. If you absolutely must use one, be sure to put the translation nearby. We have to be vigilant, because it's easy to let technical jargon creep into our questions. I found this example in a treatise purporting to show a model expert cross.

   Q: Intracranial aneurysm can give rise to a headache?

   That question passes the "short question" test but badly flunks the "plain words" test. An easy rewrite:

   Q: When a blood vessel inside your head bursts, it hurts?

   Related tip: Favor the Anglo-Saxon version of a word over the Latin version. Anglo-Saxon words are plainer, shorter, better. That's why we say "inside your head" instead of "intracranial" and "heart" instead of "cardiac." It's also why we start (instead of commence), we ask (not inquire), we walk (not ambulate), we chew (not masticate), and we build (not construct). Our foes (not adversaries) sometimes lie (not prevaricate) and buy (not purchase) witnesses. Or so they say.

9. Be careful with clichés. If I've said this once, I've said it a thousand times; I'm not going to beat around the bush here; I'll just give it to you as straight as an arrow, smooth as silk, slow as molasses, and—well, you get the idea. Clichés often say little, except to make you sound folksy and homespun. Other times clichés work well to communicate basic truths of life that everyone believes: "an accident waiting to happen,"

"hindsight is twenty-twenty," or the witness "dug his own grave." When you find yourself resorting to old chestnuts like these, just be careful that you're really communicating an idea, not just tossing around well-worn strings of words because you like the familiar ring.

10. Use truisms that communicate folk wisdom. See Appendix A on truisms and rules. Truisms differ from clichés in that truisms, the good ones anyway, have real content to deliver.

11. Advanced tip: Judiciously use literary devices that make your words sing. Can you make it rhyme? (Just spend the time . . .) Work with alliteration. Try parallel phrases. All these will make your words memorable and true. Start with the list of truisms in Appendix A, with ones like, "You snooze, you lose," "If you fail to plan, you plan to fail," or "Test, don't guess." Then adapt them to your case. People will notice.

Acknowledgments

Top lawyers generously showered me with more transcripts of worthy cross-examinations than I could use. Here are those who offered advice, comments, and transcripts, and sometimes all of the above:

Jan Baisch	Mark Mandell
Ray Chester	Randi McGinn
Charles Daniels	Denis Mitchell
Tom Demetrio	Tom Moore
Dennis Donnelly	Liz Mulvey
Jim Fitzgerald	Peter Perlman
Gary Fox	Joe Power
Rick Friedman	Joe Quinn
Jim Gilbert	Dan Rottier
Larry Grassini	Ben Rubinowitz
Jason Itkin	Tony Russell
Mike Kelly	Chris Searcy
Randy Kinnard	Shanin Specter
Tom Kline	Tyler Thompson
Jim Lees	David Wenner
Jim Leventhal	Robyn Wishart
Paul Luvera	Steve Yerrid

Robyn Wishart and David Wenner provided insightful advice, especially on the science of behavior and decision-making. My associate Dan Scialpi was particularly helpful in commenting on various chapters.

Research aid came from Gabriel Lazarus, Ed Caughlan, and Wendy Cai. Wendy especially did valuable work reading transcripts and pointing me to things that hit her eye.

Scott Suddarth generously shared his investigative techniques for finding secrets of witnesses and jury panel members.

Special thanks to Tina Ricks, my editor at Trial Guides, who helped shape, prune, and polish the original ungainly manuscript.

Sources

I tried to credit most sources in footnotes at the appropriate spots throughout the book. Here are some others.

An author who steered me to some of the fascinating modern research on the brain and behavior was Robert Sapolsky, the Stanford neurobiologist, baboon researcher, and funny guy. For a free introduction to his wit and wisdom, I recommend his Stanford "class day" commencement speech, "The Uniqueness of Humans," which as a primate researcher he could retitle as the *non*-uniqueness of humans. You can find it at https://youtu.be/hrCVu25wQ5s.

Sapolsky has three very entertaining audio courses on frontiers of brain and behavior science, stress and the body, and the neurological origins of behavior, which you can find at the Great Courses, http://www.thegreatcourses.com/tgc/professors/professor_detail.aspx?pid=124.

Here are more books I found helpful:

Daniel Kahneman, *Thinking, Fast and Slow* (Farrar, Straus & Giroux, 2011).

James L. McElhaney, *McElhaney's Trial Notebook* (ABA Press, 2005).

Ronald H. Clark, George R. Dekle Sr., and William S. Bailey, *Cross-Examination Handbook: Persuasion, Strategies, and Techniques* (Wolters Kluwer, 2011).

Larry S. Pozner and Roger J. Dodd, *Cross Examination: Science and Techniques*, 2d ed. (LexisNexis, 2004).

Index

A

Accurint/IRB database 266
adverse witnesses
    agreement cross 50, 77
    calling 297–301
    confessing fault 301–316
    money/one-sided cross
        211–230
    polarizing technique 113–117,
        231–242
agreement cross
    about 49–51, 77
    bias cross and 160
    case-building and 361–362
    contradictions cross and
        164–165
    lack of fit cross and 159
alphabetical topic index 128
American Academy of Orthopedic
    Surgeons 156
analytical thinking. *See* weapons for
    cross-examination
Andrews, William C., Jr. 225
answers to questions
    echoing technique 248
    as evidence 29
    knowing 30–33
    listening to 16, 33–35, 346–348
Armstrong, People v. 41
The Art of Cross-Examination
    (Wellman) 18
asked-and-answered objection
    290–291
assessing witness's character 92,
    94–95
authoritative literature. *See* Federal
    Rules of Evidence
Axelrod, Robert 329

B

Bailey, F. Lee 318, 346–348
Baisch, Jan 93–94, 96–103
Ball, David 156
bankruptcy records 263–264
Banner, John 344
Bartimus, Jim 186
behavior during cross-examination
    balancing act for 15–17
    for successful cross-examiner
        17–18
    whole-body techniques
        348–349
best evidence 289
betrayal mode (prisoner's dilemma)
    327–332
bias cross
    about 52–53, 62–63
    agreement cross and 160
    blending cross-examination
        types 165
    brushback pitch example 82
    checklist for areas to cover in
        depositions 270
    checklist hunting for the best
        topics 357
    contradictions cross and
        191–196
    creating 365–367
    DME example 373–377
    goals for 150–153
    money cross and 121, 191,
        211–213, 218–229
    one-sided cross and 121,
        211–218
    organizing with scoring system
        132–135
    polarizing technique and
        231–242
Blackbookonline.info website 266
Black, Roy 25–26, 37–38
body language 348–349
Boies, David 166–168
Bonaparte, Napoleon 297
Brady, William J. 94–95, 97–103

brainstorming questions 136–140
brevity in cross-examination
  24–26
brushback pitch (baseball) 82
Bryant v. Cal Dive International Inc.
  31–33, 76–77, 161–163
building the case. *See* case-building
Burn the Fat, Feed the Muscle
  (Venuto) 19

C

Cal Dive International Inc., Bryant v.
  31–33, 76–77, 161–163
Carcamo, Jose 207–210
Carmichael, Kumho Tire Co. v. 155
Carroll, Erp v. 295
case-building
  about 67
  agreement cross and 361–362
  contradiction cross and 153
  core strategies in 49–51
  developing Rules of the Road
    67–88
  goal for prior inconsistent
    statements 172–173
  ignorance or mistakes cross and
    160–164
  organizing for the case
    125–127
  organizing for the witness
    127–142
  using treatises in 107–118
  witness self-interest and
    89–106
Catholic Health Initiatives,
  Gasteazoro v. 206
Caughlan, Ed 263
Certification Matters website 265
chapter method of cross-
  examination 137
character assessment (witnesses) 92,
  94–95
checklists
  for areas to cover in depositions
    268–273
  constructing cross of DME
    360–362
  for hunting for the best topics
    356–358
  of items to subpoena 273–274
  for polarizing attacks 239–240
  of reliability facts for prior
    statements 179
  for techniques to pull it off
    358–360
Chesterton, Gilbert K. 317, 378
Christmas, James 82–87, 215–217
civil lawsuits 68, 74–75
Classmates.com website 267
Clausewitz, Carl von 141
clear rules 72–74
closing argument
  Rule of Evidence and 110
  saving ultimate point for
    41–45
Coburn v. Stevinson Chevrolet West
  Inc. 59
cognitive modes 56
common ground 330
completeness, rule of 131, 279–282
contradiction memo 129
contradictions cross
  about 53–54
  agreement cross and 164–165
  bias cross and 191–196
  blending cross-examination
    types 166
  checklist hunting for the best
    topics 357
  creating 367–369
  fixing 171–198
  goals for 153–158
  organizing for the witness
    157–158
  organizing with scoring system
    132–135
  organizing witness statements
    129
  professional norms and
    155–157
cooperation mode (prisoner's
  dilemma) 327–332
corporation searches 264
courage, necessity of 378–379

credibility of witnesses. *See* tear-down strategies for witnesses
Crime Smasher website 265–266
cross-examination
    better way 2–3
    case-building with. *See* case-building
    old way 1–2
    planning for 123–143
    ten truths about 3–4
    witness-tear-down. *See* tear-down strategies for witnesses
Cross-Examination: Science and Techniques (Pozner and Dodd) 137
cross-examiners
    choosing right weapons 47–64
    evidence rules to know 279–296
    freeing from ten commandments 23–46
    fundamental attribution and 244–246
    laying the mental foundation 11–22
Cuban missile crisis 329
Cusimano, Greg 103

D
dabbling (technique issue) 320, 334–335
damages, fair remedy for 74–75
dangling (technique issue) 318–319, 322–325
Daubert motion 155
David versus Goliath 47–49
Dawn Renae Diaz v. Sugar Transport of the Northwest, Inc., et al. 207–210
declarative statements 28
defense medical examiners (DMEs)
    constructing cross of 360–362, 369–377
    creating witness-tear-down cross 364–377
    polarizing technique 241
Department of Education 264–265

depositions
    checklist for areas to cover in 268–273
    checklist of reliability facts for prior statements 179
    digital text clips of 130
    don't-ask-if-you-don't-know-answers 31
    evidence rules and 294–295
    expert witnesses and 104
    video clips of 131
Diaz, Dawn 207–210
digital text clips 130
discovery, asking questions in 31
divorce records 264
DMEs (defense medical examiners)
    constructing cross of 360–362, 369–377
    creating witness-tear-down cross 364–377
    polarizing technique 241
doctor-patient relationship 78–81
documents, control runaway witnesses with
    runaway witnesses 343–344
document-speaks-for-itself objection 288–289, 344
Dodd, Roger J. 137
Donathan, Bette and Ben 323–325
Donathan v. The Orthopaedic & Sports Medicine Clinic 287, 324, 334
Donnelly, Dennis 339
Doyen, Michael 41
Dropbox service 132
Dru Sjodin National Sex Offender Public Website 266
Dunning-Kruger effect 377

E
Easter Sunday cross 135, 322–325
echoing technique 248
education institution databases 264–265
Eisenhower, Dwight D. 145
emotion-laden memories 14, 35
Engineers Guide USA 265

Epperly v. Perez 34, 113, 302–316, 346
Erp v. Carroll 295
evasive witnesses 35
evidence
    best evidence 289
    document-speaks-for-itself objection 288–289
    extrinsic evidence rule 279, 282–284
    leading the witness and 295–296
    out-of-court statements 284–287
    prior inconsistent statements as 292–295
    refreshed-recollection documents 289–290
    rule of completeness 131, 279–282
    witnesses' answers as 29
The Evolution of Cooperation (Axelrod) 329
expert witnesses
    depositions and 104
    juror perceptions of 27, 153, 228–230
    mining for dirt 261–276
    self-destructing 57–60
    tear-down strategies for. *See* tear-down strategies for witnesses
    turning 93–94
extrinsic evidence rule 279, 282–284
eye contact 349

F
Facebook website 267
facts
    brand-new facts 185–190
    checklist of reliability facts for prior statements 176–179
    eliciting 29–30, 32, 100
    expert witness responsibility 57
    exposing ignorant witness 199–200, 205
    facts matter premise 201–202
    organizing for the witness 136–137
    scoring system identifying 135
Farrage, James 78–80
Farrell, Daniel 186
fast cognitive mode 56
fear of cross-examination
    about 12
    realistic fear and 377–378
    technical jargon and 27
Federal Rules of Civil Procedure
    Rule 26(a) 182
    Rule 26(e)(1) 183
    Rule 30(b)(6) 295
    Rule 31(a)(4) 295
    Rule 32(a)(3) 294
    Rule 32(a)(6) 281
    Rule 43(b) 296
Federal Rules of Evidence. *See also* evidence
    about 107–110
    Friedman example 113–117
    Leventhal example 111–113
    Rule 106 281
    Rule 402 284
    Rule 403 284, 288, 290
    Rule 608(b) 282–284
    Rule 609 282–283
    Rule 611(b) 300
    Rule 611(c) 296
    Rule 612 182, 290
    Rule 705 284, 286
    Rule 801(c) 109
    Rule 801(d) 292–294
    Rule 801(d)(2) 293–294
    Rule 803(6) 293
    Rule 803(18) 109, 110
    Rule 1002 289
Feynman, Richard P. 243
fight-or-flight response 14
finger shaking 349
forbidden question 175, 179–181
Fox, Gary 191–196, 219–223

Friedman, Rick
    authoritative literature example 108, 113–117
    bias cross example 151–153
    developing case-building Rules 67
    polarizing technique 113–117, 231–242
    on principles to rules 70
Fuhrman, Mark 318, 346–348
fundamental attribution
    about 149, 243–244
    cross-examiners and 244–246
    mining for dirt 261–276
    power of public records and 246–259

G

game theory 327–334
garbage in, garbage out 97
Gasteazoro v. Catholic Health Initiatives 206
GEICO insurance company 227
GenWed website 264
Gilbert, Jim 57–59, 150, 202
goals
    how-to-succeed list for 19–21
    identifying for cross-examination 136–137
Google Scholar search engine 267
Grassini, Larry 207, 295

H

Harrison's Principles of Medicine 111
hastening (technique issue) 319, 325–326
Hay, Harry 167
head shaking 349
Healthsouth Corporation, Wade v. 80
hearsay 109, 292–294
Hill, Napoleon 21
Hogan's Heroes (TV show) 344
Holmes, Oliver Wendell 12
Hotel St. Francis, LLC, Sherman v. 149
hot quotes document 129–130
how questions 178
Huxley, Aldous 173

I

ignorance or mistakes cross
    about 52, 62, 199–200
    blending cross-examination types 165
    case-building and 160–164
    checklist hunting for the best topics 357
    corporate defendant example 207–210
    creating 364–365
    deciding which to chase 200–202
    expert witness example 202–206
    goals for 149–150
    lack of fit cross and 166–169
    organizing with scoring system 132–135
impeaching witnesses
    about 171
    with own words 30
    with prior inconsistent statements 169, 171–198
inarguable rules 72–74
index, alphabetical topic 128
informed consent 82
International Academy of Life Care Planners 74
intuitive impressions 56
Iran-Contra affair 105–106
Itkin, Jason
    case-building and 75–77, 160–164
    don't-ask-if-you-don't-know-the-answer and 31–33
    ignorance cross and 160–164, 202

J

judges
    on asked-and-answered objection 290–291
    on authoritative literature 109–110
    difficult witnesses and 220, 349

on document-speaks-for-itself
    objection 288–289
giving preliminary instructions
    28–29
on leading the witness
    295–296
perception of control 13
prolonged silence and 124
on refreshing recollection 290
rule of completeness and 281
jurors
    all-leading questions and 29
    creating impressions with
        55–56
    impact of visual displays on
        131
    misunderstanding informed
        consent 73
    objective authority and 108
    perceptions of control 13–14
    perceptions of expert witnesses
        27, 153, 228–230
    prolonged silence and 124
    stress levels of 14–17
    technical jargon and 27, 229
    tolerance for inconsistencies 157

K
Kahneman, Daniel 56, 325
Kelly, Mike 16, 148
Kennedy, John F. 329
Kinnard, Randy
    adverse witnesses and 319
    case-building and 75–78, 342
    Easter Sunday cross 135,
        322–325
    out-of-court statements and
        285–287
    patient's pain complaints
        333–334
*Kirkeminde v. Midwest Division-
    OPRMC, LLC* 186
Kumho Tire Co. v. Carmichael 155

L
lack of fit cross
    about 51–52

agreement cross and 159
blending cross-examination
    types 166
checklist for areas to cover in
    depositions 269–271
checklist hunting for the best
    topics 357
creating 363–364
DME example 369–372
fundamental attribution and
    149, 243–260
goals for 147–149
ignorance or mistakes cross and
    166–169
mining for dirt 261–276
organizing with scoring system
    132–135
sample chapter/page outline
    138–140
Lance, Kelly 149
leading questions 28–30
leading the witness 295–296
learned treatises. *See* Federal Rules of
    Evidence
Lees, Jim 245–259
Leventhal, Jim
    adverse witnesses and 319
    authoritative literature example
        108, 111–113
    controlling witness with pacing
        345–346
    defendant confessing fault
        301–316
    ignorance cross 201–206, 210
    listening to witness's answers
        example 34
    standard of care language and
        72
liability rules in cases 68–69,
    77–87
Liman, Arthur 105–106
Lincoln, Abraham 41
LinkedIn.com website 267
listening to answers 16, 33–35,
    346–348
Luvera, Paul 55
lying witnesses 16, 189–190

M
Makena Sales Co., Inc., Row v. 259
Malone, Patrick
 bias and mistakes cross 62–63
 case-building 82–87
 one-sidedness cross 215–217
marriage licenses 264
Martin, Stewart v. 152
Mattachine Society 167
McGaugh, James 14
McGinn, Randi 164
memories, emotion-laden 14, 35
Memory & Emotion (McGaugh) 14
mental foundation (cross-examiners)
 characteristics of successful
  cross-examiner 17–18
 importance of 11–12
 mental training 19–21
 positive thinking 21–22
 rules for balancing act 15–17
 stress and self-control 13–15
Midwest Division-OPRMC, LLC, Kirkeminde v. 186
Miller, Henry 107
Millhouse, Pullen v. 102
mining for dirt
 about 261–262
 checklist for areas to cover in depositions 268–273
 independent research 262–263
 sources of information 263–268
mistakes or ignorance (witnesses). *See* ignorance or mistakes cross
Mobil Oil Corporation 25
MONCO Assocs., Ltd., Patricia Rose v. 227, 326
money cross
 about 121, 211–213
 Fox example 191
 improving 218–224
 stretching money point 224–229
Morris, Errol 89
Moynihan, Daniel Patrick 199
muscle memory 137
My Cousin Vinny (film) 38, 42–45

MyLife.com website 267
MySpace website 267

N
Napoleon Bonaparte 297
narrow questions 29, 36, 38
New England Journal of Medicine 111
newspaper archives 267
Nimaroff v. Overlook Hospital 339
Nissan, Starks v. 333
Nizer, Louis 337
Noble, Elaine 168
no-explain rule 37–38
no-repeat rule 36
North, Oliver 105–106
nuclear option (body language) 349
NurSys website 265

O
O. J. Simpson murder trial 346–348
one-sided cross 121, 211–218, 373–377
opensecrets.org website 267
organizing for the witness
 adjusting plans 141–142
 analyzing and sorting statements 127–131
 brainstorming questions 136–140
 compiling materials 131–132
 contradictions cross 157–158
 scoring system 132–135
The Orthopaedic & Sports Medicine Clinic, Donathan v. 287, 324, 334
out-of-court statements 284–287
Overlook Hospital, Nimaroff v. 339

P
PACER (Public Access to Court Electronic Records) 263, 267
pacing, controlling runaway witnesses with 344–346
Patricia Rose v. MONCO Assocs., Ltd. 227, 326
Peale, Norman Vincent 22
PeekYou website 267

People v. Armstrong 41
Perez, Epperly v. 34, 113, 302–316, 346
Perlman, Peter 332
Perry v. Schwarzenegger 166
Plancher v. University of Central Florida Board of Trustees 60
planning for cross-examination
    adjusting plans 141–142
    importance of 123–125
    organizing for the case 125–127
    organizing for the witness 127–142
polarizing technique 113–117, 231–242
Polarizing the Case (Friedman) 113
positive thinking 21–22
poster boards 125–126, 130, 343
Pozner, Larry S. 137
primacy/recency strategy 238–239
principles
    identifying 93
    moving to rules from 70–72, 97
Principles of War (Clausewitz) 141
prior inconsistent statements
    asking forbidden question 175, 179–181
    brand-new facts and 185–188
    case-building goal for 172–173
    case study 191–196
    checklist of reliability facts for 176–179
    closing escape routes 181–190
    as evidence 292–295
    executing impeachment for 174–181
    favorite excuses 181–185
    getting past nitpicking 173–174
    impeachments failing for 171–172
    lying witnesses and 189–190
    writing setups for 169, 176
prisoner's dilemma 327–332
private investigators 266
problems and solutions
    about 277–278
    calling the adverse party 297–316
    controlling runaway witness 337–352
    evidence rules 279–296
    technique problems and cures 317–336
professional board certifications 265
Professional Park Pediatrics, Slayton v. 196, 222
proportional versus brief 26
Public Access to Court Electronic Records (PACER) 263, 267
publication versus statement 108–109
public records 246–259, 266
Pullen v. Millhouse 102

Q

quarreling with witnesses
    cross example 86
    technique problems and cures 319–320, 327–334
    ten commandments on 35
questions
    asking one too many 38–41
    authoritative literature 111–117
    brainstorming 136–140
    checklist of reliability for prior statements 176–179
    controlling with runaway witnesses 338–339
    don't-ask-if-you-don't-know-answers 30–33, 175, 179–181
    leading 28–30
    narrow 29, 36, 38
    for polarizing technique 240–241
    repeating 339–341
    reversing 341–342
    short 27–30
quibbling (technique issue) 319–320, 327–334

R

Records Room website 267
refreshed-recollection documents 289–290
repeating questions 339–341
researching witnesses. *See* mining for dirt
reset button 16
reversing questions 341–342
risk management
    don't-ask-if-you-don't-know-answers 31
    embracing risk in measured doses 16
    stress and self-control in 13–15
Robbins, Tony 22
Roberts, Simpson v. 63, 87, 216
Roosevelt, Teddy 378
Row v. Makena Sales Co., Inc. 259
Rules of the Road
    about 4–5, 68–70
    core strategies for cross-examination and 49–55
    developing case-building rules 67–88
    identifying 93, 95–96
    witness-tear-down 145–170
    writing better rules 395–399
runaway witnesses
    about 337–338
    controlling by closing escape doors 346–348
    controlling by listening to 346–348
    controlling by sidestepping the bait 348
    controlling documents 343–344
    controlling the question 338–339
    controlling with agreement 342–343
    controlling with pacing 344–346
    controlling with your body 348–349
    controlling yourself 338
    not recommended control tips 349–350
    repeating questions 339–341
    reversing questions 341–342
Ruskin, John 39
Russell, Bertrand 377–378
Russell, Tony 224–227, 326

S

Sanction (program) 130
SCC (State Corporation Commissions) 264
Schultz, Sergeant 344
Schwarzenegger, Perry v. 166
scoring system 132–135
self-control
    about 13–15
    achieving better 15–17
    perception of 13–14
    quarreling with witness and 35
self-interest (witnesses)
    about 89
    cross-examination example 97–102
    finding core weakness 102–104
    game theory on 330–331
    key points of 90–91
    looking out for number one 90–91
    sizing up witnesses 105–106
    studying 361
    three-step analysis 92–96
    turning an expert witness 93–94
sequencing strategies for cross-examination 61
sex offenders 266
Shaw, George Bernard 23
Sherman v. Hotel St. Francis, LLC 149
short questions 27
Simon, David 211
Simpson v. Roberts 63, 87, 216
Sinclair, Upton 227
sizing up witnesses 105–106
Skip Smasher database service 265
Slayton, Julie 193
Slayton, Levi 192–196

Slayton v. Professional Park Pediatrics
   196, 222
slow cognitive mode 56
Spear, Allan 167–168
speed in cross-examination
   importance of 123–125
   organizing for the case
      125–127
   organizing for the witness
      127–142
sponsors, witnesses and 50, 104
standard of care language 72, 81, 286
Starks v. Nissan 333
State Corporation Commissions
   (SCC) 264
statements, out-of-court 284–287
statement versus publication
   108–109
Steuer, Max 36
*Stevinson Chevrolet West Inc.,
   Coburn v.* 59
Stewart v. Martin 152
stop signal 349
strategies for cross-examination.
   See tear-down strategies
   for witnesses; weapons for
   cross-examination
stress
      about 13–15
      modulating 15–17
stretching technique 224–229,
   325–326, 346
subpoena, checklist of items to
   273–274
Suddarth, Scott 263–267
*Sugar Transport of the Northwest,
   Inc., et al., Dawn Renae Diaz v.*
   207–210
summary and analysis (key topics)
   129
Sun Tzu 11, 123, 231

T
tear-down strategies for witnesses
   about 67, 145–147
   agreement cross. *See* agreement
      cross

bias cross. *See* bias cross
contradictions cross.
   See contradictions cross
creating 362–369
ignorance or mistakes cross.
   See ignorance or mistakes
   cross
lack of fit cross. *See* lack of fit
   cross
mining for dirt 261–276
money cross. *See* money cross
one-sided cross. *See* one-sided
   cross
planning for cross-examination
   123–143
polarizing technique 113–117,
   231–242
technique problems and cures
   about 317
   categories of issues 318–320
   curing the ailments 320–335
ten commandments of
   cross-examination
   about 23–24
   brevity in 24–26
   don't-ask-if-you-don't-know
      30–33, 175, 179–181
   leading questions 28–30
   listening to witness's answers
      33–35, 346–348
   never ask one question too
      many 38–41
   no-explain rule 37–38
   no-repeat rule 36
   plain words 27–30
   quarreling with witness 35
   rewritten list 45
   saving ultimate point for closing
      41–45
   short questions 27–30
text clips 130
Think and Grow Rich (Hill) 22
Thinking, Fast and Slow (Kahneman)
   56, 325
timeouts 17
tit-for-tat strategy 328–329
topic index 128

Index   415

traffic tickets 263
treatises. *See* Federal Rules of Evidence
Trial Director (program) 130
Triangle Shirtwaist Factory case 36
Trotsky, Leon 67
truisms for trial lawyers 383–393
Twain, Mark 69
Twitter website 267

U

University of Central Florida Board of Trustees, Plancher v. 60

V

Venuto, Tom 19
video clips 130–131
visual displays
    digital text clips 130
    poster boards 125–126, 130, 343
    video clips 130–131

W

Wade v. Healthsouth Corporation 80
Walker, Vaughn 166
wandering (technique issue) 318, 321–322
Washington Post 25
weapons for cross-examination
    about 47
    blending 61–63
    core strategies 49–54
    creating impressions with jurors 49–50, 55–56
    David versus Goliath 47–49
    knowing when to stop 55
    launching 54–55
    planning 123–143
    self-destructing witnesses 57–60
    sequencing 61
    using witnesses to set up rule or norm 60–61
Wellman, Francis 18, 36
Wenner, David 103–104
what questions 177

when questions 177
where questions 178
Whistler, James (artist) 39–40
Whitman, Walt 171
whole-body techniques 348–349
who questions 177
why questions
    about 178
    asking repeatedly 301
    risks with 112, 255
    setting up cross with 193
witnesses
    adverse 50, 77, 113–117, 211–230, 297–316
    analyzing statements of 127–131
    answers as evidence 29
    controlling 29, 337–352
    evasive 35
    expert. *See* expert witnesses
    finding core weakness 102–104
    impeaching 30, 169, 171–198
    leading 295–296
    listening to answers of 16, 33–35, 346–348
    lying 16, 189–190
    mining for dirt 261–276
    no-explain rule 37–38
    no-repeat rule 36
    quarreling with 35, 86, 319–320, 327–334
    researching. *See* mining for dirt
    runaway 337–352
    self-destructing 57–60
    self-interest. *See* self-interest (witnesses)
    sizing up 105–106
    sponsors and 50, 104
    tear-down strategies for. *See* tear-down strategies for witnesses
    using to set up rule or norm 60–61

Y

Yerrid, Steve 60, 75

Younger, Irving 23–26, 37–38, 41–42

Z
Ziegler, Edward 246–259
Ziglar, Zig 22

About the Author

Patrick Malone learned how to ask questions and get answers as an award-winning investigative journalist. Now he is a leading attorney working on behalf of seriously injured people in lawsuits against hospitals, doctors, drug companies, government agencies, and other defendants. Over the last three decades, he has won a long string of exceptional results for his clients. Malone is the author of *Winning Medical Malpractice Cases: With the Rules of the Road Technique* and is coauthor of the best-selling advocacy book, *Rules of the Road: A Plaintiff Lawyer's Guide to Proving Liability*. He also wrote a book for consumers: *The Life You Save: Nine Steps to Finding the Best Medical Care—and Avoiding the Worst*. Patrick Malone is a graduate of Yale Law School and is a member of the Inner Circle of Advocates and a fellow of the International Academy of Trial Lawyers. He is also on the board of trustees of the Pound Civil Justice Institute. Malone has been recognized as a leader in the law by *Lawdragon 500 Leading Lawyers in America*, *Super Lawyers*, and *The Best Lawyers in America*. Malone grew up in Wichita, Kansas, the oldest of seven children in an Irish Catholic family. Malone and his staff work out of offices in Washington, DC, a few blocks north of the White House, and they represent clients throughout Maryland, Virginia, and the District of Columbia.